Major League
Umpires' Performance,
2007–2010

ALSO BY ANDREW GOLDBLATT
AND FROM McFARLAND

*The Giants and the Dodgers:
Four Cities, Two Teams, One Rivalry* (2003)

Major League Umpires' Performance, 2007–2010

A Comprehensive Statistical Review

Andrew Goldblatt

McFarland & Company, Inc., Publishers
Jefferson, North Carolina, and London

LIBRARY OF CONGRESS CATALOGUING-IN-PUBLICATION DATA

Goldblatt, Andrew.
Major league umpires' performance, 2007–2010 :
a comprehensive statistical review / Andrew Goldblatt.
    p.   cm.
Includes bibliographical references and index.

ISBN 978-0-7864-6058-8
softcover : 50# alkaline paper ∞

1. Baseball umpires — United States.   2. Baseball — Umpiring — United States.
3. Baseball — Statistics.   4. Baseball — United States — History.   I. Title.
GV876.G65 2011   796.357'3 — dc22   2011002277

BRITISH LIBRARY CATALOGUING DATA ARE AVAILABLE

© 2011 Andrew Goldblatt. All rights reserved

*No part of this book may be reproduced or transmitted in any form
or by any means, electronic or mechanical, including photocopying
or recording, or by any information storage and retrieval system,
without permission in writing from the publisher.*

On the cover: New York Yankees catcher Wil Nieves, center, throws the ball around the diamond
as Arizona Diamondbacks' Carlos Quentin, right, reacts after being called out on strikes
by home plate umpire Bill Welke, left, during the eighth inning in Major League Baseball,
Wednesday, June, 13, 2007, at Yankee Stadium in New York (AP Photo/Julie Jacobson)

Manufactured in the United States of America

*McFarland & Company, Inc., Publishers
Box 611, Jefferson, North Carolina 28640
www.mcfarlandpub.com*

Contents

Preface 1

Introduction 5

The Umpires 19

Appendices

1. Highest and Lowest Runs per Nine Innings (R/9), 2007   183
2. Highest and Lowest Runs per Nine Innings (R/9), 2008   183
3. Highest and Lowest Runs per Nine Innings (R/9), 2009   183
4. Highest and Lowest Runs per Nine Innings (R/9), 2010   184
5. Highest and Lowest Walks per Nine Innings (BB/9), 2007   184
6. Highest and Lowest Walks per Nine Innings (BB/9), 2008   184
7. Highest and Lowest Walks per Nine Innings (BB/9), 2009   185
8. Highest and Lowest Walks per Nine Innings (BB/9), 2010   185
9. Highest and Lowest Strikeouts per Nine Innings (K/9), 2007   186
10. Highest and Lowest Strikeouts per Nine Innings (K/9), 2008   186
11. Highest and Lowest Strikeouts per Nine Innings (K/9), 2009   186
12. Highest and Lowest Strikeouts per Nine Innings (K/9), 2010   187
13. Highest and Lowest Strikeout-to-Walk Ratio (K/BB), 2007   187
14. Highest and Lowest Strikeout-to-Walk Ratio (K/BB), 2008   187
15. Highest and Lowest Strikeout-to-Walk Ratio (K/BB), 2009   188
16. Highest and Lowest Strikeout-to-Walk Ratio (K/BB), 2010   188
17. Runs per Nine Innings (R/9), 2007–2010   188
18. Walks per Nine Innings (BB/9), 2007–2010   189
19. Strikeouts per Nine Innings (K/9), 2007–2010   190
20. Strikeout-to-Walk Ratio (K/BB), 2007–2010   191

Index 193

Preface

We're 30 years into the sabermetric revolution, yet the impact of umpires on major league games remains among the least examined subjects in baseball. We know more about the impact of ballparks and weather.

For years I wondered how much the umpires' interpretation of the strike zone varied, and to what extent that variation influenced results. Over the winter of 2009 I charted each umpire's plate performance for the 2007, 2008, and 2009 regular seasons, recording:

- Date of game
- Visiting team
- Home team
- Innings called (in sixths of an inning, since for an umpire each inning lasts six outs)
- Runs scored
- Unintentional walks
- Intentional walks
- Strikeouts

I learned that the difference between strike zones could be huge. For instance, after factoring out intentional walks, Paul Schrieber granted 7.69 bases on balls per nine innings over those three years, whereas Doug Eddings granted just 5.27 — a difference of some 45 percent. And Schrieber, perhaps because he put nearly two-and-a-half more runners on base, saw 9.69 runs per nine innings cross the plate as opposed to 9.18 for Eddings. I had to tell the world.

But I wanted to do it for a general audience, in hopes of raising interest in umpires. When a fifth starter sprains his ankle, it makes the news. When an umpire struggles along with a bad back or misses six weeks with a concussion, there is no announcement and few fans care. (Legally, Major League Baseball may not disclose employees' medical information, but the umpires themselves, through their union or individually, may do so.) This is a shame. Umpires matter. They should be recognized and honored. This book is intended to help the average fan get to know the umpires as individuals and to encourage rational, informed discussion of their performance. For those reasons, as well as a desire to conceal my ignorance of statistical method, I have kept the metrics simple. Hardcore data crunchers are welcome to build on this study or, if truth demands, to knock it down.

When I wrote my last baseball book in 2001 and 2002, I did almost all my research in libraries. This time I did almost all my research on the Internet. Going into this project,

I shared the popular prejudice that Internet research is inferior because it precludes the kind of bookshelf browsing that leads to serendipitous discoveries of source material. I still think there's truth to that. But I've learned that by surfing the net I can find information I never would have stumbled upon in a year's worth of roaming the stacks. Plus it's nice to do research while your cat sleeps on your lap. Something's lost, but something's gained.

For the 2007, 2008, and 2009 seasons, I used Retrosheet as my source. The folks at Retrosheet ask that people using their data include the following language: "The information used here was obtained free of charge from and is copyrighted by Retrosheet. Interested parties may contact Retrosheet at www.retrosheet.org." I'm willing to go further. Retrosheet is the greatest resource for baseball researchers in the universe, and the people behind it cannot be thanked enough for their dedication and generosity.

I continued to track umpire performance while writing the book in 2010. Because Retrosheet wouldn't post 2010 data until a month or two past my deadline, I worked from the daily box scores at ESPN. I chose ESPN over other sites because it included pitch-by-pitch accounts of every game, indispensable when the home plate umpire suffers an injury or illness and has to be replaced. The pitch-by-pitch account helped me correctly attribute innings called, strikeouts, walks, etc.

I used several other web sites virtually every day. Baseball Prospectus is a magnificent creation. Its umpire page is so comprehensive that I used it to double-check the accuracy of my database. It is also the source of all references to umpire slash stats. My one complaint is that when multiple umpires work home plate, Baseball Prospectus credits only one with the results for the game. This can be significant. On September 1, 2010, Tom Hallion called pitches for the game between Baltimore and Boston until there were two out in the bottom of the ninth, when he was struck by a foul ball and had to leave. Lance Barksdale replaced him and saw just three pitches before the game ended. Baseball Prospectus credited the entire game to Barksdale.

For details about ejections I used The Left Field Corner, home of an umpire ejection fantasy league (I didn't know such a thing existed either). It contains accurate accounts of every ejection going back to 2007, and provides links to Major League Baseball videos so you can watch the toss and come to your own conclusions. I used the *New York Times* site mostly to confirm what I read elsewhere, but sometimes as a primary source, and used Baseball-Reference to confirm team, league, and seasonal statistical data. I didn't make much use of Brooks Baseball, but its Pitch f/x tool is amazing and deserves mention. Nor did I make much use of the umpire biographies at The Official Site of Major League Baseball, as they are both out of date and dull—with the sole exception of the one for Jim Reynolds, who admitted to the *Washington Post* that he listed his hobbies as bocce, archery, and haberdashery because their first letters spelled "bah," his young nephew's favorite word.

Sources follow each entry. Dates in parentheses indicate when websites were accessed.

I am grateful to David Vincent for providing data on ejection totals going back 40 years. I also wish to thank Lisa Benninger, John Bergez, Frances Cave, Leon Nehmad,

Janice Schachter, Leila Shockley, David K. Smith (not the Retrosheet guy, but the longtime friend), and Colleen Whitney for their support. Most of all I wish to thank my wife Christa, my first, best reader and many wonderful things besides.

SOURCES

Baseball Prospectus, http://www.baseballprospectus.com/.
Baseball Reference, http://www.baseball-reference.com/.
Brooks Baseball, http://www.brooksbaseball.net/.
ESPN MLB, http://espn.go.com/mlb/.
The Left Field Corner, http://cascreamindude.livejournal.com/.
The New York Times, http://www.nytimes.com.
The Official Site of Major League Baseball, http://mlb.mlb.com/index.jsp.
Retrosheet, http://www.retrosheet.org/.

Introduction

"Boys, I'm one of those umpires that misses 'em every once in a while. So if it's close, you'd better hit it," Hall of Fame umpire Cal Hubbard reputedly warned batters. On the one hand, it's a humble admission of fallibility. On the other, it's a not-so-subtle reminder that the home plate umpire decides what's a ball and what's a strike.

Section 2.00 of the *Major League Rule Book* defines the strike zone as "that area over home plate the upper limit of which is a horizontal line at the midpoint between the top of the shoulders and the top of the uniform pants, and the lower level is a line at the hollow beneath the kneecap." But even the most experienced umpire can't be expected to follow this definition to the letter. The strike zone isn't marked by lines like the end zone in football or the three-second lane in basketball. It varies according to each batter's height, and changes as the batter steps toward the pitch. Pitchers complicate the home plate umpire's job by aiming for the strike zone's upper, lower, inner, and outer edges with pitches that sink, dive, or dart. And so the strike zone becomes a matter of judgment.

Purists bemoan this fact. *Why won't the umpires call the rule book strike zone? How can they get so many pitches wrong?* they ask. It is, perhaps, the dark side of the sabermetric impulse, a longing for a kind of test tube baseball where variables like weather, ballpark dimensions, and umpires can be minimized or eliminated so players can be more cleanly evaluated. Or it could just stem from the conviction that too many games are decided by bad calls, a belief fomented by home team announcers crying "We was robbed!" during the season and network announcers fixating on super-slow-motion replays of close calls during the postseason. As umpires themselves say, they're expected to be perfect from the start and then get better.

The day is coming when machines will be able to judge balls and strikes, fair or foul balls, and safes or outs with near-total accuracy. If they can do it more cheaply than umpires, the parsimonious characters in charge of the game (hereafter referred to as the Lords of Baseball in tribute to Harold Parrott, the Brooklyn Dodger functionary whose book by that name dispels any illusion that ownership ever cared about more than money) may embrace the new technology. And in some ways it *will* be better: no more mortifying mistakes like the one made by Jim Joyce on June 2, 2010, when he erroneously ruled that Cleveland's Jason Donald beat out a ground ball with two outs in the ninth, denying Detroit Tiger pitcher Armando Galarraga a perfect game.

But in some ways it will be worse, because every fan who recalls Joyce's gaffe most likely also recalls getting into a conversation about it with someone otherwise indifferent to baseball. Much of the nation followed as Joyce and Galarraga turned the moment into a touching lesson in good sportsmanship. And Americans probably learned more about jurisprudence (especially the importance of precedent) from the debate over whether to retroactively change Joyce's call than from the last 20 years of Senate hearings for Supreme Court nominees. This is what sets baseball apart from other sports. Since the publication of *Casey at the Bat* and probably earlier, it has cherished, even celebrated, failure. You've heard it before: The best hitters fail 70 percent of the time, no other sport keeps track of errors, and so forth. And that's good for baseball, because however scorned failure may have become in our society, it's something we can all relate to. It stimulates our sympathy (or schadenfreude) and gets us talking to each other. Replacing umpires with machines will not destroy baseball. But it will make baseball less rich, less human, less worth talking about.

If the Lords of Baseball recognize that as a threat to their bottom line, their innate conservatism may incline them against replacing umpires. That has been the case so far. In August 2008 they broke a barrier by permitting umpires to review replays of disputed home runs. After a flurry of blown calls in the 2009 and 2010 postseasons, they came under pressure to expand the use of instant replay. But they held fast. During the 2009 postseason Commissioner Bud Selig said, "I don't really have any desire to increase the amount of replay, period." Just the same, the new contract ratified by the umpires in January 2010 allowed him to authorize the use of instant replay for more than disputed home runs.

If Selig didn't expand the use of instant replay after *l'affaire Joyce,* it's probably safe to assume that for the next several years, and perhaps longer, human beings will continue to decide close plays. Which means the rental car pitchmen masquerading as national broadcasters will continue to complain about the lopsided strike zone and blown calls on the basepaths. They should be conceded this much: Umpires owe it to us to be absolutely impartial and as accurate as they can be. *But we owe it to umpires to accept that they are human,* and that they bring their subjective judgment with them, especially when they work home plate. It's time we regarded umpires not as failed robots, but as dynamic actors whose impact on the game can be measured, analyzed, and enjoyed.

Over the last decade the Lords of Baseball have tried to make the umpires' strike zones as identical as fast food hamburgers. Using technology like QuesTec, a network of video cameras installed in many parks, they track each pitch, compare what a computer says the pitch was with what the umpire says it was, and send the umpire the results. The aim is to coax umpires into conformance with the rule book strike zone. The real effect is to make umpires cautious. Rather than be scolded for missing pitches, they shrink their strike zone, calling only obvious strikes. "It was a running joke: 'We're playing in a park with QuesTec, so it's going to be a three-and-a-half-hour game,'" said former pitcher John Smoltz. On top of that, due to camera angle problems and other technical challenges, neither QuesTec nor its successor, the Zone Evaluation System, is absolutely definitive, so the Lords of Baseball must continue to concede a certain amount of subjectivity to the umps.

In early 2003, a few months after going to work for the Boston Red Sox, godfather of sabermetrics Bill James chatted online with fans via *USA Today's* web site and was asked whether anyone kept statistics on umpires. He said that STATS Inc., a private firm he once worked with, collected umpire data, but "MLB didn't really like us printing them." Only in May 2010 did word leak that a number of major league teams have commissioned studies of umpires. "We do have their tendencies in the dugout on the wall. The name of the umpire and his tendencies, what they call and what part of the zone they call strikes," confirmed Ron Washington, manager of the Texas Rangers. The studies often include biographical information. Oakland Athletics manager Bob Geren said, "We like to get the players to know who's going to be there, get to know them and give them a little bit of background, so the players can say hello."

Also paying close attention to the umpires' home plate performance are gamblers. Go to just about any sports gambling web site and you will find the umpires' won-lost record for the home team and the average number of walks, strikeouts, and runs in their games. One bettors' web site declares that the home plate umpire is the third most important person on the field, behind the two starting pitchers. Don't place your money until you know who the home plate umpire will be, you are told. These sites notice when, say, Tim McClelland calls 11 straight games in which the home team wins, as happened in early 2010.

Fortunately, more wholesome web sites are also following umpire performance. The Internet abounds with articles about the umpires' plate judgment. Some of those articles overlap the subject matter of this book.* The level of erudition varies, with the best work done by experienced sabermetricians and the worst generally produced by blogging partisans of particular teams.

No survey of interest in umpire performance can omit Bruce Weber's 2009 book *As They See 'Em: A Fan's Travels in the Land of Umpires*, even though it's not really about performance. Instead, Weber definitively answers the question of what it's like *to be* an umpire. Weber shows how hard the job is and what a struggle it is to break in, climb the minor league ladder, and reach the majors (it's easier to make it as a player). He reminds us that umpires travel twice as much as players and are often booed, seldom cheered. They are scandalously underpaid in the minor leagues, and in the majors even the highest-paid among them earns less than a rookie player. Reading Weber's masterpiece should cure all but those raised by wolves of the temptation to shout "Kill the umpire!"

Players are the closest observers of umpires, and because baseball is their livelihood they regard the umps pragmatically, leaving rule book idealism to those on the sidelines. Former first baseman Wally Joyner, who played most of his career for the Angels, Royals, and Padres, once asked a *Baseball Digest* writer how many umpires there were. When told there were 68, he said, "Well, that's 68 strike zones." Pitchers Greg Maddux and Tom Glavine, who racked up 355 and 305 career wins respectively, were notorious for exploiting the outside corner, seeing how far off the plate they could put the ball and still get a strike

---

*Superior examples include Jonathan Hale's "A Strike Zone of Their Own" for Hardball Times; J.C. Bradbury's "Overhauling Umpires" for Sabernomics; and Jeff Zimmerman's "Pitcher and Hitter Friendly Umpires" for Beyond the Box Score.

from the ump. Hall of Fame hitter Tony Gwynn, ejected just twice in his 2,440-game career, knew it was a waste of time to complain. "I had to expand my strike zone a little because Maddux and Glavine were great at hitting the center of the glove. When they hit the glove dead center, the umpires would start calling it a strike," he explained. So he adjusted, and wound up with a career average of .429 against Maddux and .312 against Glavine.

Using four easily grasped statistics, we can measure the differences between umpires and become more knowledgeable about what's happening on the field. Just as we note the weather before game time and think, "The wind's blowing out, we may see a bunch of home runs," we should note who will be calling balls and strikes and think, "He's got a big strike zone, we'll probably see more strikeouts." And because game management skills also matter — another common complaint about umpires is that they're too argumentative — we can use a fifth easily grasped stat (discussed a bit later) for insight into umpire temperament.

The first statistic is *runs per nine innings (R/9)*. It's derived much like a pitcher's earned run average (ERA). Take the number of runs scored while an umpire is behind the plate, multiply by nine, and divide by the number of innings the umpire has called. R/9 differs from a pitcher's ERA in two important respects. First, it doesn't distinguish between earned and unearned runs; all runs are counted. Second, an umpire's inning is six outs as opposed to three, because the umpire is calling the game for both sides. So when you read that Umpire X called 300 innings last year, that's equivalent to Pitcher Y throwing 600 innings.

The second statistic is *walks per nine innings (BB/9)*. It too is derived like a pitcher's ERA. Take the number of walks an umpire has granted while behind the plate, multiply by nine, and divide by the number of innings the umpire has called. To eliminate the distortion created by intentional walks, which are called by managers rather than umpires, they have been subtracted from each umpire's seasonal totals. The difference can be substantial. In 2009, managers ordered 29 intentional walks in the 310 innings called by Mike Everitt, but only nine in the 297 innings called by Dana DeMuth. Everitt's BB/9 was 6.53, DeMuth's 7.12, more than half a walk per nine innings apart. If intentional walks had been left in, their BB/9s would have been virtually identical, 7.39 to 7.37, masking the difference in the size of their strike zones.

The third statistic is *strikeouts per nine innings (K/9)*. Again, the concept is the same as a pitcher's ERA. Take the number of strikeouts that occur while the umpire is behind home plate, multiply by nine, and divide by the number of innings the umpire has called. It's tempting to distinguish between swinging strikeouts, where the batter tries to hit the ball but misses, and called strikeouts, where the batter lets the ball go by and the umpire declares it a third strike. The latter would seem a purer indication of the umpire's plate judgment. But at-bats are more complicated than that. A called strike on a close pitch early in the count can prompt a batter to swing and miss at a similar pitch for strike three. Which pitch mattered more? Ultimately, a strikeout results from three failures by the batter (or successes by the pitcher), not one, and it seems a stretch to argue that the nature of the last is either unrelated to or is more significant than the nature of the first two.

The fourth statistic is *strikeout-to-walk ratio (K/BB)*. This one is *not* calculated like a pitcher's ERA. Instead, the total number of strikeouts is divided by the total number of walks. This gives us further insight into the size of an umpire's strike zone. Usually, if an umpire's BB/9 is high (meaning he calls more walks than his peers), his K/9 is low (he presides over fewer strikeouts than his peers). It also works in reverse: A lower BB/9 is usually paired with a higher K/9. But the relationship is not ironclad. Sometimes an umpire has both a lower than usual BB/9 and K/9, or a higher than usual BB/9 and K/9. In these cases, the K/BB ratio makes it easier for us to determine whether the umpire's plate judgment favors hitters or pitchers.

To better understand the meaning of an umpire's R/9, let's look to history. The 1930 season is widely considered the best for hitters. As a group, National League batters hit .303, led by Bill Terry of the New York Giants, whose .401 made him the last National Leaguer ever to hit .400. In the American League the collective batting average was .288, and the Yankees, led by Babe Ruth and Lou Gehrig, scored 1,062 runs. The major league R/9 for 1930 was 11.28.

The mirror image of the 1930 season was 1968. Bob Gibson of the St. Louis Cardinals compiled a 1.12 ERA, lowest since the Dead Ball Era, and Dennis McLain of the Detroit Tigers became the last pitcher to win 30 games. In the National League, only four batters hit 30 or more homers, and in the American League, only Carl Yastrzemski hit over .300. The major league R/9 for 1968 was 6.84.

So all the R/9 action, if you will, occurs along a spectrum 4.44 runs wide. In that narrow context, a difference of one run is significant, and a difference of two runs is huge. When we look at the R/9 of all umpires who called 500 or more innings from 2007 through 2010, the difference between the most hitter-friendly umpire (Gerry Davis at 10.18) and the most pitcher-friendly umpire (Mike Estabrook at 8.13) is 2.05 runs!

Another way to look at it — and the way we will look at it here — is that umpires can post R/9s significantly above or below average. Since 2007, the annual R/9 has been falling as the major leagues emerge from the Steroid Era:

	2007	2008	2009	2010	*Four-Year Average*
R/9	9.67	9.38	9.33	8.86	9.31

Gerry Davis's R/9 is eight percent higher than the average umpire's. Estabrook's R/9 is 14 percent lower than the average umpire's and *25 percent* lower than Davis's. This is a greater difference than the one between home games in Colorado's Coors Field (10.41 runs per game in 2009, even with the humidor) and San Francisco's AT&T Park (8.02 runs per game in 2009). So if you like 1930-vintage slugfests, try to see a game when Davis wears the mask. But if you prefer 1968-style pitching duels, wait for Mike Estabrook to come to town — or Andy Fletcher, whose R/9 is next lowest at 8.28.

How do we account for such wide discrepancies in R/9? Random variation would explain differences over a few games, and maybe over a full season, but over four full seasons? It's fair to assume that something in the way Gerry Davis calls balls and strikes encourages hitting, while something in the way Mike Estabrook calls balls and strikes helps pitchers. And it makes intuitive sense that an umpire with a higher than average R/9 has a hitter-friendly, i.e. small, strike zone, and that an umpire with a lower than average R/9 has a pitcher-friendly, i.e. large, strike zone. A small strike zone increases offense by creating more baserunners through walks, by allowing hitters to be more selective, and by forcing pitchers to throw the ball over the plate, where it's more likely to get clobbered. A large strike zone decreases offense by taking away baserunners who might otherwise walk, by forcing hitters to swing at close pitches or risk striking out, and by crediting pitchers with strikes on pitches that nick the edge of the plate or miss entirely.

The size of an umpire's strike zone can be inferred from his BB/9 and K/9. If an umpire has a higher than average BB/9 and a lower than average K/9, he has a small strike zone. He's calling more walks and watching over fewer strikeouts, which favors hitters. If an umpire has a lower than average BB/9 and a higher than average K/9, he has a large strike zone. He's calling fewer walks and presiding over more strikeouts, which favors pitchers.

So in English-major mathematics, here's what we'd expect:

Higher than average R/9 = Higher than average BB/9 + Lower than average K/9
Lower than average R/9 = Lower than average BB/9 + Higher than average K/9

But is that what we get?

In 2010, BB/9 dropped in tandem with R/9. But in the two years prior, BB/9 crept up while R/9 went down, *contrary* to what we'd expect. The trend for K/9 fully corresponded with the drop in R/9, rising every year, and K/BB remained stable until 2010, when it increased in favor of pitchers, just what we'd expect in a year when R/9 dropped nearly half a run from the season before:

	2007	2008	2009	2010	Four-Year Average
BB/9	6.12	6.24	6.42	6.05	6.21
K/9	13.34	13.65	13.97	14.26	13.81
K/BB	2.18	2.19	2.18	2.36	2.22

So the 2008–2009 rise in BB/9 notwithstanding, from the forest perspective we can see that the drop in R/9 since 2007 corresponds with a reduction in walks and an increase in strikeouts.

But what about at tree level? The paradigm certainly holds true for Gerry Davis and Mike Estabrook. Davis's four-year BB/9 is six percent higher than average and his four-year K/9 is five percent lower than average, marks of a hitters' umpire. Estabrook's four-year BB/9 is 14 percent lower than average (only three umpires have a lower BB/9 than he) and his four-year K/9 is half a percent higher than average, consistent with a pitcher's umpire.

(If you're thinking that in the scheme of things these percentage differences are minor, think again. Baseball is a game of small tolerances. The drop in offense from 2009 to 2010 was .47 runs per nine innings, little more than five percent. In real terms, that meant nearly 800 fewer walks, nearly a thousand fewer hits, and more than 400 fewer homers. If an umpire with an average strike zone could call every single major league game, the difference between him and an umpire whose strike zone favored pitchers by five percent would be equivalent to all the homers hit by the top ten power hitters of 2010 plus all the base hits accumulated by Ichiro Suzuki, Robinson Cano, and Carlos Gonzalez. And the difference between a Gerry Davis and a Mike Estabrook, as we have seen, is much greater than five percent.)

But the paradigm doesn't always hold. Sometimes the relationship between an umpire's R/9 and strike zone is the opposite of what it should be. For the period under study, Tim Welke's R/9 was 10.06, fifth highest of all umpires and eight percent above average. But his BB/9 was 6.14, one percent *below* average, and his K/9 was third highest of all umpires at 14.50, five percent *above* average. In other words, he gave pitchers plenty of strike zone, but the hitters rampaged anyway. So the size of an umpire's strike zone, as determined by his BB/9 and K/9, is not a consistent guide to the number of runs that will score when he's behind the plate.

In fact, the correlation is surprisingly weak. From 2007 through 2010 there were 289 umpire seasons of 150 or more innings called, and in those 289 seasons, BB/9s correlated with R/9s 58 percent of the time. That's better than a random result, but not by much. The R/9-K/9 correlation is just 52 percent, barely above random; we're safer concluding that K/9 is irrelevant to R/9 than trying to assign some significance to it.

When the size of the umpire's strike zone fails to explain his R/9, slash statistics often do. Slash stats are the three averages most commonly used to assess hitting performance: batting average, on-base percentage, and slugging percentage. Batting average is the classic measure of hitting prowess, calculated by dividing hits by at-bats. On-base percentage reveals how often hitters reach base without making an out. The formula is (hits + walks + hit by pitch) divided by (at-bats + walks + hit by pitch + sacrifice flies). Slugging percentage measures power, and is derived by dividing total bases by at-bats. Slash stats are often represented in succession and separated by slashes, which explains the name. For the four years under study, the major league slash stats are .263/.332/.415. To give those numbers historical context, in 1930, the great hitters' season, the slash stats were .296/.356/.434. In 1968, the great pitchers' season, the slash stats were .237/.299/.340.

So when we look at Tim Welke's sky-high 11.29 R/9 in 2009, we know it can't be solely due to his BB/9, which at 7.25 was a full walk per game higher than average. One extra baserunner per game isn't going to result in two extra runs per game. And we know it can't be due to a low K/9, either, because his 14.58 rate was four percent *higher* than average. Then we look up his slash stats. Batters hit .275/.349/.451 when he worked the plate. Their slugging percentage was higher than what Babe Ruth and cohort achieved in 1930! That explains the high R/9. But it gives rise to a new question: How could the hitters have done so well while protecting a larger than average strike zone? We would need to study many other variables before answering. Even then, would we truly have an answer, or would we be imposing our need for explanations on a random result?

Consider the slash stats of Laz Diaz and Joe West in 2010. Hitters slashed at a .256/.325/.402 rate for Diaz, .255/.325/.400 for West. Batting average and slugging percentage were virtually identical. On-base percentage *was* identical. If slash stats reliably correlated to R/9, Diaz and West should have seen a very similar number of runs cross the plate. But Diaz's R/9 was 8.52, West's 8.06, a difference of nearly half a run. Baseball may be a game where small differences change outcomes, but no way such trivial differences change results that profoundly. Sometimes another statistic, such as home run rate (HR/9) or a comparison of innings called to pitches seen, can help clear up the contradiction, and when that's the case the statistic is included. But in baseball as in life, there's more mystery than we'd like to admit.

Umpires aren't evaluated by plate judgment alone. Their work at first, second, and third base is important too. But it's hard to come by reliable data for basework, despite some tantalizing hints that calls in the field can vary as much as strike zone judgment. In 2000, Michael Wolverton published an article (available at Baseball Prospectus) showing that some umpires are twice as likely to call a base stealer out at second as their peers. In August 2010 ESPN's *Outside the Lines* conducted a study of 184 games and concluded that 20 percent of close fair-or-foul and out-or-safe calls were incorrect. Most likely someone has done an extensive study on the subject, but if it's been published it's languishing in some obscure corner of the Internet—or hasn't been posted at all. So there will be no evaluation of the umpires' work on the basepaths here.

Another important measure of umpire performance is game management, which incorporates a number of skills, among them the ability to keep the details straight (runs, outs, balls and strikes, ground rules, batting orders, substitutions), the ability to keep a game moving, and the ability to minimize conflict. Over the last decade the Lords of Baseball have focused heavily on the pace of games, prodding umpires to make games go faster. But the fans and the media tend to focus more on conflict management. For years, umpires have reputedly had hair-trigger tempers. A number of them have been accused of provoking arguments and focusing attention on themselves—a professional taboo, as almost all umpires agree that a good game is one in which they *aren't* noticed.

We can measure conflict management by a fifth statistic, *ejection rate,* the number of ejections divided by the number of games in which the umpire worked (at any base, not just home plate). We can express ejection rate as a percentage, i.e., Marvin Hudson had an ejection rate of two percent from 2007 through 2010, matching the average for that period.

The belief that umpires have become excessively confrontational has been around for nearly 20 years. "It has been a violent change. It's worse now than ever, and it's very, very wrong. You can't even talk to umpires anymore. You ask about a ball or strike, politely, and they react with aggression," Cookie Rojas, an infielder who came up in 1962, complained while working as a Florida Marlin coach in 1996. Chicago Cub first baseman

Mark Grace put it even more bluntly: "The umps will mark their territory, just like animals do."

Former umpire Mark Hirschbeck defended himself and his colleagues. "A player plays with intensity, and he's a gamer. An umpire umpires with intensity, and he's a red-ass. Where's the fairness?" Bruce Froemming, who worked a record 37 years as a major league umpire and frequently was accused of pugnacious behavior, said, "Nobody wants nine innings of peace more than we do. But if we are treated with abuse, we'll take action. In your job, your home, your church, you wouldn't allow somebody to curse you, would you? So why should we?"

The umpires' belligerence on the field was often associated with their confrontational tactics off the field. Like the players, the umpires unionized in the 1960s. In 1978 they hired an aggressive Philadelphia lawyer named Richie Phillips to represent them. They staged walkouts in 1979, 1984, 1990, 1991, and 1995. The umpires felt underpaid, unappreciated, and besieged, especially after Roberto Alomar spat on umpire John Hirschbeck (Mark Hirschbeck's brother) in 1996 and the Lords of Baseball responded with what the umpires considered inadequate punishment. "Tolerance in baseball is leading to total anarchy," proclaimed Jerry Crawford and colleague Don Denkinger in a 1997 spring training statement. Phillips declared, "Umpires will no longer bend over backward to keep players in the game. Players who engage in aberrant behavior can expect an immediate ejection and little conversation, so that should lessen confrontation." Indeed — just as nuclear weapons can lessen bedbug infestations.

Matters came to a head in 1999, the last year of a four-year contract between the umpires and the Lords of Baseball. The contract prohibited umpires from striking, but they felt an urgent need to demonstrate their discontent. Phillips hit on the idea of having all the umpires resign just as the pennant races were heating up. Union president Crawford and his leadership team deemed it a brilliant stratagem, so word went out to the membership: Submit your resignation. Most umpires obeyed, but several, led by John Hirschbeck, realized that far from being a clever tactic that got around the prohibition against strikes, the mass resignation was an invitation to the Lords of Baseball to fire any umpire they wished. An internecine struggle ensued, with Hirschbeck's side prevailing. The union withdrew the resignations. But it was too late. The Lords of Baseball accepted the resignations of 22 umpires, one-third of the union membership.

This watershed moment in umpire history had a number of ramifications that, taken together, helped improve the umpires' collective reputation. The old union was decertified and Richie Phillips was sent packing. The new union, the World Umpires Association, headed by John Hirschbeck until 2009 and then by Joe West, negotiated with the Lords of Baseball in a more adult manner. A flood of young umpires lacking the old sense of grievance came into the game. Eleven of the umpires whose resignations were accepted eventually returned, usually as humbler individuals. The separate National and American League umpiring staffs were merged to reduce insularity (the National League umps had been particularly militant against management). And the Lords of Baseball took steps to address performance standards, including the aforementioned pitch-tracking systems.

Introduction

These days the most common complaint about umpires is that they get calls wrong. You seldom hear, as you did 15 or 20 years ago, that umpires are getting a lot of calls wrong *and* are fat and mean — although some old timers, including Joe Torre, think that as far as the mean part goes, things haven't changed. "I'm not saying they should take abuse, but strike three with men on base, the player throws his helmet, and all of a sudden, it's 'You're out of here,'" he complained after Paul Emmel ejected him on September 11, 2010. Six days later Torre announced his retirement.

Perhaps Torre had a point. The ejection rate from 1990 through 1999, when umpires were supposedly so abusive, was 2.26 percent. The ejection rate from 2000 through 2009, when umpires were supposedly less confrontational, was 2.21 percent — virtually indistinguishable. But a closer look at the numbers from 2000 through 2010 reveals an encouraging trend. Remember that a lot of new umpires arrived in late 1999. "They test you the first three or four years. It's the nature of the beast," said veteran umpire Dale Scott. The ejection rate peaked in 2003 at 2.9 percent, as many of the new umpires were working their fourth full season. Since then the ejection rate has been heading downward. From 2007 through 2010 it dropped to a flat two percent. So it could be that we are just beginning to reap the benefits of a less confrontational umpiring corps. (Skeptics tempted to argue that the drop in ejections is due to fewer steroid-fueled rages by players should keep in mind that most ejectees are managers and coaches.)

Remember too that not all ejections stem from disputes with the umpire. Sometimes the players fight with each other, and the umpires have to banish the combatants to restore order. This can unfairly inflate an ejection rate. On September 1, 2010, pitcher Chris Volstad of the Florida Marlins hit Nyjer Morgan of the Washington Nationals with a pitch. The night before, Morgan had plowed into Florida catcher Brett Hayes on a play at the plate, separating Hayes's shoulder. Volstad's retaliation should have evened things out. But then Morgan stole second and third with his team losing by 11 runs. The next time Morgan batted, Volstad threw behind him. Morgan charged the mound. He got in one punch (a miss) before Marlin first baseman Gaby Sanchez flattened him and a brawl ensued. Home plate umpire Marvin Hudson ejected Morgan, Volstad, and Florida manager Edwin Rodriguez. When Sanchez took his turn at the plate, Doug Slaten of the Nationals beaned him, so Hudson ejected Slaten and Washington manager Jim Riggleman. That made five ejections in one game. Prior to that evening, Hudson had a season ejection rate under one percent and a career ejection rate of 1.7 percent, both well below average. The incident raised his season ejection rate to 4.4 percent, which would lead you to think him a screaming hyena if you didn't know the Volstad-Morgan story.

When there is an argument over a call, umpires differ in what they consider ejectionable behavior. Joe West does not tolerate profanity. No surprise that he has a high ejection rate. Ed Hickox, whose career ejection rate is slightly lower than average, follows the more common rule of thumb. "They can say, 'Eddie, that was a horseshit call.' They're not talking about me, they're talking about my call. But if they say, 'Eddie, you're a horseshit umpire,' then that's automatic because they're getting personal, directing it at you."

An umpire's ejection rate gives us a glimpse into his on-field personality. Is he a totalitarian, someone who doesn't just need to prevail, but needs to crush dissent and humiliate anyone who opposes him? Or is he a benevolent dictator, someone who maintains that what he says goes, but is open to discussion and can acknowledge a mistake? Taste in umpire demeanor varies, but as a group the players clearly prefer the benevolent dictators. *Sports Illustrated* conducted player polls in 2003 and 2006, and *ESPN The Magazine* conducted a poll in 2010. In each, the players were asked whom they considered the best and worst umpires. The results were consistent. Umpires who readily admit mistakes like Jim Joyce and Tim McClelland are widely admired. My-way-or-the-highway types like Joe West are not.

Umpires with an ejection rate of 2.2 percent have an average temperament. Umpires with a higher ejection rate have more totalitarian leanings. Those with a lower ejection rate behave more like benevolent dictators. Since 2007, the most totalitarian umpires have been Bill Hohn (despite a relatively peaceful 2010) and Bob Davidson. The most benevolent dictators have been Randy Marsh (who retired after 2009), Brian Gorman, Mike Reilly, and Bruce Dreckman. Curiously, the umpire players most dislike, C.B. Bucknor, has one of the lowest ejection rates among umpires working in 300 or more games since 2007.

Umpires have a hierarchy. On top are the 17 crew chiefs. They are the leaders of the four-man crews who work regular season games and the six-man crews who work postseason games. They earn their supervisory positions on merit rather than seniority. In addition to other perks, they enjoy the most flexibility in vacation scheduling and coordinate the crew's on-field choreography, no small matter if they're hurting or don't run well (crew chiefs tend to be older). They also have the most responsibility. They review replays of disputed home run calls. They intercede when a manager or player ejected by a crewmate won't leave the field. And they speak to the press after a crewmate has made a controversial call. All crew chiefs belong to the World Umpires Association (WUA), although the recently retired Jerry Crawford never got over the shock of 1999 and the decertification of his old union (the Major League Umpires Association) and declined to join the WUA.

The middle class consists of 51 major league umpires, all of whom belong to the WUA. Like the crew chiefs, they receive four weeks of in-season vacation per year, meaning they work about 135 games out of a 162-game schedule. Although terms of the five-year contract ratified in January 2010 were not disclosed, it's believed that umpire salaries start around $120,000 and range up to $350,000, not including a per diem allowance of at least $340 per day for hotels, meals, rental cars, and other expenses. The cost of flying first class is covered by the Lords of Baseball, who keep the umpires' schedules confidential as a security measure. Like the crew chiefs, regular major league umpires are tenured. Unless they commit some grave offense (consorting with known gamblers, for instance) they cannot be fired, regardless of what the Lords of Baseball, the players, or anyone else thinks of their skills.

The lower class consists of some 20 Triple-A call-up umpires who do not belong to the union (although they may belong to the Association of Minor League Umpires, or AMLU). If they were players, we would label them prospects. They normally work in the minors, but when a major league umpire goes on vacation or needs time to heal from an injury, one of them comes up as a replacement. Triple-A call-ups do not get vacations and are often exploited by the Lords of Baseball, sometimes working more games than the union umpires (although in 2010 the Lords eased up on the abuse). They don't complain because they know they're prime candidates for a major league job and don't want to ruin their chances. Before the 2010 season began, four Triple-A call-ups were promoted to the major leagues: Rob Drake, Chad Fairchild, James Hoye, and Adrian Johnson. Leading candidates for openings in 2011 and beyond include (in order of 2010 plate innings worked) Scott Barry, Mike Estabrook, Todd Tichenor, Brian Knight, Angel Campos, Dan Bellino, and D.J. Reyburn.

Regardless of his place in the hierarchy, every umpire who called at least one major league game in either 2009 or 2010 is profiled in the next section of this book. Each profile begins with a chart that shows the number of games at home plate, the number of six-out innings worked at home plate, and then R/9, BB/9, K/9, and K/BB. To quickly gauge an umpire's performance, keep these numbers in mind:

$$9.30 \quad 6 \quad 14 \quad 2.20$$

That's roughly the average R/9, BB/9, K/9, and K/BB for the period.

For further reference, the section after the umpire profiles contains charts ranking the highest and lowest R/9s, BB/9s, K/9s, and K/BBs for each season under study. The section also contains a complete ranking, from highest to lowest, of R/9, BB/9, K/9, and K/BB for the entire four-year period. Only those umpires who called 150 innings or more are included in seasonal rankings. When ranking umpires over the four-year period under study, only those who called 500 innings or more are included. That's equivalent to 17 or 18 games behind home plate in a season and between 56 and 60 games behind home plate over four years. That may not seem like much, but keep in mind that 150 innings for an umpire translate to 300 innings for a pitcher (who works three-out innings) and 500 umpire innings equal 1,000 pitcher innings. Think you're safe evaluating a pitcher's season on the basis of 300 innings, and his career on the basis of 1,000 innings? Then you should feel safe evaluating an umpire on the basis of 150 innings per season and 500 innings overall. Besides, most umpires work much more than that. The typical major league umpire spends about 300 innings behind home plate each year and roughly 1,200 innings over four years.

In addition to an analysis of the umpire's behind-the-plate stats, the profile reviews his game management skills by comparing his ejection rate to the norm. The profile also includes highlights and controversies from the umpire's career and quotes ranging from why he ejected someone to what he thinks of instant replay to how he regards his profession. Finding quotes isn't always easy. Most umpires eschew the spotlight and either mumble clichés or avoid the media altogether. Interestingly, though, some will speak to their hometown newspaper or college alma mater. Most of the umpires are from small towns in the middle of the country — six were born in Kentucky, eight in Ohio, and eight in Michigan, for instance — and their neighbors often regard them as celebrities, according them a level of respect the national media don't. In friendly surroundings they sometimes let down their guard, candidly acknowledging their humanity. Rob Drake, an evangelical Christian, might have best expressed their chief predicament: "Every time I walk on the baseball field I want to be perfect. Every morning when I wake up, I pray that He will give me the strength to live a sin-free life. The problem is that both are impossible."

SOURCES

Associated Press. "GMs Pass on Expanding Instant Replay." ESPN.com, November 10, 2009. (August 10, 2010.) http://sports.espn.go.com/mlb/news/story?id=4642344.

Batard, Dan Le. "Making the Call on Umpires Becoming More Confrontational." Knight Ridder/Tribune News Service via Access My Library.com, September 7, 1996. (August 14, 2010.) http://www.accessmylibrary.com/coms2/summary_0286-6384396_ITM.

Bradbury, J.C. "Overhauling Umpires." Sabernomics.com, October 28, 2009. (August 14, 2010.) http://www.sabernomics.com/sabernomics/index.php/2009/10/overhauling-umpires/.

Gwynn, Tony. "The Book on Maddux, Glavine." ESPN.com, April 17, 2002. (August 21, 2010.) http://assets.espn.go.com/mlb/columns/gwynn_tony/1369978.html.

Hale, Jonathan. "A Zone of Their Own." Hardball Times.com, November 28, 2007. (August 14, 2010.) http://www.hardballtimes.com/main/article/a-zone-of-their-own/.

Jackson, Tony. "Joe Torre: Umpires Getting Hair Triggers." ESPN.com, September 12, 2010. (September 13, 2010.) http://sports.espn.go.com/los-angeles/mlb/news/story?ie=5564550.

James, Bill. "Fantasy Baseball: Bill James." *USA Today,* March 26, 2003. (August 10, 2010.) http://cgi1.usatoday.com/mchat/20030325004/tscript.htm.

Miller, Stuart. "A Slow Burn Over a Reluctance to Call High Strikes." *New York Times,* August 8, 2010. (August 10, 2010.) http://www.nytimes.com/2010/08/09/sports/baseball/09highstrike.html.

Quinn, T.J., and Willie Weinbaum. "Study Shows 1 in 5 Close Calls Wrong." ESPN.com, August 15, 2010. (August 15, 2010.) http://sports.espn.go.com/espn/otl/news/story?id=5464015.

Ropeik, David. "The Men in Black (or Light Blue)." Boston.com, September 28, 2005. (August 17, 2010.) http://www.boston.com/sports/baseball/redsox/articles/2005/09/28/the_men_in_black/.

Walker, Ben. "Getting a Jump on the Ump: Some Major League Teams Compile Scouting Reports on the Men in Blue." *Washington Examiner,* May 10, 2010. (August 10, 2010.) http://www.washingtonexaminer.com/nation/getting-a-jump-on-the-ump-some-major-league-teams-compile-scouting-reports-on-men-in-blue-93316919.html.

Wolverton, Michael. "Tough Cops ... and Other Ones." BaseballProspectus.com, September 18, 2000. (August 10, 2010.) http://www.baseballprospectus.com/article.php?articleid=779.

Zimmerman, Jeff. "Pitcher and Hitter Friendly Umpires." Beyond the Box Score.com, March 24, 2010. (September 15, 2010.) http://www.beyondtheboxscore.com/2010/3/24/1386512/pitcher-and-hitter-friendly-umpires.

The Umpires

Lance Barksdale

BORN: March 8, 1967
FIRST MAJOR LEAGUE GAME: May 29, 2000
FAVORS: Hitters, strongly
THEY HATE HIM IN: Florida

	2007	2008	2009	2010	Totals
Games	35	34	35	34	138
Innings	309.33	297.17	308.83	291.33	1,206.67
R/9	9.78	9.30	9.73	9.02	9.46
BB/9	6.84	8.00	6.94	5.78	6.89
K/9	12.83	13.30	13.23	15.32	13.65
K/BB	1.88	1.66	1.91	2.65	1.98

It's unusual for umpires to call many games in which there are more walks than strikeouts. The norm, remember, is fewer than half as many walks as strikeouts. In 2008, Lance Barksdale called six games with more walks than strikeouts. He called another three games in which there were an equal number of walks and strikeouts. No surprise, then, that he led the majors in 2008 with an astonishing 8.00 BB/9.

Barksdale was also generous with free passes in 2007 and 2009. Overall, his 2007–2009 BB/9 of 7.25 ranked fourth highest. He was also consistently below average in strikeouts during that period. The high BB/9s and low K/9s resulted in a three-year K/BB ratio of 1.81, fifth lowest overall. The numbers made a convincing argument that Barksdale had one of the tightest strike zones in the major leagues. But in 2010 Barksdale did an about-face, strongly favoring pitchers. His BB/9 dropped by more than a full walk per game and his K/9 rose by more than two strikeouts per game. His four-year K/BB rose to a more moderate 1.98. That's still the ninth lowest for the period under study, so despite 2010 he remains a hitters' umpire.

Barksdale's hitter-friendly strike zone has not resulted in many additional runs. In 2007 his 9.78 R/9 was a scant one percent above average, and in 2008, the year of his 8.00 BB/9, his R/9 was actually one percent *below* average. In 2009 the small strike zone manifested itself more logically, resulting in four percent more runs. Overall, though, in his 1,206.67 innings from 2007 to 2010, his hitter-friendly ways resulted in just 21 runs more than average.

The only major league umpire born in Mississippi, Barksdale is also among the smallest, listed at 5'10" and 175 pounds. Among active umpires, only Jerry Meals weighs less. You might think this would lead to Little Man Syndrome and a need for Barksdale to prove himself among the much larger bodies that inhabit the major league universe, but his career ejection rate is 2.4 percent, only slightly above average. And Barksdale would not have had any ejections at all in 2010 if not for vuvuzelas and a wily veteran.

The South African horns known as vuvuzelas created a sensation during the 2010

World Cup soccer championship, and on June 19, 2010, the Florida Marlins gave away 15,000 of them for a game against the Tampa Bay Rays. The resulting din made it nearly impossible to hear. With the game tied in the bottom of the ninth, Marlin manager Fredi Gonzalez shouted a lineup switch to Barksdale. Gonzalez intended for Brian Barden to bat third and Wes Helms to bat ninth. Somehow Barksdale got them reversed. When Barden led off with a walk, Tampa Bay manager Joe Maddon argued that Barden was batting out of order. Barksdale agreed and called Barden out. Gonzalez argued, earning a thumb from Barksdale. "He screwed it up. I told him three times who I wanted to hit. I thought we had it straightened out," Gonzalez said afterward. Answering for Barksdale, crew chief Tom Hallion blamed the vuvuzelas. "It was the most uncomfortable baseball game I've been a part of in a long time because of that," Hallion said. The game went 11 innings and the Marlins lost.

The wily veteran was Derek Jeter of the New York Yankees. On September 15, 2010, he decoyed Barksdale into awarding him first base on a flubbed bunt. Jeter half-squared, then pulled his bat back, but the ball hit his bat on the knob and trickled toward the pitcher. Instead of running to first, Jeter wheeled away from the batter's box and clutched his arm. Barksdale declared that Jeter had been hit by the pitch and sent him to first. Joe Maddon, winner of the vuvuzela argument, was the loser this time. He argued, correctly, that the ball hit Jeter's bat, not Jeter's arm. Barksdale stuck by his call and tossed Maddon.

On May 13, 2009, Barksdale became the first umpire to have a home run call overturned by instant replay. In the top of the first inning at St. Louis, Pirate first baseman Adam LaRoche pulled a pitch from Joel Pineiro over the right field wall. The ball hit a railing or screen and bounced back onto the field. Barksdale, working first base, ruled it a home run. But the Cardinals challenged the call. They were right. The replay showed that the object the ball hit was defined by the ground rules as in play. Crew chief Randy Marsh called LaRoche out of the dugout and put him back on second base. No harm. The Pirates won anyway.

SOURCE

Capozzi, Joe. "Players, Umpires Blast 'Awful, Awful' Florida Marlins Vuvuzelas." *Palm Beach Post,* June 20, 2010. (October 15, 2010.) http://blogs.palmbeachpost.com/marlins/2010/06/20/florida-marlins-manager-fredi-gonzalez-umpire-screwed-up-lineup-change-in-9-8-loss/.

Lance Barrett

BORN: October 3, 1984
FIRST MAJOR LEAGUE GAME: October 1, 2010
FAVORS: Way too early to tell
THEY HATE HIM IN: Nowhere yet

	2007	2008	2009	2010	Totals
Games	0	0	0	1	1
Innings	0	0	0	9	9
R/9	0.00	0.00	0.00	11.00	11.00
BB/9	0.00	0.00	0.00	9.00	9.00
K/9	0.00	0.00	0.00	15.00	15.00
K/BB	0.00	0.00	0.00	1.67	1.67

Barrett was named a Triple-A call-up in 2010, only his second year at the top minor league level. It was a sign that the Lords of Baseball saw a lot of potential in the 6'5", 225 pound Texan. But he didn't get called up until the last weekend of the season, for a meaningless series between the Chicago Cubs and Houston Astros. Crew chief Tim Tschida and Alfonso Marquez ended their seasons early, leaving Barrett and fellow rookie David Rackley to work with Bob Davidson and Tim Timmons, both of whom are known for short fuses. Neither Barrett nor Rackley ejected anybody.

On October 2, 2010, the next to last day of the season, Barrett made his major league debut behind home plate. The very first batter, Chicago's Jeff Baker, earned Barrett's first major league base on balls. Three batters later, the Cubs' Xavier Nady became the first victim of a called strike three from Barrett. Nady had good reason to keep the bat on his shoulder, because Barrett started off with a tight strike zone. He issued six walks in the first three innings. Thereafter, either he widened up or the pitchers sharpened up, because he finished the game with 15 strikeouts, six of them called. Behind Carlos Zambrano, the visiting Cubs won, 8–3.

Because Barrett works in the International League, he will most likely be found working games in the Midwest and on the East Coast if he remains a Triple-A call-up.

Ted Barrett

BORN: July 31, 1965
FIRST MAJOR LEAGUE GAME: May 28, 1994
FAVORS: Pitchers
THEY HATE HIM IN: Hell

	2007	2008	2009	2010	Totals
Games	34	34	34	35	137
Innings	307.17	305	299.17	305.5	1,216.83
R/9	10.08	8.17	8.48	10.08	9.21
BB/9	6.15	5.46	5.99	6.04	5.91
K/9	13.45	14.67	12.85	14.32	13.82
K/BB	2.19	2.69	2.15	2.37	2.34

Barrett is among the game's biggest umpires, standing 6'4" and weighing 255 pounds. Only Joe West admits to weighing more. Conventional wisdom has it that big, tall umps like Barrett have trouble calling the low strike, forcing pitchers to come up, which leads to more hard-hit balls and higher scores. That's not the case with Barrett. Although his R/9 has a crater-like character, starting at a high 10.08 in 2007, plunging almost two full runs in 2008, staying down in 2009, then returning to 10.08 in 2010, overall he's more congenial to pitchers. His 13.82 K/9 from 2007 through 2010 is right at the major league average, and his BB/9 of 5.91 is five percent below average. That gives him a higher than normal K/BB ratio, which helps explain why his total R/9 is slightly below average.

Also, if Barrett forced pitchers to throw higher strikes to get a call, it would cause more balls to leave the park. Only in 2010 was that the case. His rate of home runs per nine innings (HR/9) was very close to the norm in 2007 and 2008, and was way below the norm in 2009. But in 2010 his HR/9 soared to 12 percent above the norm. Remarkably, Barrett's BB/9, K/9, and K/BB were all exactly average that year. So by contributing to high slash stats of .272/.337/.429, the extra homers were the main reason Barrett's R/9 jumped to third amongst umps in 2010.

Barrett is more open than most umpires about his personal life. He was born in Pasco, Washington, but spent his childhood in upstate New York and the San Francisco Bay Area. He took up boxing and was good enough to spar with George Foreman and Evander Holyfield. His father, horrified by his son's career path, offered to pay for umpire school. Tempted by a free vacation in Florida, Barrett accepted. Turned out he had the knack, and five years later, a rapid rise by modern standards, he reached the major leagues.

Barrett is deeply religious, professing the kind of muscular Christianity popular in the nineteenth century. "A Christian can be a football player, and a good one. He can knock an opponent flat on his back. He just needs to help him up afterwards," he told an interviewer for the World Umpires Association. An ordained minister, he earned a master's in biblical studies from Trinity University in 2007 and is highly active in Calling for Christ, a ministry for umpires. He's often asked to lead the umps in prayer before union meetings. "It's kind of funny because I pray and ten seconds later, harsh words start flying," he said. Perhaps he's motivated by the well-worn joke, told even by some umpires, about Satan challenging God to a winner-take-all baseball game. "You must be crazy," God says, "Here in heaven I've got the greatest players of all time." To which Satan smiles and says, "Yes, but I've got the umpires."

Barrett's size and cheek-turning disposition serve him well on the field. His ejection rate for the period under study is less than half that of his peers. His career rate is much higher (2.4 percent), but it's distorted by one game. On April 24, 2005, Barrett was calling balls and strikes for the Boston Red Sox and Tampa Bay Devil Rays. A beanball war broke out in the seventh inning, leading to a brawl. Barrett ejected four men that inning and two more in the eighth when the beanballing resumed. Thus in the span of two innings he accumulated one-eighth of all the ejections he's amassed over a 17-year career. Barrett's most notorious ejection occurred on August 14, 2007, when he threw

Atlanta manager Bobby Cox out of a game against the San Francisco Giants. It was Cox's 132nd ejection, making him the most ejected man of all time. For 75 years the record had belonged to John McGraw, legendary manager of the New York Giants. "Just routine arguing balls and strikes. Nothing out of the ordinary from other ejections," Barrett said after the game.

Barrett was behind the plate when David Cone of the New York Yankees hurled a perfect game against the Montreal Expos — the first interleague perfecto — on July 18, 1999 at Yankee Stadium. He was also calling the pitches on August 7, 2004, when Greg Maddux, in his second stint for the Chicago Cubs, earned his 300th win.

SOURCE

Williamson, Dana. "Growing Number of Umpires Are 'Calling for Christ.'" BPSports.net, August 15, 2007. (October 15, 2010.) http://www.bpsports.net/bpsports.asp?ID=5643.

Scott Barry

BORN: August 3, 1976
FIRST MAJOR LEAGUE GAME: June 4, 2006
FAVORS: Hitters, strongly
THEY HATE HIM IN: Philadelphia

	2007	2008	2009	2010	Totals
Games	8	30	40	33	111
Innings	71.17	261.33	346.33	293	971.83
R/9	12.39	10.23	8.99	9.71	9.79
BB/9	8.98	6.82	7.20	5.90	6.83
K/9	12.77	13.02	13.36	13.42	13.24
K/BB	1.42	1.91	1.86	2.28	1.94

When Barry came up in 2006 for an abbreviated stint (he worked 20 games, five behind home plate) he gave no indication he would be a hitter's umpire. Pitchers were credited with 21 strikeouts in each of his first two games behind the plate. His R/9 over 43.33 innings was a measly 7.89. In 2007 he was called up for a second tour of the bigs and was a completely different umpire. His R/9 soared to 12.39, propelled by a BB/9 that was nearly half again the standard. On July 20, 2007, he granted 15 bases on balls in a game between the Tampa Bay Devil Rays and New York Yankees.

But the Lords of Baseball liked what they saw and installed Barry as a *de facto* regular umpire. He worked 900 innings behind home plate from 2008 through 2010, and for the most part his numbers reflect the general trend of fewer walks and more strikeouts. But even in 2010, when his BB/9 fell significantly, his K/BB ratio was lower than average.

Overall he has the ninth highest BB/9 and the ninth lowest K/9 of the 77 umpires who worked 500 or more innings during the period under study. His cumulative K/BB of 1.94 is fifth lowest of all umpires. That puts him solidly in the hitters' camp, which is also reflected in his four-year R/9 of 9.79, five percent higher than average. Based on the number of games he has worked as a Triple-A call-up, Barry is very likely to receive one of the three or four major league umpiring jobs that come available in 2011. Hitters should rejoice.

Barry has a slow fuse. He worked 155 games in 2009, and only James Hoye put in more innings behind the plate. Yet he had just one ejection, Boston manager Terry Francona in the aftermath of a serious fight between the Red Sox' Kevin Youkilis and Detroit pitcher Rick Porcello. He had three ejections in 2010, but two came on one play, a disputed strike call against the Washington Nationals' Ryan Zimmerman that ended with Zimmerman and his manager, Jim Riggleman, sent to the showers. The other came in the 14th inning of the August 24 game between the Houston Astros and Philadelphia Phillies. Barry was at third base. Responding to appeal requests from home plate umpire Greg Gibson, Barry called two check-swing strikes on Phillie slugger Ryan Howard, including strike three. Howard glared at Barry after the first call, and Barry glared back, matching Howard's body language by putting his hands on his hips. After the second call, Howard threw his bat and helmet in anger, whereupon Barry bounced him. Replays showed that Barry got the calls right, but that didn't stop former Phillie pitcher Mitch "Wild Thing" Williams from blogging on Major League Baseball's web site that Barry deserved a reprimand — one of the milder things said about Barry by Phillie fan bloggers.

Although they wouldn't agree in Philadelphia, Andre Ethier of the Los Angeles Dodgers may have provided the best description of Barry's comportment after Barry ruled foul his liner down the right field line on August 1, 2009. Replays showed the ball landed fair. Ethier screamed at Barry, who said nothing. But later in the game, after Ethier apologized for his outburst, a contrite Barry apologized for missing the call. "You have to give him a lot of credit for owning up to that," Ethier told the *Los Angeles Times*.

SOURCE

Hernandez, Dylan. "Dodgers Fall to Derek Lowe and Braves." *Los Angeles Times,* August 2, 2009. (October 16, 2010.) http://articles.latimes.com/2009/aug/02/sports/sp-dodgers-braves2.

Damien Beal

BORN: April 26, 1973
FIRST MAJOR LEAGUE GAME: August 24, 2007
FAVORS: Pitchers, if the tiny sample size is indicative
THEY HATE HIM IN: Nowhere yet

	2007	2008	2009	2010	Totals
Games	0	6	8	0	14
Innings	0	52.5	69	0	121.5
R/9	0.00	8.23	8.74	0.00	8.52
BB/9	0.00	6.86	6.00	0.00	6.37
K/9	0.00	15.60	12.52	0.00	13.85
K/BB	0.00	2.27	2.09	0.00	2.17

A Triple-A call-up, Beal appeared in a couple of games at third base in 2007. He didn't get his first shot behind the plate until May 8, 2008, when he called a game between the Milwaukee Brewers and Florida Marlins. His first home plate assignment of 2009 was also a game involving the Brewers and Marlins. Later in 2009 he called three Brewers-Pirates games. It's unusual for a full-time ump to handle plate duties for a team more than three times a season. For a part-timer to call balls and strikes for the same team five times in 14 starts? That's way strange. It certainly wasn't the Brewers' idea. They lost four of the five games.

Based on the few games he's called, Beal looks like the epitome of plate judgment. His BB/9, K/9, and K/BB are almost exactly equal to the major league averages for the combined 2008 and 2009 campaigns. He's classified as a pitchers' umpire because his R/9 is nine percent lower than average for those two seasons. Further analysis of his low R/9 reveals that his home run rate (HR/9) is six percent lower than average for 2008 and 2009, meaning another couple of home runs should have been hit during the games he called. But even if both homers were grand slams, they wouldn't have gotten him to an average R/9. The low R/9 is more likely an anomaly attributable to the small sample size, and could disappear if he's given more work.

Despite his promise as a plate umpire, it appears unlikely Beal will get much chance to raise that low R/9. After a cup of coffee in April, he did not see any major league action in 2010. At this point he is a long shot for a big league job. He turned 37 shortly after the 2010 season began and spent his eighth year at the Triple-A International League. There are numerous veteran Triple-A call-ups ahead of him, and several rookie umpires got more time in the majors than he did in 2010, suggesting they may have passed him as well.

Beal is one of the few African American umpires at baseball's upper levels. Born in Baton Rouge, he attended Louisiana's Southern University, which also helped launch the major league careers of Lou Brock, Trenidad Hubbard, Rickie Weeks, and Fred Lewis.

SOURCE

Schiefelbein, Joseph. "Beal Joins Three Other Ex-Jaguars in Majors." MEAC/SWAC Sports Main Street, August 31, 2007. (October 16, 2010.) http://meacswacsports.blogspot.com/2007/08/beal-joins-three-other-ex-jaguars-in.html.

Wally Bell

BORN: January 10, 1965
FIRST MAJOR LEAGUE GAME: June 16, 1992
FAVORS: Pitchers, slightly
THEY HATE HIM IN: Lance Berkman's house

	2007	2008	2009	2010	Totals
Games	33	36	38	34	141
Innings	291.83	324	335.33	302.5	1,253.67
R/9	10.15	9.11	9.42	8.75	9.35
BB/9	6.41	5.86	6.33	5.36	5.99
K/9	13.45	13.75	14.17	15.20	14.14
K/BB	2.10	2.35	2.24	2.84	2.36

Bell started as a National League umpire in 1992 but almost didn't make it to the millennium, weathering two career crises in 1999. First he needed bypass surgery. Then his union told him to resign. Bell survived the heart operation, and maintains that his proudest moment as an umpire was returning to work after that ordeal. The resignation was dicier. It was a poorly-conceived negotiating ploy by the union, and Bell, reminded by the health scare not to take his job for granted, soon thought better of it. Within days he and Jeff Nelson became the only National League umps to rescind their resignations. The move quite possibly saved their careers. Twenty-two of their more stubborn colleagues, most of them National Leaguers, were fired.

Although Bell's backtracking made him unpopular among union die-hards, he found a home under the wing of John Hirschbeck, who led the rebellion against the old union and served as first president of the new (and current) umpires' union. Bell joined Hirschbeck's crew and has been an exemplary employee since. His career ejection rate is 1.6 percent, more than 25 percent lower than average, and he didn't eject anyone in 2010. Since 2001 he's missed only one week of work (in 2007), and in 2010 he bounced right back from a July 30 bout of heat exhaustion that forced him to leave a game. He ranks fourth in innings behind the plate from 2007 to 2010, behind only James Hoye, Rob Drake, and Chris Guccione, all of whom were overworked Triple-A call-ups for part of that period. And his 9.35 R/9 from 2007 through 2010 is only .04 from average, less than half a percent.

Bell's game-calling stats from 2007 through 2009 were all within one percent of the major league norm. In 2010 he joined the trend toward pitchers, reducing his BB/9 by nearly one walk per nine innings and increasing his K/9 by roughly the same amount. His 2010 K/BB soared to fourth highest of all umpires. The extreme 2010 dropped his four-year BB/9 to three percent lower than average and raised his K/9 to two percent higher than average, both of which favor pitchers. For that reason he rates as a pitchers' umpire. But given the uncharacteristic nature of his 2010, it would come as no surprise if he shows more generosity to hitters in the future.

Bell endured considerable criticism for trying to finish an August 4, 2008 game between the Houston Astros and Chicago Cubs while tornado sirens blared. The game had already been delayed nearly three hours after the fifth inning by an epic rainstorm. Acting as crew chief in Hirschbeck's absence, Bell called the teams back on the field at 10:24 P.M. They managed to play the sixth, seventh, and part of the eighth before Astro first baseman Lance Berkman rebelled. As the wind picked up and lightning struck closer, he first removed the metal chain around his neck, then fled for the dugout. "You have to be an idiot to stand outside during a lightning storm. That's just common sense," he told the Associated Press. (In fairness, Berkman was referring to himself as an idiot, not Bell.) Rather than demand the Astros put a first baseman on the field or forfeit, Bell suspended play and, a few minutes later, called the game with the Cubs ahead 2–0. "I would never put any team or player or umpire in harm's way," he explained, but "this time of year with the playoffs and teams in contention, we know it's tough. I don't really want to be here at midnight, but that's our job, that's what you do."

When Roger Clemens won his 350th game, a 5–1 Yankee win over the Minnesota Twins on July 2, 2007, Bell worked home plate. It was the first time in 44 years an umpire had presided over a pitcher's 350th victory (Bill Jackowski called Warren Spahn's 350th on September 29, 1963). Prior to that, Bell's most significant interaction with Clemens had been a lowlight for the ace hurler. Those who remember the 2000 Yankee-Met World Series may recall that Clemens tried to spear Met catcher Mike Piazza with a shattered bat. Charlie Reliford capably handled that situation, but on June 15, 2002, Clemens came to bat at Shea Stadium for the first time since the 2000 Series. Met pitcher Shawn Estes greeted Clemens with a fastball behind the knees, a purpose pitch if ever there was one. Bell, the home plate umpire, immediately warned both benches, preventing a beanball war. But he couldn't save Clemens from an 8–0 shellacking that commenced when Clemens failed to cover home on an Estes sacrifice that advanced Rey Ordonez from second to third. Ordonez alertly scored, and the distracted Clemens was done for.

SOURCE

Walker, Ben. "Umpire Recovering from Five-Bypass Surgery." *Los Angeles Times,* May 2, 1999. (October 16, 2010.) http://articles.latimes.com/1999/may/02/sports/sp-33353.

Dan Bellino

BORN: October 10, 1978
FIRST MAJOR LEAGUE GAME: June 25, 2008
FAVORS: Pitchers
THEY HATE HIM IN: Chicago — how could he treat his homeboys this way?

	2007	2008	2009	2010	Totals
Games	0	0	8	24	32
Innings	0	0	71	216.83	287.83
R/9	0.00	0.00	8.11	9.21	8.94
BB/9	0.00	0.00	5.32	6.02	5.85
K/9	0.00	0.00	16.48	14.32	14.85
K/BB	0.00	0.00	3.10	2.38	2.54

The Chicago-born Bellino participated in just one major league game in 2008, substituting at third base for Mike Winters during an interleague contest at Wrigley Field. The Cubs won. But in 2009, Bellino got three starts behind home plate at Wrigley and the Cubs lost them all, scoring a total of four runs. He also called a pair of games on the South Side. The White Sox salvaged a split. Of Bellino's three other appearances behind home plate in 2009, one was in Milwaukee, so through 2009 he had called only two big league games beyond a 90-mile radius of his hometown.

That changed in 2010, as the International League-based Bellino replaced veteran Paul Schrieber in Joe West's crew for most of the second half. Only two of his starts behind home plate were in Chicago. The rest ranged from Boston to San Diego. Bellino was still giving his hometown teams fits, however, as the White Sox went 0–3 in games when he called balls and strikes, and the Cubs lost the only game he called for them.

Bellino's 2010 statistics put his strike zone squarely in the middle. His BB/9 was half a percent lower than average and his K/9 was half a percent above average, making his K/BB a scant one percent above average. His R/9 was four percent higher than average, somewhat anomalous in that his slash stats weren't that far from the norm: batting average eight points higher, on-base percentage six points higher, and slugging percentage three points *lower*. Most likely a full season of work — another ten starts behind home plate — would have brought his R/9 down a bit.

Bellino can be found on YouTube telling an interviewer that "the integrity of baseball is the most important part of umpiring." On June 9, 2009, Milwaukee outfielder Mike Cameron called Bellino's integrity into question. Cameron was in the midst of appealing a suspension for bumping umpire Marvin Hudson three days earlier, and was batting with runners on first and second and two out in the third inning. Bellino, starting just his second major league game behind home plate, called him out on strikes. Cameron looked back as if to say, "You're getting even for what I did to Hudson, aren't you?" but held his peace. Bellino didn't say anything either and the incident ended.

Thanks to Cameron's silence, Bellino's first big league ejection didn't come until April 23, 2010. With Tampa Bay losing 6–1 to Toronto, Grant Balfour of the Rays threw a 1–2 pitch low to Adam Lind. Balfour's catcher, Dioner Navarro, disagreed with the call. He stood up, turned around, and said so. His chest protector may have grazed Bellino in the process. Bellino unhesitatingly ejected him. Bellino amassed three more ejections in 2010, giving him a higher than average ejection rate, not surprising given that he's a new umpire and players and managers are testing him.

One of those tests came on August 25, when Bellino called strike three on a plainly unhappy Adrian Beltre of the Boston Red Sox. Beltre claimed that when he went to play defense, he engaged in trash talk with Felix Hernandez of the Seattle Mariners, the former teammate who had just struck him out. Bellino believed Beltre was jawing at him, so he threw Beltre out of the game. When Boston manager Terry Francona protested, Bellino tossed him as well. "I figure if a guy's old enough to throw you out, he's old enough to get yelled at," Francona said.

Bellino is the in-a-hurry, high-achiever type. While working as a minor league umpire he earned an MBA and graduated from law school. "There's no question that law school has been a major help," he told *Street & Smith's Sports Business Journal*. "My baseball rule book is, geez, 80 pages. That's one night's reading in law school." Why did he go into umpiring when a career in law would have been a surer bet? "I wouldn't love it as much," he said. Based on the volume of work he received in 2010 and his solid sense of the strike zone, Bellino is likely to land a major league job, although he probably won't get one of the openings that come available in 2011.

SOURCE

Hyman, Mark. "Behind the Plate or Approaching the Bench, He's a Special Case." *Street & Smith's Sports Business Journal,* August 16, 2004. (October 16, 2010.) http://www.sportsbusinessjournal.com/article/40272.

Cory Blaser

BORN: December 8, 1981
FIRST MAJOR LEAGUE GAME: April 24, 2010
FAVORS: Way too early to tell
THEY HATE HIM IN: Colorado and Oakland

	2007	2008	2009	2010	Totals
Games	0	0	0	2	2
Innings	0	0	0	17.5	17.5
R/9	0.00	0.00	0.00	6.17	6.17
BB/9	0.00	0.00	0.00	4.11	4.11
K/9	0.00	0.00	0.00	19.03	19.03
K/BB	0.00	0.00	0.00	4.63	4.63

In his third season with the Pacific Coast League, Blaser finally got the call to the big leagues. "I went to umpiring school just after I had turned 20, and I had always thought to myself that if I could just work one game in the big leagues then it will all have been worth it," he told MLB.com in May 2010. He realized his dream and more. Not only was his first day in the big leagues in his home state of Colorado, but he got to work *two* games as the Florida Marlins and Colorado Rockies made up for a rainout by playing a doubleheader. Blaser handled first base in the afternoon game and third base in the nightcap. "It's something I will cherish forever, but at the same time it makes me even hungrier," he said.

Blaser's first integrity test came a few weeks later, when he was again working first base at a Rockie game, this time against the Philadelphia Phillies. With the score tied in the bottom of the ninth, Colorado's speedy Eric Young Jr. led off with a grounder into the hole at short. The play at first was bang-bang, and Blaser called it in favor of the Phillies. Colorado manager Jim Tracy bounded from the dugout to argue and quickly became vehement. Blaser unhesitatingly tossed him. Acting crew chief Brian O'Nora had to step between Blaser and Tracy and prod Tracy to leave. Even with the benefit of replays from multiple angles, it was impossible to determine whether Blaser got the call right, so Tracy had no grounds to argue. The Rockies wound up winning in the tenth.

Blaser returned to the majors on August 9, 2010, for a series between Oakland and Seattle. It was the Mariners' first game under new manager Daren Brown, and to celebrate they turned a 5–4–3 triple play. Blaser made the call on the third out, which batter Mark Ellis hotly disputed. "I was safe. There's not really anything else to say," Ellis grumbled afterward. The next night Blaser called his first major league game. This too was memorable, as Felix Hernandez of the Mariners went eight shutout innings and struck out 13. Hernandez was nearly matched by Oakland's Brett Anderson, who went seven and gave up just one run, striking out seven. Blaser called only two walks, but that didn't necessarily signal that he's an extreme pitchers' umpire, because he called only four of the game's 21 strikeouts; the rest were swinging. Mark Ellis went 0-for-3 with three strikeouts.

Blaser was brought back to the majors for the final week of the 2010 season and called an uneventful game between the Cleveland Indians and Chicago White Sox.

SOURCE

Hill, Benjamin. "Umps Follow Same Road as Players." MLB.com, May 14, 2010. (October 16, 2010.) http://www.minorleaguebaseball.com/news/article.jsp?ymd=20100514&content_id=10030356&vkey=news_milb&fext=.jsp.

C.B. Bucknor

BORN: August 23, 1962
FIRST MAJOR LEAGUE GAME: April 4, 1996
FAVORS: Hitters, slightly
THEY HATE HIM IN: Every major league clubhouse

	2007	2008	2009	2010	Totals
Games	34	33	35	34	136
Innings	296.83	288.83	310	315.5	1,211.17
R/9	10.04	8.60	9.35	9.73	9.44
BB/9	5.85	5.92	6.85	6.36	6.26
K/9	12.92	13.87	14.28	13.75	13.71
K/BB	2.21	2.34	2.08	2.16	2.19

C.B. Bucknor is the most hated umpire in baseball.

Sports Illustrated conducted a poll of 550 major league players in 2003 and asked whom they considered the worst umpire. Bucknor won hands-down, named by nearly 21 percent. The only other ump to finish in double figures was Bruce Froemming, the legendary, expletive-spouting veteran who retired in 2007. *Sports Illustrated* repeated the poll in 2006, this time gathering 470 player responses. Bucknor and Froemming again finished one-two, with Bucknor repeating his 21 percent tally. In June 2010 *ESPN The Magazine* polled a hundred players, 50 in each league, and they voted Bucknor the game's poorest umpire. Fans don't like Bucknor either. He so provoked otherwise mild-mannered Toronto Blue Jay partisans that in 2006 they started an on-line petition to get him fired.

Why is C.B. Bucknor so reviled? That's hard to answer, because his critics are either incoherent or rendered so by his actions. Take Curt Schilling, whose Red Sox were enraged by a pair of bad calls Bucknor made at first base during the opening game of the 2009 American League Division Series. The next morning, Schilling titled his blog "Why C.B. Bucknor Is Not a Good Umpire." First he wrote that a bad ump is always fighting with coaches and players — only to back off a paragraph later by saying, "I don't think C.B. is that guy." Then Schilling wrote that a bad ump causes both hitters and pitchers to complain — and proceeded to talk about Joe West, with not a word about Bucknor.

Bucknor has a slow fuse. From 2007 to 2010 he threw out only six disputants, giving him an ejection rate for the period of slightly more than one percent. Even in 2003 and 2006, when the players trashed him to *Sports Illustrated,* he had just two ejections. In 2010, the year of the ESPN survey, he had three ejections, a middling total. So Schilling was right to reconsider: Bucknor *isn't* the kind of guy always fighting coaches and players.

The numbers suggest that Bucknor's problem may be inconsistency. Look at his annual R/9s. In 2007 he was at 10.04. Then he dipped all the way to 8.60. In 2009 he went back up to 9.35, and in 2010, while the major league R/9 was dropping nearly half a run, his went *up* to 9.73. His BB/9 held steady in 2007 and 2008, but then in 2009 he called an additional walk per game, and though his BB/9 came down in 2010, it was still five percent higher than average. His K/9 shot up by a full strikeout in 2008, went up again in 2009, then fell in 2010.

Yet when you combine Bucknor's results for the last four years, he comes close to the middle in every statistical category. Of the 77 umpires who called 500 or more innings from 2007 to 2010, Bucknor ranked 30th in R/9, 35th in BB/9, 44th in K/9, and 47th in K/BB. This may be what Curt Schilling and his fellow clubhouse pundits are groping for: Although Bucknor's aggregate numbers put him in the middle of the pack, they may be a synthesis of extremes rather than evidence of steady performance.

Players may also resent that Bucknor is unafraid of making controversial calls — calls that can make him the focus of the game. Remember the New York Mets' epic collapse in September 2007? They led the National League East by seven games on September 12 and wound up losing the division to Philadelphia. The Mets' fall was foreshadowed on August 29, when they had runners on first and third with one out in the ninth and trailed the Phillies by one run. Met batter Shawn Green grounded to Phillie shortstop Jimmy Rollins, who tossed to second in hopes of starting a double play. But second baseman Tad Iguchi's throw to first was wide, and the tying run scored — until Bucknor, working second base, called runner's interference on Marlon Anderson, the Met going from first to second, and ruled that Iguchi would have completed the double play. Not only did Bucknor's call nullify the tying run, it ended the game. "You can't end a game on a call like that," fumed the Mets' Billy Wagner. Responded crew chief Joe West, "C.B. made a great call, a gutsy call and didn't back down." Nor was it the first time Bucknor had made such a call. On May 25, 2004, he ended a one-run game between the Detroit Tigers and Kansas City Royals the same way. This time the runner was Detroit's Carlos Guillen. Bucknor conceded that Guillen was in the baseline, but "there wasn't any doubt. The runner said he slid before the bag, but it was quite obvious he was way past the bag" in a blatant attempt to block out Royal second baseman Desi Relaford.

Hailing from Jamaica, Bucknor is one of three foreign-born major league umpires. The others are Angel Hernandez and Alfonso Marquez.

SOURCE

Schilling, Curt. "Why C.B. Bucknor Is Not a Good Umpire." Curt Schilling's Official Blog, October 9, 2009. (October 16, 2010.) http://38pitches.weei.com/sports/boston/baseball/curt-schilling/general/2009/10/09/why-c-b-bucknor-is-not-a-good-umpire/.

Angel Campos

BORN: August 22, 1973
FIRST MAJOR LEAGUE GAME: May 3, 2007
FAVORS: Hitters
THEY HATE HIM IN: Tampa Bay

	2007	2008	2009	2010	Totals
Games	6	27	27	25	85
Innings	54	232.5	242.17	218.17	746.83
R/9	9.83	11.30	8.96	10.07	10.07
BB/9	6.17	6.00	5.57	7.30	6.25
K/9	14.67	14.79	14.38	14.04	14.42
K/BB	2.38	2.47	2.58	1.92	2.31

If you're looking for evidence that the size of an umpire's strike zone has little to do with the number of runs scored, look no further than Triple-A call-up Angel Campos. His totals from 2007 through 2009 showed that he had one of the biggest strike zones in the major leagues, with a K/9 of 14.59 and a K/BB ratio of 2.51. Yet his R/9 was 10.08, six percent *higher* than average. His 11.30 R/9 in 2008 led the majors. Still, there *does* tend to be a correlation between runs scored and strike zone size, and the odds finally caught up with Campos in 2010. His R/9 matched his career average at 10.07 and was fourth highest of all umps. But this time there was symmetry as his K/BB of 1.92 was fifth lowest, a consequence of his walk rate rocketing up by 1.73 and his strikeout rate dipping by .34.

Even though 2010 evened things out somewhat, Campos's four-year R/9 is more than seven percent higher than the major league average, ranking him the fourth most run-friendly umpire to work 500 innings or more behind home plate from 2007 to 2010. Over the same period, he has the fifth highest K/9. The likely explanation for this contradictory combination is that he has a high strike zone, something of a surprise in that he is only 5' 9". High strike zones usually lead to both more home runs and more strikeouts. In 2008, Campos's HR/9 was 2.44, miles above the major league average of 2.03. His home run rate dropped in 2008, but in 2010 it took off again, to 2.32 compared to a league-wide 1.92.

Campos's temper appears to run hot and cold. In 2007 he didn't eject anyone. In 2008 he had six ejections. In 2009 he instigated just one ejection, but in 2010 amassed four in only 103 games. Three of his four 2010 ejections concerned called strike threes. On April 15 he rang up Derrek Lee of the Cubs, whose protests earned him a dismissal. Twelve days later Campos called strike three on James Loney of the Los Angeles Dodgers, who argued briefly, walked away, but threw his batting glove in disgust, prompting Campos to run him. "I think it was unnecessary and just unfortunate that it happened — on the part of the umpire, not James," said Dodger manager Joe Torre. And on July 4 Campos took the bat out Cincinnati slugger Joey Votto's hands in the first inning of a game against the Cubs. Votto made the mistake of throwing his helmet after losing a brief argument with Campos. Replays showed that Campos might have made a mistake on the pitch to Loney, but was right on the other two. The fourth ejection of 2010 came on August 24, after Campos called Evan Longoria of the Tampa Bay Rays out at second on a steal attempt. Campos ruled that Longoria beat the throw but came off the bag while Los Angeles Angel shortstop Erick Aybar was still tagging him. Tampa manager Joe Maddon disagreed and was banished.

On September 11, 2010, Campos was getting ready to work the plate in a game between the Minnesota Twins and Cleveland Indians when he fell ill. He was rushed to the hospital and diagnosed with appendicitis. The appendectomy prematurely ended his season. Even so, he finished fifth among Triple-A call-ups in innings behind the plate in 2010, meaning he remains a serious contender for promotion to major league status.

On July 24, 2008, Campos called one of the most impressive (if unrecognized) pitching duels of recent years. Tim Redding of the Washington Nationals and Matt Cain of the victorious San Francisco Giants each went the distance in a 1–0 game. Neither gave up a walk. The game was played in two hours flat.

SOURCE

Gurnick, Ken. "Loney Ejected for Arguing Balls and Strikes." MLB.com, April 27, 2010. (October 16, 2010.) http://mlb.mlb.com/news/article.jsp?ymd=20100427&content_id=9622454&key=news_mlb&fext=.jsp&c_id=mlb.

Victor Carapazza

BORN: July 6, 1979
FIRST MAJOR LEAGUE GAME: April 9, 2010
FAVORS: Too early to tell
THEY HATE HIM IN: Also too early to tell

	2007	2008	2009	2010	Totals
Games	0	0	0	7	7
Innings	0	0	0	60.17	60.17
R/9	0.00	0.00	0.00	7.78	7.78
BB/9	0.00	0.00	0.00	6.43	6.43
K/9	0.00	0.00	0.00	13.16	13.16
K/BB	0.00	0.00	0.00	2.05	2.05

"I was pretty good in the field but couldn't hit. You realize you are not going to get to the ultimate level. I loved the game so much." That's typically how an umpiring career is born: Injury or lack of ability causes an ambitious player to try an alternative route to the big leagues. But Carapazza's path wasn't as direct as the one taken by most of his colleagues. Four years elapsed between the end of his playing days and his arrival in umpire school. He enlisted in the Air Force first and was stationed mostly stateside, but also in Kuwait. "When I got to umpire school, I loved umpiring. It's the best job in the world. Oh my God, I love it to death," he told the *Sarasota Herald Tribune* in 2006.

After two years in the Pacific Coast League, Carapazza transferred to the International League in 2010, presumably to be closer to his family in Tennessee. Shortly before the season began he was named a Triple-A call-up. He worked his first big league game behind home plate on June 5. Jon Lester led the Boston Red Sox to an 8–2 win over the host Baltimore Orioles. Carapazza's first called strike three was on Ty Wigginton of the Orioles. The first beneficiary of a Carapazza ball four call was Dustin Pedroia of the Red Sox, at the expense of Oriole starting pitcher Jeremy Guthrie.

Carapazza didn't get another home plate assignment until after the All-Star break. On July 18 he worked the game between Pittsburgh and Houston. The Pirates' Paul Maholm tossed a three-hit shutout but recorded just one strikeout (called). Roy Oswalt took the loss. Later in July, Carapazza called games between Washington and Milwaukee and between Chicago and Houston. Of the eight teams competing in Carapazza's first four home plate assignments, seven had losing records. Major League Baseball was breaking him in slowly.

Over the last couple weeks of the 2010 season the Lords of Baseball took another look at Carapazza. He worked the plate for two Florida Marlin games. The Fish won both, making six times out of seven the home team won when Carapazza called balls and strikes. Although his sample size is too small to draw conclusions from, in 2010 he showed a hitter-friendly strike zone. Hitters failed to capitalize on it, though, compiling a low 7.78 R/9. The contradiction didn't seem to worry his big league supervisors. Of all rookie umpires, only Al Porter was assigned more innings behind the plate than Carapazza.

Lots of players are superstitious. Umpire Carapazza is too. "I always carry Halls Cough Drops in my left pocket. Whether I have a cold or not and whether it's hot or cold outside, I always have them." That's because he once lost his voice during a minor league game. "I try and do things very hard, crisp, and assertive," he explained.

SOURCE

Pentz, Perry D. "The Minor Leagues: Behind the Scenes." *Sarasota Herald Tribune,* July 22, 2006. (October 17, 2010.) http://www.heraldtribune.com/article/20060722/SPORTS/607220595?p=1&tc=pg.

Mark Carlson

BORN: July 11, 1969
FIRST MAJOR LEAGUE GAME: June 11, 1999
FAVORS: Pitchers
THEY HATE HIM IN: His doctor's office — guys who have been through what he has medically shouldn't be doing what he does

	2007	2008	2009	2010	Totals
Games	34	1	35	35	105
Innings	305.83	8.5	308	305.5	927.83
R/9	8.89	5.29	8.50	10.19	9.16
BB/9	5.41	6.35	6.49	6.83	6.25
K/9	14.07	9.53	14.26	14.08	14.09
K/BB	2.60	1.50	2.20	2.06	2.26

It started as numbness and tingling down his arms, along with problems turning his neck. The diagnosis: disc degeneration. As the symptoms worsened, he tried all sorts of non-invasive treatments, including steroids. By spring 2008 he could barely function, so after the first week of the season, Mark Carlson underwent surgery to remove three herniated discs and fuse his bottom cervical vertebrae with his top thoracic vertebra. Anyone familiar with spinal issues will recognize how serious an operation that was.

What caused his neck to deteriorate? "I've taken multiple foul balls and fast pitches to the face and neck, which obviously caused some problems, but that's just one part of the wear and tear of baseball," Carlson said. "It's also different beds and pillows, traveling on airplanes every three days — it all takes a toll on the body." There was no guarantee the surgery would permit him to work as an umpire again, but happily he made a strong recovery.

Pitchers were particularly glad to see Carlson back, because it's hard to find a more textbook example of pro-pitcher game calling than Carlson's 2007, which featured a BB/9 11 percent below average and a K/9 five percent above average, leading to an R/9 eight percent below average. Strike zones don't get much more generous or produce more favorable results for hurlers. And though Carlson's walk rate increased substantially after 2007, he remained favorable to pitchers, posting the second lowest R/9 among umpires from 2007 through 2009.

But in 2010 Carlson showed more sympathy for hitters. His walk rate rose five percent, his strikeout rate dropped slightly, and his R/9 increased by an amazing 1.69 to 10.19, second in the league. A home run rate of 2.56, way above the league average of 1.92 and second among all umpires (Sam Holbrook was tops at 2.68), undoubtedly had as much to do with the jump in R/9 as his slightly smaller strike zone. On July 24, 2010, former pitcher Mike Krukow, now an announcer for the San Francisco Giants, told his television audience that Carlson wasn't giving pitchers knee-level strikes anymore. So pitchers may not be as fond of Carlson as they once were. But even after 2010, his four-year totals lean their way in every category.

One pitcher definitely not fond of Carlson is the Chicago Cubs' Carlos Zambrano. On May 27, 2009, the volatile Zambrano was leading the Pittsburgh Pirates 2–1 in the seventh inning at Wrigley Field. It's unlikely Zambrano had any simmering complaints about the strike zone: Carlson had dinged him for just two walks (Zambrano's 2009 BB/9, after factoring out intentional passes, was 3.83) and called five third strikes for him. With a runner on third and one out, though, Zambrano let loose a 58-footer that bounced away from catcher Geovany Soto. Zambrano ran home to cover the plate and took Soto's throw, but Carlson ruled that Pirate baserunner Nyjer Morgan slid under Zambrano's tag. That was it. The beefy Cub ace went crazy, bumping Carlson and poking a finger within inches of Carlson's nose. Carlson threw him out, whereupon Zambrano heaved the ball into the outfield, threw his glove, and slammed a plastic cooler with a bat while Cub manager Lou Piniella tried to calm him down. Replays showed that Joliet native Carlson had been absolutely right: Morgan had slipped his left hand past Zambrano's tag and scored. Major League Baseball suspended Zambrano for six days and fined him $3,000. Even Zambrano deemed the punishment fair.

Perhaps Carlson's service in the Marine Corps helped him stand up to Zambrano. Although he isn't known for a short fuse, he doesn't take a lot of guff either. His career ejection rate of 2.6 percent is nearly 20 percent higher than average.

Kevin Causey

BORN: August 13, 1978
FIRST MAJOR LEAGUE GAME: September 2, 2006
FAVORED: R/9 says pitchers, K/BB says hitters, statisticians say sample size too small
THEY HATED HIM IN: Milwaukee

	2007	2008	2009	2010	Totals
Games	0	9	5	0	14
Innings	0	80.5	43.5	0	124
R/9	0.00	10.51	6.00	0.00	8.93
BB/9	0.00	6.71	6.41	0.00	6.61
K/9	0.00	10.96	14.28	0.00	12.12
K/BB	0.00	1.63	2.23	0.00	1.84

A Triple-A call-up, Causey worked four major league contests in 2006 and one in 2007 before getting a real chance in 2008, when he saw action in 52 games. In 2009 he got into another 24 big league games. But of his 81 total games, only 14 were behind the plate.

Like a talented but raw pitcher, Causey was inconsistent. His 2008 numbers, compiled over nine plate appearances, evidenced a very small strike zone. The BB/9 of 6.71 was eight percent higher than average, and the K/9 of 10.96 was an extreme 20 percent lower than average. His K/BB of 1.63 would have ranked him third lowest had he kept it up through 150 innings. Not surprisingly, his R/9 was 12 percent above average.

When Causey returned for five plate appearances in 2009, he was completely different. His BB/9 fell to average and his K/9 rose to just slightly above average, indicating a much larger strike zone. His R/9 plunged, despite the fact that every team he called games for, with the exception of the Cincinnati Reds, had a higher than average ERA (the Reds were right at average).

Here's another way to look at the contrast between his two seasons. In six of the nine games Causey called in 2008, ten or more runs scored. In *none* of the five games he called in 2009 did ten or more runs score. His highest run total in 2009 was nine — and that game was between the Baltimore Orioles and Cleveland Indians, the teams with the worst pitching staffs in the majors.

The Milwaukee Brewers were particularly unappreciative of Causey's enlarged 2009 strike zone. On July 17, Causey called runner's interference on Mike Cameron to end a bases-loaded rally in a game the Brewers trailed by three. The Brewers were still smarting from that call two days later, when Causey worked the plate. It seemed to them that Causey called every down and away pitch a strike. The fifth called strike three against them ended the game, and though the victim, Craig Counsell, kept his feelings to himself, coach Dale Sveum harangued Causey until Brian Runge interceded. After the game, Brewer manager Ken Macha defended Sveum's outburst. "Dale goes in every inning and sees where the strikes are at. He felt the guy's strike zone was a bit erratic." Brewer right fielder Corey Hart put it this way: "You want to try to adjust but you probably can't get to those pitches anyway." Sveum was suspended three games and fined for his tirade.

Evidently the Lords of Baseball saw something about Causey they didn't like either, because they released him prior to the 2010 season. He had worked six seasons in the Triple-A International League. He spent 2010 working college games in Virginia and vicinity and serving as an umpiring consultant to the Virginia Babe Ruth Umpires Association.

Source

Haudricourt, Tom. "Caught Looking a Bit Frustrated." *Milwaukee Journal-Sentinel,* July 19, 2009. (October 17, 2010.) http://www.jsonline.com/sports/brewers/51146292.html.

Gary Cederstrom

Born: October 4, 1955
First Major League Game: June 2, 1989
Favors: Pitchers
They hate him in: Detroit

	2007	2008	2009	2010	Totals
Games	33	35	32	35	135
Innings	287.67	313	281	307.67	1,189.33
R/9	9.64	8.60	8.87	8.72	8.94
BB/9	6.41	5.23	6.18	6.29	6.02
K/9	14.02	13.54	14.64	14.07	14.05
K/BB	2.19	2.59	2.37	2.24	2.34

In 2007 Cederstrom came closest of all umpires to the major league average R/9. Since then he has followed the trend toward fewer runs, his R/9 hanging in the high eights. Cederstrom's 2007 K/BB was also closer to average than any other umpire's. But in 2008 his K/BB rose dramatically, to ninth highest. The inflated K/BB was more a reflection of what he *wasn't* calling than what he was: His combined walks and strikeouts per nine came to less than 19 in 2008, as opposed to well over 20 in every other year under study, and most of the missing calls were walks. Since then Cederstrom's K/BB has gradually fallen to its 2007 level, which due to the trend toward pitching is now below average. When the numbers from all four seasons are aggregated, Cederstrom comes out strongly pro-pitcher, having the 12th lowest R/9 of the 77 umpires who called 500 or more innings from 2007 through 2010. His strike zone ranks just inside the top third for size, his K/BB for the period coming in at 26th.

The only umpire from North Dakota, Cederstrom is a big, burly guy with a slow fuse. His career ejection rate is just 1.4 percent, considerably below average. He was named a crew chief in 2008, having solidified his claim to the honor on October 18, 2007, when Fox aired an audio replay of a confrontation between pitcher Josh Beckett of the Boston Red Sox and Kenny Lofton of the Cleveland Indians during the fifth game of the American League Championship Series. Beckett had long despised Lofton's habit of showily dropping his bat after receiving a walk. Leading off the top of the fifth, Lofton worked the count from Beckett to 3–0. Thinking the next pitch low, Lofton did his bat-dropping thing and started toward first. Except Cederstrom called the pitch strike one. Lofton hit a routine fly to left on the next pitch. As Lofton trotted toward first, Beckett screamed at him. Lofton took the challenge and headed toward the mound. The benches cleared.

But Cederstrom took control before a single punch was thrown. "Josh, not a word, not a word, not a word!" he commanded the Red Sox hurler, who obediently shut up. "You pitchers get your sprints in, now run all the way back [to your respective bullpens]!" Cederstrom said to the players who had run onto the field. They did. Cederstrom quickly restored order without ejecting a single player. Nor were there any more hit batsmen. Beckett went on to pitch eight innings and earn the victory, keeping the Red Sox alive. They won the next two games to reach the World Series, and then they won their second Fall Classic in four seasons.

Cederstrom also owns up to mistakes instead of insisting on infallibility. He made a crucial error on June 26, 2010, at the end of a 4–3 game between the Atlanta Braves and Detroit Tigers. The Tigers had two out with the bases loaded and Johnny Damon at bat in the bottom of the ninth. Atlanta reliever Peter Moylan went 3–2 on Damon. His next pitch was outside, which should have been a game-tying ball four, but pitchers' friend Cederstrom called it strike three to end the game. Cederstrom watched replays afterward and realized he had made a mistake. In a private phone call with Tigers manager Jim Leyland, he apologized.

The next morning, Leyland disclosed Cederstrom's apology to the media. Cederstrom could have made Leyland's betrayal of confidence the subject, but took the high road. "My timing was fast. Whenever you have fast timing as an umpire, you usually get in trouble," he said. Leyland, whose pitcher Armando Galarraga had been denied a perfect game by an errant Jim Joyce call earlier in the month, still nursed a grudge. "You have to turn the page. You can't do anything about it," he acknowledged, but then fumed, "That's just not acceptable in those situations. It's just not acceptable. That's just the way it is." That afternoon, Leyland got into an argument with Fieldin Culbreth over an out call at first base. After Culbreth ejected Leyland, Cederstrom guided Leyland across the field to the Tigers' dugout. Leyland harangued Cederstrom the entire way, gesturing angrily, but Cederstrom remained stoic.

When Rickey Henderson stole his 939th base to break Lou Brock's major league record, Cederstrom was the ump who called him safe at third.

SOURCE

Associated Press. "Tigers Again on Wrong End of Close Call." ESPN.com, June 27, 2010. (October 17, 2010.) http://sports.espn.go.com/mlb/news/story?id=5333815.

Delfin Colon

BORN: August 22, 1969
FIRST MAJOR LEAGUE GAME: July 28, 2008
FAVORED: Hitters, if the small sample size reflected his true tendencies
THEY HATED HIM IN: Houston

	2007	2008	2009	2010	Totals
Games	0	2	6	0	8
Innings	0	17.5	52.5	0	70
R/9	0.00	13.37	10.97	0.00	11.57
BB/9	0.00	4.63	5.31	0.00	5.14
K/9	0.00	14.91	12.86	0.00	13.37
K/BB	0.00	3.22	2.42	0.00	2.60

Time ran out on Colon. He turned 40 in 2009, was still a Triple-A call-up, and had participated in just 46 big league games. He was older than two dozen other umpires, including five (Bruce Dreckman, Alfonso Marquez, Brian Runge, Mike Wegner, and Hunter Wendelstedt) who had been carrying union cards for years. Still, it came as a surprise when he was released. "I felt like I was just getting started. I was looking forward to this year [2010], getting more games," he said. "It was pretty devastating. And it happens not because you're not doing the job but because they have so many guys coming up that they have to make room for them."

The 6'5" Colon worked half of his eight big league plate appearances in Houston. Though born in Puerto Rico, he resided in Houston and considered it his hometown. His first major league home plate assignment came on July 30, 2008, in Minute Maid Park. "When I was doing the plate, it probably took me about three innings to get the nerves all lined up and be able to control myself," he said of that day. "It's the atmosphere, the stadium, the fact that instead of four cameras you have 18 cameras on you, and there is not that much room for a mistake." He didn't do his hometown team any favors. The Astros lost three of the four games he called at Minute Maid.

On May 21, 2009, working home plate for the third time in Houston, Colon got into a shouting match with Astro first baseman Lance Berkman and manager Cecil Cooper. Berkman tried to score on a two-out single to left and was thrown out. Colon called the play correctly, but Berkman and Cooper argued that Berkman got his left hand on the plate as he slid past the tag. Colon tossed them both, the only ejections of his big league career. Although the Astros were leading at the time 3–1, they lost the game, with Berkman's replacement, Darin Erstad, whiffing in his only at-bat. "It was quick, but I don't think it was completely unjustified," Berkman later said of his ejection. Cooper was less contrite. "Tonight, overall, we got shafted by some poor umpiring," he said.

The other big controversy in Colon's brief career came on July 26, 2009, in Seattle. With the score tied 2–2 in the top of the fifth, Mariner starter Jason Vargas faltered badly against the Cleveland Indians. He walked Grady Sizemore. He threw a wild pitch. He foolishly went for the lead runner on a sacrifice bunt, and everyone was safe. And then, according to Colon, he hit Indian first baseman Ryan Garko with a pitch to load the bases. Mariner manager Don Wakamatsu argued that Garko hadn't even been grazed. Colon stood by his call (replays showed the ball did nick Garko's elbow, but Garko did not try to avoid the pitch). Three pitches later, Jhonny Peralta hit a grand slam to decide the game.

Colon spent 2010 in the independent Atlantic League. "I didn't think about it twice. I thought that for me it would be a good experience. One year, see what happens, and we'll go from there," he told My Central Jersey.

Source

Dunleavy, Ryan. "Delfin Colon Makes Atlantic League Umpiring History." MyCentralJersey.com, May 1, 2010. (October 17, 2010.) http://blogs.mycentraljersey.com/patriots/2010/05/01/delfin-colon-makes-atlantic-league-umpiring-history.

Chris Conroy

BORN: July 22, 1974
FIRST MAJOR LEAGUE GAME: September 29, 2010
FAVORS: Sample size too small
THEY HATE HIM IN: Nowhere yet

	2007	2008	2009	2010	Totals
Games	0	0	0	1	1
Innings	0	0	0	8.5	8.5
R/9	0.00	0.00	0.00	3.18	3.18
BB/9	0.00	0.00	0.00	3.18	3.18
K/9	0.00	0.00	0.00	21.18	21.18
K/BB	0.00	0.00	0.00	6.67	6.67

If Conroy makes it, he'll become only the second active major league umpire born in Massachusetts. (The other is Jim Reynolds.) The New Englander was named a Triple-A call-up in his fifth year at the top minor league rung, having toiled a year in the Pacific Coast League before switching to the International League in 2007. He called balls and strikes during the Triple-A All-Star game on July 14, 2010, then worked the Triple-A championship game on September 21. Scarcely a week later he made it to the big time, working third base for a contest between the Milwaukee Brewers and New York Mets at Citi Field. The 36-year-old veteran minor league ump told the *Berkshire Eagle*, his hometown newspaper, that "We came around the corner, and there was Citi Field. I almost kind of started tearing up a little bit — remembering everything me and my wife and my family have gone through over 11 years just to get to this point."

Conroy said a big league game behind home plate "would be a pretty cool experience." He got that experience when he was sent to Baltimore to work the season-ending series between the Tigers and Orioles. He called balls and strikes on October 2. Armando Galarraga, the pitcher who lost his perfect game to a bad call by Jim Joyce, started for Detroit and went the distance, but lost, 2–1, to Brian Matusz and three Oriole relievers. Conroy evidently gave the pitchers a generous strike zone, as they compiled 20 punchouts, although only four were called. Jhonny Peralta of the Tigers earned Conroy's first called strike three. The Tigers' Austin Jackson earned Conroy's first base on balls.

"I just got on the reserve list this season," Conroy told the *Berkshire Eagle*. "Maybe doing a handful of games down the stretch will help me get some more next year."

Source

Herman, Howard. "Local Umpire Gets Called to Bigs." *Berkshire Eagle*, October 1, 2010. (October 13, 2010.) http://www.berkshireeagle.com/ci_16222220.

Eric Cooper

BORN: December 18, 1966
FIRST MAJOR LEAGUE GAME: June 17, 1996
FAVORS: R/9 says hitters, K/BB says pitchers
THEY HATE HIM IN: Atlanta

	2007	2008	2009	2010	Totals
Games	32	34	31	34	131
Innings	283	300.5	283	297.67	1,164.17
R/9	9.70	9.64	9.60	8.92	9.46
BB/9	5.53	5.30	5.82	5.62	5.57
K/9	13.58	13.15	14.09	14.63	13.86
K/BB	2.46	2.48	2.42	2.60	2.49

Eric Cooper is allergic to walks. In each of the years under study his BB/9 scored well below average: nine percent below in 2007, 15 percent below in 2008 (he had the third lowest BB/9 of all umpires that season), nine percent below in 2009, and seven percent below in 2010. His overall BB/9 is fifth lowest among the 77 umpires who called 500 or more innings from 2007 through 2010. As if that isn't bad enough for hitters, in 2009 and 2010 his strikeout totals spiked. That combination of a low walk rate and an increasing strikeout rate gives him the ninth-largest strike zone of all active umpires.

So do the hitters begrudge him? Hardly. Cooper's total R/9 is actually two percent above the norm. It ranks 28th overall, only a few thousandths of a percentage point below Lance Barksdale's. That's amazing considering that Barksdale's BB/9 is 1.32 higher. In fact, going by K/BB, Cooper's strike zone is 25 percent larger than Barksdale's! Yet even in 2010, when it plunged by two-thirds of a run, Cooper's R/9 remained above average. One possible explanation is that even though Cooper's strike zone is much larger than Barksdale's, it's also more consistent. Note that his BB/9s are all within a ten percent range. Barksdale's, by contrast, deviate considerably from year to year.

A consistent strike zone can be a boon to pitchers as well as hitters. Over one stretch of three home plate appearances in 2009, Cooper presided over a walkless complete game by Roy Halladay of the Toronto Blue Jays, a perfect game by Mark Buehrle of the Chicago White Sox, and an eight-inning complete game by Matt Cain of the San Francisco Giants in a rain-shortened contest. Cooper had also called Buehrle's 2007 no-hitter. "I'm certainly aware of the situation, especially late in the game, just because of the way the fans are reacting," Cooper said after Buehrle's perfecto. "But it doesn't differentiate how I call the game. I have the same approach whether the score is 0–0 or 10–0, or whether there is a perfect game or no-hitter going. I try to call strikes strikes and balls balls." On April 4, 2001, Cooper called a no-hitter for Hideo Nomo of the Boston Red Sox against the Baltimore Orioles. Buehrle's perfect game made Cooper the only active umpire to call three no-hit games.

But for every sublime moment like a no-hitter, there is an embarrassing one. On May 20, 2009, Cooper created embarrassment for manager Cecil Cooper of the Houston Astros (no relation). The Astros sent center fielder Michael Bourn to the plate to lead off a game against the Milwaukee Brewers. He smacked a single. Up stepped second baseman Kaz Matsui. Would he take a few pitches to let Bourn steal? Would he bunt? Would he swing away? None of the above. Matsui stood impassively as Ken Macha, manager of the Milwaukee Brewers, conferred with umpire Cooper at home plate, and then was stunned when Cooper turned to him and called him out. He hadn't even seen a pitch! But Astro manager Cecil Cooper had submitted a lineup card in which Matsui, not Bourn, led off. The Astros had batted out of turn. As manager Cooper sat mortified in the dugout, not even daring to argue, umpire Cooper dismissed Matsui and brought Bourn back to the plate for real.

Cooper embarrassed himself on August 7, 2009. He was calling a 2–2 game between Atlanta and Los Angeles when the Dodgers' Rafael Furcal led off the bottom of the fifth by singling. That brought up Andre Ethier. With the count 3–1, Ethier took a close pitch from Atlanta's Jair Jurrjens as Furcal tried to steal. "Ball!" cried Cooper — and then raised his right fist to signal a strike as Atlanta catcher Brian McCann threw to second and nailed Furcal. Which was it, a ball or a strike? Two men on, or two men out? Hard to imagine a bigger boo-boo from an umpire. When Cooper clarified that the pitch was ball four, putting Dodgers on first and second with nobody out, the reaction from Atlanta's umpire-baiting manager, Bobby Cox, was predictable. Cooper knew he'd done wrong. "I shouldn't have used my right hand when I raised it. I know there was some confusion in the dugout. I explained that to Bobby and I understand that there *should* have been some confusion in the dugout," he said after the game.

But Cooper also has a short fuse. His lifetime ejection rate is over three percent, well above average. He let Cox imitate his strike call only so many times before sending the Atlanta skipper to the showers. The Dodgers went on to score three runs that inning, but the Braves eventually won in the 12th, mellowing Cox's post-game reaction. "These guys are scrutinized so much that you hate to say anything," he reflected sympathetically.

SOURCE

Bowman, Mark. "Cooper Provides Explanation About Friday's Fifth-Inning Confusion." MLBlogs Network, August 8, 2009. (October 17, 2010.) http://markbowman.mlblogs.com/archives/2009/08/cooper_provides_explanation_ab.html.

Derryl Cousins

BORN: August 18, 1946
FIRST MAJOR LEAGUE GAME: April 6, 1979
FAVORS: Hitters
THEY HATE HIM IN: The vicinity of Scott Kazmir

	2007	2008	2009	2010	Totals
Games	33	35	34	34	136
Innings	298.83	317.83	304.17	302.33	1,223.17
R/9	8.91	9.26	8.85	9.94	9.24
BB/9	6.42	6.77	6.81	6.67	6.67
K/9	13.55	12.77	13.73	14.41	13.60
K/BB	2.11	1.89	2.02	2.16	2.04

Cousins is the oldest active umpire, and given the credo his fraternity lives by (it's a good game if nobody notices you), it's a tribute that after more than 30 years in the majors few fans know who he is. The first big league game he ever appeared in, between the Minnesota Twins and Oakland Athletics, was also his first behind home plate. As if that wasn't unusual enough, he didn't credit Athletic pitchers with a single strikeout, although in fairness to Cousins, the A's starter was junkballer Rick Langford. Nor are there any signs that Cousins is slowing down. He hasn't missed significant time since 2004. He had a bit of scare on September 15, 2009, when he was struck on the knee by a loaded can of soda thrown from the stands during a fight between the Toronto Blue Jays and host New York Yankees, but X-rays revealed no broken bones and he was back on the field the next day.

Cousins's chart is further proof of the weak correlation between the size of an umpire's strike zone and the number of runs that score in the games he calls. Cousins has a consistently small strike zone. His walk totals range from five to ten percent above average each year. His strikeout totals range from a hair above average (2007 and 2010) to as much as six percent below average (2008). His overall K/BB ratio ranks 14th lowest of all umpires who worked 500 or more innings from 2007 through 2010. That suggests hitters should prosper when he stands behind home plate. Yet except for 2010, his annual R/9s are *below* average, and his cumulative R/9 of 9.24 is slightly lower than the norm. Perhaps hitters get a bit too relaxed with him back there.

Another possibility is that Cousins is too streaky to be predictable. Once or twice a year, it seems, he makes a conscious effort to call more strikes. In his first three games behind the plate in 2007, there were just 17 walks (BB/9 of 5.67) and 60 strikeouts (K/9 of 20!). After calling 21 walks in an 11-inning game between Detroit and Oakland on June 3, 2008, he called just 12 over his next three plate assignments, games that saw 44 strikeouts. Over his final six starts behind the plate in 2009, which spanned 52 innings, he called just 31 walks (BB/9 of 5.37) while calling or acknowledging 92 strikeouts (K/9 of 15.92). One last example: in mid– and late May 2010 he recorded a K/9 of 10.53, then over an equal number of innings in early June 2010 recorded a K/9 of 17.66. Cousins called 155 strikes in the May games, 190 strikes in the June games.

Despite the occasional spasms of pitcher-friendliness, Cousins's reputation as a hitters' umpire is well established, to the point where some players call him "Shoebox" for the size of his strike zone. On June 11, 2008, the pressure of pitching with Cousins behind the plate got to Scott Kazmir of the Tampa Bay Rays. Kazmir was going for his seventh straight win. Through six innings he had struck out eight Los Angeles Angels — all swinging, none called. Leading 2–1 in the seventh, Kazmir fanned Gary Matthews, Jr., and Mike Napoli swinging. But the pressure and fatigue finally wore him down. Two singles and a walk later, he blew the lead. He placed the blame on Cousins, as did his manager, Joe Maddon, who earned an ejection for questioning Cousins's plate judgment.

According to Kazmir, not only was Cousins squeezing the plate, he was giving hitters make-up calls for earlier pitches he had called strikes. Kazmir believed Cousins was determined to give the Angels' Reggie Willits first base during that crucial seventh inning, in which Willits indeed received a walk. "As soon as Willits got up, it was like, 'you can swing if you want to, but if not, just take your base,'" Kazmir said, claiming he had two strikes called balls during that at-bat. "I never said anything like this about an umpire, but that was just a crucial part of the game and you just don't do that." Kazmir said he received a few make-up calls himself, including one pitch "literally almost in the dirt" that was called a strike in the sixth inning. "It's like it was already predetermined, like he already had it in his head what he was going to call," Kazmir said. Despite his status as a crew chief, Cousins chose not to address Kazmir's allegations. "I didn't know he's been around that long. I've got nothing to say," he shrugged.

Earlier in his career, Cousins's reaction would have been harsher. From 1985 through 1987 he was the most combative umpire in the American League, leading the circuit in ejections. Since then he's calmed down considerably. Prior to 1988, his ejection rate was four percent. From 1988 on, his ejection rate has been two percent, slightly lower than average. In both 2009 and 2010 he had just one ejection.

Cousins was behind home plate in San Diego on August 4, 2007, when Barry Bonds of the San Francisco Giants hit his 755th home run, tying Henry Aaron's all-time record.

Source

Topkin, Marc. "Kazmir Rages at Umpire's Strike Zone After Rays Lose to Angels." *St. Petersburg Times*, June 12, 2008. (October 17, 2010.) http://www.tampabay.com/sports/baseball/rays/kazmir-rages-at-umpires-strike-zone-after-rays-lose-to-angels/619527.

Jerry Crawford

Born: August 13, 1947
First Major League Game: May 15, 1976
Favored: Hitters, by a lot
They hated him in: Pre-game pitchers and catchers meetings

	2007	2008	2009	2010	Totals
Games	16	23	25	23	87
Innings	135.5	194.33	208	206	743.83
R/9	10.23	11.21	10.43	8.56	10.08
BB/9	6.58	7.69	8.18	7.25	7.50
K/9	12.55	12.23	14.80	12.67	13.13
K/BB	1.91	1.59	1.81	1.75	1.75

Like slugfests? Then you should be lamenting the retirement of Jerry Crawford. From 2007 through 2009 he had a 10.66 R/9, higher than the R/9 for the American League in 1927, when Babe Ruth hit 60 homers; higher than the R/9 for the American League in 1941, when Ted Williams hit .406 and Joe DiMaggio hit in 56 straight games; higher than the R/9 for the American League in 1961, when expansion led to an offensive explosion, including Roger Maris's 61 homers; and higher than the R/9 for the National League in 1998, when Mark McGwire and Sammy Sosa broke Maris's home run mark. Although Crawford's style was the same in 2010, hitters inexplicably failed to take advantage, and that dropped Crawford's R/9 to third among umpires who called 500 or more innings from 2007 through 2010, behind Gerry Davis and Tim McClelland.

Why did so many runs score when Crawford wore the mask? Not much mystery there. He had an extremely small strike zone. From 2007 through 2010 he had the second highest BB/9 of all umpires, the seventh lowest K/9, and the second lowest K/BB. Even in 2009, when his strikeout rate spiked—more than two per nine innings higher than 2008 and 2010—he still logged a K/BB ratio 17 percent lower than the major league average. But then, how many umpires averaged more than eight walks per game in 2009? Only three: Tim Tschida, McClelland, and Crawford. If the players refer to Derryl Cousins as "Shoebox" for the size of his strike zone, they should have called Crawford "Matchbox."

In 2010 Crawford was the second oldest active umpire (behind Cousins) and the most senior in terms of service. Age was taking its toll, however, and he missed significant time in each of the years under study, due mostly to back trouble. He aggravated his back injury working home plate during an August 14, 2007 game between the Houston Astros and Los Angeles Dodgers and had to leave; he worked second base the next day, worked second again two days later, but was done for the season after that. In 2008 his back forced him out of an August 1 contest between Milwaukee and Atlanta; after missing more than two weeks, he worked three games, then went out for another three weeks. In 2009 the back got him twice: in a June 21 game between the Tampa Bay Rays and New York Mets, costing him a month, and in an August 26 Tampa Bay-Toronto game, an inning after he had been hit in the mask by a foul ball, although this time he missed only five days. In 2010 he was hit in the ribs by a foul ball while working home plate in a game between San Diego and Florida; that and the chronic back problems kept him on the sidelines for most of May and July. "All my off-time I'm rehabbing," he said.

Crawford's worst work experience had nothing to do with his own pain. He was handling first base duties on April 1, 1996, opening day in Cincinnati, when home plate umpire and friend John McSherry collapsed and died of a heart attack just seven pitches into the game. "I don't think he ever heard me when I got to him, when I was talking to him," Crawford said afterward. At first, Crawford told Cincinnati manager Ray Knight he would be willing to go on with the game, but Knight said neither his players nor the Montreal Expos in the visiting clubhouse were in any shape to perform. So Crawford postponed the game, came back the next day, and handled home plate duties.

Crawford also suffered through some very hard days in 1999, but for more prosaic reasons. He was president of the umpires' union when its executive director, attorney Richie Phillips, recommended the umpires resign as a negotiating tactic. Crawford strongly favored the move, even after the Lords of Baseball began accepting the resignations and support for the tactic evaporated. Eventually Crawford's union was dissolved and replaced with the World Umpires Association. Crawford refused to join the new union.

The 1999 union debacle was the unfortunate consequence of an extreme attitude that mirrored the extreme tightness of Crawford's strike zone. Joe Torre wrote an opinion piece about umpires for the *New York Times* in 1988. It was mostly innocuous, written by a jobless manager reluctant to offend potential employers. Yet he singled out Paul Runge and Jerry Crawford as umpires whose confrontational attitudes changed the profession.

Torre speculated that Crawford's approach was learned at home. Crawford's father, Shag, was a National League umpire from 1956 through 1975, and is perhaps best remembered as the horrified umpire standing behind Juan Marichal of the San Francisco Giants as Marichal raised his bat and brought it down on the head of Los Angeles Dodger catcher John Roseboro on August 22, 1965, the signature moment of the Giant-Dodger rivalry in California.

Jerry Crawford would no doubt dispute Torre's contention, and he can point to a career ejection rate of 1.8 percent, some 20 percent below average, as proof that he wasn't as confrontational as Torre alleged. A crew chief since 1998, Crawford told his hometown *Philadelphia Inquirer* in August 2010 that his father did get him and his brother, a referee in the National Basketball Association, started in the profession, but that "His real advice was the game doesn't owe you anything and you owe the game everything and to go about it that way. And really, I did. That's how I went about it." He worked his last game in Philadelphia on August 22, 2010, and was given a huge pregame ovation. "I was very moved," Crawford admitted. Then in the second inning he called a Washington National batter safe at first on a close play. "I hear a guy going, 'Ah, you missed that one.' And everything was normal again," he laughed.

SOURCE

Parrillo, Ray. "Philly Native Son Jerry Crawford Umps Final Game in Hometown." *Philadelphia Inquirer*, August 22, 2010. (October 18, 2010.) http://www.philly.com/inquirer/breaking/sports_breaking/20100822_Philly_native_son_Jerry_Crawford_umps_final_game_in_hometown.html.

Fieldin Culbreth

BORN: March 16, 1963
FIRST MAJOR LEAGUE GAME: August 13, 1993
FAVORS: Hitters, although it doesn't translate into runs
THEY HATE HIM IN: The Society of 6'10" Future Hall of Famers

	2007	2008	2009	2010	Totals
Games	34	34	34	34	136
Innings	301.17	305.83	300.67	299.67	1,207.33
R/9	9.56	8.80	8.71	9.64	9.18
BB/9	5.50	6.95	6.88	6.01	6.34
K/9	12.94	13.39	13.23	13.76	13.33
K/BB	2.35	1.93	1.92	2.29	2.10

"Seems to expand zone on 3–2, as he punches out hitters he normally calls a ball [on] in different counts," reads one team's report on Culbreth. Perhaps so, but it's not reflected in the numbers. Culbreth's K/9 came in below average for every year of this study, and he has the 13th lowest K/9 of the 77 umpires who worked 500 or more innings behind home plate from 2007 through 2010. No wonder Culbreth, when asked to comment about the team's report, said "I'd rather not get involved in that. It doesn't matter."

Culbreth's chart suggests that umpire statistics in general don't matter. In 2007 his BB/9 was ten percent below average and his R/9 was just one percent below average, so there was something of a correlation. (Remember that high BB/9s encourage offense, while low BB/9s discourage offense.) In 2008 his BB/9 jumped to 11 percent above average, but his R/9 went *down* by three-quarters of a run. In 2009 his BB/9 stayed high, and his R/9 stayed low. Then in 2010 he cut his BB/9 drastically — and in a year when offensive production declined by nearly half a run per game, his R/9 went *up* almost a full run! Further evidence that life — or at least baseball — cannot be explained by statistics alone.

Culbreth is one of the nice guys in the umpire corps. His career ejection rate is 1.6 percent, well below the norm. Since 2006 he's thrown out only four people. He didn't eject anyone in 2007 or 2009. In 2008 he ran Detroit Tiger designated hitter Gary Sheffield for arguing a called strike three (replays show the pitch was very close but that Sheffield was correct) and Cleveland Indian manager Eric Wedge for arguing that a call of unintentional runner's interference against the Seattle Mariners in an extra-inning game should have been called intentional, and hence a double play against the Mariners (the replays showed Culbreth was right). In 2010 Culbreth ran two managers, Ozzie Guillen of the Chicago White Sox and Jim Leyland of the Detroit Tigers. Guillen went for arguing that the Seattle Mariners' Jack Wilson shouldn't have been allowed to score from first after a White Sox fan interfered with a fair ball in the right field corner. Leyland made a forced departure after arguing an out call at first base. Note that in four full seasons and more than 1,200 innings behind home plate, Culbreth needed to eject someone over a disputed pitch call just once.

The most famous ejection of Culbreth's career occurred on September 16, 2005. The New York Yankees were playing the Toronto Blue Jays in Canada. Trailing the Boston Red Sox in the standings by a game and a half with 17 to play, the Yankees sent Randy Johnson to the mound. In his previous start Johnson had pitched seven strong innings, allowing just one hit and two walks while striking out eight. But with Culbreth behind the plate, he felt squeezed. After hitting the first batter and walking the second, he went 3–2 on the third batter, Vernon Wells. "I called a pitch on Wells and had the ball rather inside, and Randy questioned the pitch and was looking at me and yelling a bit. At that point, he was told that was enough, because he was starting to get pretty animated," Culbreth said.

Wells homered to give the Jays a 3–0 lead. Johnson held his peace until the second inning, when Culbreth called a ball on an inside pitch that Johnson thought a strike. "Randy immediately came off the mound and had some choice words to say. I told him to knock it off and get back on the mound. He screamed again, an expletive, and 'just call it a strike,' and at that point he also screamed out, 'and the pitch on Wells was an expletive strike as well.' And at that point, I ejected him. I would think that he knows that when he came off the mound and was saying the things he was saying, that he had to be putting himself in a position to be ejected."

The Yankees rallied to win, 11–10, and perhaps because of that Johnson was contrite the next day. "I know I was wrong for my actions," he said.

A native of South Carolina, Culbreth told his hometown *Spartanburg Herald-Journal* in 2008 that "I think people have the impression that if I miss a call, I go home and it's no big deal. That's not the truth. It totally eats me up to the point where it's probably unhealthy." But when it comes to working in the major leagues, "It's everything you think it would be. It's exciting. It's huge. There's not enough adjectives to explain what working in any major league sport is like."

Fieldin is a family name. He is Fieldin Henry Culbreth III, and his son is Fieldin Henry Culbreth IV.

Source

"USC Upstate Welcomes Major League Baseball Umpire to Sports Officiating Class." *University of South Carolina Upstate,* February 26, 2007. (October 18, 2010.) http://www.uscupstate.edu/press/article.aspx?id=6156.

Phil Cuzzi

BORN: August 29, 1955
FIRST MAJOR LEAGUE GAME: June 4, 1991
FAVORS: Pitchers, strongly
THEY HATE HIM IN: Minnesota and the South Side of Chicago

	2007	2008	2009	2010	Totals
Games	35	33	34	35	137
Innings	305.33	295.5	303	309.17	1,213
R/9	10.52	8.59	8.79	8.50	9.10
BB/9	5.90	5.82	6.03	5.41	5.79
K/9	13.15	15.56	14.38	14.79	14.46
K/BB	2.23	2.67	2.38	2.73	2.50

Every few years, major league umpires botch a slew of calls when everyone is watching, triggering a national debate about the quality of their work. The most recent cluster came during the 2009 playoffs, and no umpire, not even the widely reviled C.B. Bucknor, faced more opprobrium than Phil Cuzzi. Working left field during the second game of the American League Division Series between the Minnesota Twins and New York Yankees, Cuzzi was put on the spot when Twin superstar Joe Mauer started the 11th inning with a slicing fly ball down the left field line. The Yankees' Melky Cabrera gave chase and tipped the ball with his glove before it landed fair and bounced into the stands for a ground-rule double.

Cuzzi called it a foul ball.

Mauer returned to the batter's box without complaint and hit a single, but Cuzzi's glaring mistake cost the Twins a run. The next two batters also singled. Had Mauer been on second, where he belonged, he would have scored. Instead he advanced only as far as third (he suffered from a hip injury and was unable to take two bases on a single) and was forced at home on a ground out. The Twins failed to score. Then the first batter for New York in the bottom of the 11th, Mark Teixeira, homered, giving the Yankees what proved an insurmountable 2–0 series lead.

Said Twin closer Joe Nathan, "You see on the replays [Cuzzi's] probably about ten feet from the call, and the ball was not on the line. It was a good eight inches inside the line, so I don't know how he missed it." The replay showed Cuzzi was farther from the play than Nathan thought, but straddling the line so he had an excellent angle. So how did he miss it? "We're not used to playing that far down the line," he told his hometown paper, the *Newark Star-Ledger,* the next day. "The instant the ball is hit, we usually start running. I think I may have been looking too closely at it. I never had a feel for where the left fielder was on the play." That said, "There is no excuse. I missed the play. It's a terrible feeling. As badly as many people on that field may have felt, I don't think any of them had a worse night's sleep than I did."

The blown call prompted reporters and bloggers to plumb Cuzzi's past. They discovered that even though he made his major league debut in 1991 and saw additional action in 1992 and 1993, he was never more than a Triple-A call-up — and had been fired from his minor league job in November 1993. He was working as a hotel concierge in Short Hills, New Jersey, when Leonard Coleman, president of the National League, spent a night there in 1996. Cuzzi accosted Coleman in the lobby and asked for a second chance. Coleman assigned him to Class A minor league games, and Cuzzi worked his way back up, returning to the majors in 1999 as a replacement for the union umpires whose resignations had been accepted. None of these details improved Cuzzi's reputation.

Cuzzi has a quick temper. In 2003 he issued 12 ejections. In 2007 he led the majors with ten. His career ejection rate is 3.6 percent, significantly higher than the major league norm of 2.2 percent. But he had just one ejection a year in 2008, 2009, and 2010, so he may be settling down. Even so, put him in the same park as the combustible manager of the Chicago White Sox, Ozzie Guillen, and watch the sparks fly. "From 1985 to now, I don't see any umpire [disrespect] players and managers the way that guy does," Guillen said after Cuzzi ejected him for disputing a checked swing call on July 31, 2007. "If they're willing to fine me for what I say, I'm willing to pay that money because I called him a lot of things I'm not supposed to say." Cuzzi ejected Guillen again on April 7, 2008 for disputing balls and strikes. "I just let him know I don't like him the first day I see him, and I think he feels the same way about me," Guillen said. Major League Baseball fined Guillen for his remarks.

Whatever Guillen may think, his pitchers probably like Cuzzi. The New Jersey ump has one of the biggest strike zones in the game. His BB/9 is consistently below the major league average and ranks 12th lowest of all umpires who called 500 or more innings from 2007 through 2010. He had the highest K/9 of all umpires in 2008 and has the fourth highest for the period under study. Cuzzi's overall 2.50 K/BB ratio is eighth highest of all umpires. Except for 2007, the large strike zone has had an impact on the number of runs scored in the games he calls, as his R/9 has been down in the eights.

Cuzzi seemed determined to make his strike zone smaller when the 2009 season began. In his first three games behind the plate he called 35 walks for a BB/9 of 12.11. But then he went back to old habits, posting a BB/9 of 5.46 the rest of the way. Without those first three games, his BB/9 would have been third lowest among the 68 umpires who called 150 or more innings in 2009. Instead, he finished 21 from the bottom — still in the lower third. In 2010 he didn't seem to worry as much about his strike zone, and over one four-game stretch (August 28 through September 17) he presided over 81 strikeouts in 35 innings, a K/9 of 20.83!

Source

Lamberti, Mike. "Cuzzi Is Safe at Home After Long Run on Bases." Old Belleville.org, August 1999. (October 18, 2010.) http://www.oldbelleville.org/cuzzi.html.

Kerwin Danley

Born: May 25, 1961
First Major League Game: June 12, 1992
Favors: Hitters
They hate him in: The headquarters of Major League Baseball's health insurance provider

	2007	2008	2009	2010	Totals
Games	34	26	10	34	104
Innings	303.5	220.5	85.17	295	904.17
R/9	9.61	8.94	9.83	9.61	9.47
BB/9	5.96	6.24	6.45	7.02	6.42
K/9	12.37	13.06	13.31	15.32	13.59
K/BB	2.08	2.09	2.06	2.18	2.12

Danley missed a lot of time in 2008 and 2009 due to head injuries. On April 26, 2008, he was behind the plate during a game between Colorado and Los Angeles when the Dodger battery, pitcher Brad Penny and catcher Russell Martin, got crossed up on signs. Penny threw a high 96 mile-per-hour fastball and Martin missed it. "Look out!" Martin cried when he realized he wouldn't catch the ball. "I could see it coming. I couldn't do anything about it," said Danley. The pitch hit him on the jaw and knocked him out. Danley comes from Los Angeles, and his mother was in the stands. She rode with him to the hospital. He was released the next morning, but needed six weeks to shake off the headaches and fuzz.

Nearly a year later, on April 21, 2009, Danley was again working the plate, this time in a game between Texas and Toronto, when Ranger designated hitter Hank Blalock's bat shattered on a pop-up and the barrel nailed Danley in the face mask. This time Danley remained conscious, but the injury was worse — a concussion — and he missed four months. "It didn't sound good, it was a pretty loud thump," said Blue Jay catcher Rod Barajas. "I was hoping he'd get right back up and shake it off but his eyes were closed and he wasn't making any movements and he wasn't talking."

Danley's chart shows a very clear trend: His BB/9 and K/9 are going up every year. It's hard to imagine that continuing. In 2010 his BB/9 was fifth highest and his K/9 was fourth highest, and neither can go much higher without jeopardizing his credibility. (The only other umpire to make the top ten in both categories was Mike Winters.) Based on his K/BB ratios, Danley eased up on pitchers in 2010, but still favored hitters. His prohitter leanings become more obvious when looking at his overall results. His BB/9 ranks 20th, his K/9 54th, and his K/BB 55th out of 77, all indicative of a small strike zone. His aggregate R/9 of 9.47 is 26th overall, so the hitters are taking advantage of his largesse.

Although Danley's career ejection rate is just below average, he has mellowed considerably over time and now has one of the slowest fuses of all active umpires. From 2004 through 2010 he issued only six dismissals, less than 40 percent of the norm. In 2006, 2007, and 2009 he didn't eject anyone at all. One of his few victims was first base coach Rick Renteria of the San Diego Padres. On July 17, 2010, Danley was working first base and Renteria was giving him a hard time for not calling a balk on the Arizona Diamondbacks' Rodrigo Lopez, who was trying to keep the Padres' Scott Hairston close. After some brief back-and-forth, Danley exiled Renteria, suggesting that Renteria had broken the rule against personalizing disagreements with umpires.

Prior to Renteria, Danley hadn't ejected anyone since Cleveland Indian manager Eric Wedge on July 13, 2008, more than two years earlier. Again the issue was a balk. In the top of the second Danley, working home plate, called a balk on Indian pitcher Jeremy Sowers. Although Wedge never left the dugout, he gave Danley plenty of grief, and eventually Danley heard enough. Replays showed that Danley called the balk correctly.

Danley's most embarrassing day as an umpire probably came on October 23, 2008, his first World Series appearance behind home plate. In the bottom of the second, Rocco Baldelli of the Tampa Bay Rays tried to check a swing on a 3–2 pitch. Danley put his arm in the air, suggesting Baldelli had struck out, but then sent Baldelli to first on a walk, creating confusion. "It was [Danley's] intention to go to first base for help on a half-swing that he had as ball four. He just gave a confusing mechanic," baseball executive Mike Port explained. Danley had another bad moment in the top of the ninth. Jimmy Rollins of the Philadelphia Phillies was grazed by a pitch from Tampa Bay's David Price. But Danley ruled that Rollins wasn't hit. Rollins popped out and the Phillies' last-ditch rally fizzled, leading to a 4–2 loss.

Danley's best day as an umpire might have come on August 6, 1999, when he was at first base for a game between the San Diego Padres and Montreal Expos. In the top of the first, future Hall-of-Famer Tony Gwynn singled to center field. It was the 3,000th hit of Gwynn's storied career. Danley gave Gwynn a big hug, an unusual, even inappropriate, display of emotion for an umpire.

What few onlookers knew was that Danley and Gwynn were teammates on the San Diego State University baseball team.

Source

Shaikin, Bill. "The Pitch Struck Umpire Out." *Los Angeles Times*, May 3, 2008. (October 18, 2010.) http://articles.latimes.com/2008/may/03/sports/sp-ump3.

Gary Darling

Born: October 9, 1957
First Major League Game: June 3, 1986
Favors: Pitchers
They hate him in: The San Francisco Bay Area

	2007	2008	2009	2010	Totals
Games	33	34	28	34	129
Innings	290.33	293.67	245.33	305.17	1,134.5
R/9	9.05	10.33	8.55	9.08	9.28
BB/9	5.46	6.07	5.91	5.78	5.80
K/9	13.08	13.18	14.42	15.78	14.12
K/BB	2.40	2.17	2.44	2.73	2.44

You're in your fourth full season as a major league umpire, so you've been around the track a few times. You're working home plate during an early August game between two teams that are long shots to win the division. The home team (let's call it Cincinnati) is losing by four in the bottom of the eighth when the second baseman, not exactly blessed with power, pulls one over the right field fence very, very close to the foul pole. Fair or foul? It's the first base umpire's call. He's closer to the foul pole and has a lot more experience than you. He says home run. But then he does something strange. He comes to you and asks, "Do you think it was fair?" You say no, and overrule his call. The hometown fans boo. The manager, a known hothead (let's call him Lou Piniella) goes bananas. You eject him.

After the game, the manager accuses you of bias. "All year, we haven't gotten a call from him and I don't think we'll get a call from him the rest of the year. When it comes to the Cincinnati Reds, he doesn't call a game the way it's supposed to be called."

How do you handle these intemperate remarks? Do you:

A. Not respond. Such comments do not merit a response.
B. Laugh it off and tell reporters to consider the source.
C. Work through Major League Baseball's front office to issue a statement explaining the basis for your call, expressing regret that the manager didn't see things the same way, and denying any bias whatsoever.
D. File a $5 million defamation lawsuit against the bastard.

The umpire in this situation was Gary Darling, the game took place on August 3, 1991, and you guessed it: His answer was D.

Fair to say that back then Darling had a serious attitude problem. He meted out ten ejections in 1991 and an astonishing 15 in 1992, leading the National League both seasons. Since then he has calmed down. He had just one ejection in 2007, one in 2008, three in 2009, and three in 2010. Five of the eight recent ejectees worked for the San Francisco Giants or Oakland Athletics, interesting in that Darling was born in the Bay Area. On April 29, 2008, Darling banished San Francisco manager Bruce Bochy for arguing a balk call. On August 12, 2009, Darling thumbed Bochy in the second inning for arguing a pickoff play at first base, then tossed Bochy's replacement, Ron Wotus, in the ninth over another close play at first. Four days later, Darling booted Oakland manager Bob Geren for arguing a safe call on a stolen base attempt by Jayson Nix of the Chicago White Sox. On August 3, 2010, Darling got Geren again, this time over a rundown play from which Geren wanted two outs but was granted only one.

Behind the plate, Darling is consistently reluctant to call balls, as his BB/9 is below average every year and 13th lowest of the 77 umpires who worked 500 or more innings from 2007 through 2010. For this reason alone he can be seen as a pitchers' umpire, but then look at his K/9. Not only has it gone up every year, but in 2010 it reached the stratosphere, ranking second highest in the majors. Darling's overall 2.44 K/BB ratio is 13th highest, a sure sign of an ample strike zone. With the exception of 2008, Darling's R/9 reflects that large strike zone. When you take out his 2008 innings and runs, his R/9 drops to 8.92, well below average for the 2007, 2009, and 2010 seasons.

So how did Darling's lawsuit turn out? The arguments were simple. "Come on, where's your sense of the first amendment, your sense of freedom of speech — your sense of humor?" asked Piniella's attorney. Responded Richie Phillips, head of the umpires' union and an attorney himself, "It's not freedom of speech to impugn an umpire's integrity. His livelihood is based on his honesty and reputation." Anyone with a legal background will recognize that the defense had a stronger case, but you don't need a legal background to know that extra-legal issues factor into these situations. The Lords of Baseball did not want the media focused on a lawsuit between an umpire and a manager. Three weeks after the incident, Piniella recanted his belief that Darling was biased, and after the season the two sides settled out of court. Terms were not disclosed, but they clearly included kissing and making up. "I have high regard for Gary Darling's integrity and deeply regret comments that may have maligned his character in any way," said Piniella. "Lou is a great guy. We've always been great friends," chirped Richie Phillips.

Darling was named a crew chief in 2004.

SOURCE

Chass, Murray. "Umpire's Suit Against Piniella Is Settled Out of Court." *New York Times*, December 19, 1991. (October 18, 2010.) http://www.nytimes.com/1991/12/19/sports/baseball-umpire-s-suit-against-piniella-is-settled-out-of-court.html.

Bob Davidson

BORN: August 3, 1952
FIRST MAJOR LEAGUE GAME: May 31, 1982
FAVORS: Pitchers
THEY HATE HIM IN: A better question might be, where *don't* they hate him?

	2007	2008	2009	2010	Totals
Games	34	34	33	36	137
Innings	304	306	290.17	332.67	1,232.83
R/9	9.30	8.03	10.20	8.31	8.83
BB/9	6.01	6.44	6.17	5.92	6.13
K/9	12.58	13.76	13.68	14.20	13.57
K/BB	2.09	2.14	2.22	2.40	2.21

Davidson is the game's angry old man. His career ejection rate of 4.4 percent is twice the major league norm. He led the National League in ejections in 1990 (16) and 1993 (15). And he isn't mellowing with age. Since 2007 his ejection rate has swelled to 5.3 percent while the collective rate of his peers has gone down. His 11 ejections in 2010 were the most by any umpire. On September 7, 2010, he even ejected a fan, although apparently with some cause. The intoxicated 44-year-old loner was harassing St. Louis Cardinal catcher Yadier Molina, hollering a homophobic slur at him. "Molina, I thought he was going to go toward [the fan] and I said, 'I'll take care of it,'" explained Davidson. Molina did not dispute Davidson's account. Nor did the fan, whose best defense was, "You'd think these guys would have tougher skin than that."

A hint of parody has crept into Davidson's temper. On August 14, 2009, the Cleveland Indians were in Minnesota for a game against the Twins. After six turns at bat they were losing 9–0. Minnesota had a runner on first and nobody out when Justin Morneau swung at a 3-2 pitch and apparently tipped it. Home plate umpire Davidson ruled it a foul-tip strike three. But Twins manager Ron Gardenhire asked Davidson to inspect the ball, and when Davidson saw dirt on it, he consulted with his colleagues and concluded that the ball hit the ground before it landed in the catcher's mitt. He changed his ruling to a foul ball and brought Morneau back to bat.

That enraged Eric Wedge, manager of the Indians. The two had a titanic argument, the bills of their caps butting as they shouted and pointed fingers at each other — and every now and then a flash of pleasure crossed Davidson's face. A couple of mornings later, as Wedge was speaking to the media, Davidson wandered past. "Hey Wedgie, tell them that's one of the best arguments I've ever had," he called out. "Thanks, Bob. I know you've had a few of them over the years. That's old school, right?" Davidson's response was wistful and perhaps genuine. "No one does that anymore. Coxie [Atlanta manager Bobby Cox] does that. Leyland [Detroit manager Jim] does it. That was great. I called my wife and said, 'You know what, I had more fun tonight than I've had in a long time.'"

Turned out that not only were they screaming at each other over a minor moment in a blowout, but their argument was based on a false premise. Replays showed that Morneau hadn't foul-tipped the ball. He missed it cleanly, and should have been out on strikes regardless of where the ball landed.

Davidson took his reputation global in 2006. He was assigned to work the inaugural World Baseball Classic, and was behind the plate for a second round game between Japan and the United States. The score was tied in the eighth when Akinori Iwamura, playing for his native Japan, hit a fly ball to left with a runner on third. Randy Winn of the American team caught the ball. His throw home was off line, and Japan took a 4–3 lead. That is, until Buck Martinez, manager of the American team, argued that the runner on third left the bag before Winn made his catch. Brian Knight, the umpire closest to the play, ruled against Martinez. But then Davidson overruled Knight. As home plate umpire, the call was technically his to make. The run came off the board and the American team went on to win. Sadaharu Oh, the legendary slugger who managed the Japanese team, couldn't hide his outrage: "It's unimaginable that this could happen in the United States, where baseball is so famous and popular." A few days later Davidson further fueled the world's doubts about his integrity when he called a home run off the foul pole by Mexico's Mario Valenzuela a double. Valenzuela scored anyway and Mexico won, so Davidson's ruling had less consequence.

When it comes to plate judgment, Davidson isn't at all controversial. His overall 6.13 BB/9 is just one percent below average and his 13.57 K/9 is two percent below average. The most he strayed from the norm in any plate ratio during the period under study was a 12.58 K/9 in 2007, which was six percent below average. Otherwise he comes close to the middle year after year. That hasn't prevented his R/9 from gyrating wildly, from four percent below average in 2007 to 14 percent below average in 2008 to nine percent above average in 2009 back down to six percent below average in 2010. As you would expect, that has more to do with the hitters than with Davidson. In 2007 their slash stats were .262/.326/.410, three or four percent below normal. In 2008 a 35 point drop in slugging percentage contributed to the precipitous drop in R/9. In 2009 the slash stats jumped to .268/.334/.437, accounting for the leap to a 10.20 R/9. In 2010 they dropped back to .257/.327/.370, the slugging percentage a full 33 points below normal, due in large part to a home run rate of just 1.32 per nine innings (the league norm was 1.92).

Davidson is often referred to as "Balking" Bob due to his penchant for making that unusual call.

Sources

Turner, Jamie. "What Grudges? Wedge, Umpire Davidson Laugh Off Friday's Rhubarb." *Cleveland Plain Dealer,* August 16, 2009. (October 18, 2010.) http://www.cleveland.com/tribe/index.ssf/2009/08/what_grudges_wedge_umpire_davi.html.

To watch the argument between Davidson and Wedge, go to http://mlb.mlb.com/video/play.jsp?content_id=6106301.

Gerry Davis

BORN: February 22, 1953
FIRST MAJOR LEAGUE GAME: June 9, 1982
FAVORS: Hitters, by a lot
THEY HATE HIM IN: Christian Dior's Umpwear Division

	2007	2008	2009	2010	Totals
Games	35	33	34	34	136
Innings	310.83	282.67	303.5	303	1,200
R/9	11.81	10.12	9.79	8.94	10.18
BB/9	7.44	6.81	6.55	5.58	6.60
K/9	12.48	13.47	12.93	13.40	13.06
K/BB	1.68	1.98	1.97	2.40	1.98

More runs score when Davis is behind the plate than any other current ump. The last time the major leagues as a whole compiled an R/9 higher than Davis's 10.18 was in 2000, when the collective R/9 was 10.28. Remember 2000? It was the heart of the Steroid Era. Batters hit over a thousand more home runs than they did in 2010.

But since compiling an absolutely outrageous 11.81 R/9 in 2007—the highest for any season of 150 or more innings in this study, and more than half a run more than the R/9 for 1930, the best hitters' season on record—Davis has been steadily coming back to earth. Each year since 2007 his R/9 and BB/9 have gone down. In 2010 his R/9 was just one percent above average. His BB/9 sank well below average, although his K/9 remained low (seventh lowest among his peers) so his K/BB remained within sniffing range of the norm. Even with that sober 2010, Davis's four-year performance establishes his strike zone as one of the smallest in the game. He has the 15th highest BB/9, sixth lowest K/9, and eighth lowest K/BB ratio of all current umpires.

Davis is an innovator, creator of a plate stance that is apparently gaining ground within the profession. There are many elements to the Gerry Davis stance, but the key is that the umpire spreads his legs far apart, keeps his knees straight, and rests his hands on his lower thighs to put his head at strike zone level. By contrast, the traditional home plate stance has the umpire crouch at the knees or even put a knee on the ground. The Gerry Davis stance greatly reduces stress on the knees and back. (It also aligns the umpire's nose with the inside corner, making pitches along that border particularly easy to judge.)

It has certainly worked for Davis. He is among the oldest umpires in the major leagues, but has never suffered a significant injury. He was hit in the mask by a pitched ball on July 26, 2008, and had to leave the game, but was back in action within a week.

Davis has also developed his own line of umpiring equipment. Some of it is engineered to facilitate his home plate stance. If you go to his web site you can purchase a starter kit — hat, mask, chest protector, shirt, pants, belt, shin guards, socks, shoes, ball bag, indicator (for balls, strikes, and outs) and plate brush — for $366.90.

Davis currently lives in Wisconsin, but was born in baseball-mad St. Louis. When he first came up he was challenged by Cardinal manager Whitey Herzog. Davis was working the plate on August 1, 1982, when he called a balk on Cardinal pitcher Joaquin Andujar. Herzog argued and Davis ejected him. It was the only ejection of Davis's rookie season. "He's done about six or eight of our games, and he's afraid he's going to give us a call," Herzog alleged, adding that Davis's presumed fear of favoring his hometown team should disqualify him from working Cardinal games. Davis let the remark go, and the incident blew over. In his 29-year career Davis has let a lot blow over. He has a 1.8 percent ejection rate, slightly below average. Since 2007 his ejection rate has plunged to 1.1 percent.

That forbearance has earned Davis the trust of Major League Baseball. He was appointed a crew chief in 1999, and in 2009 the Lords of Baseball named him the crew chief for the World Series, a sensitive assignment in light of the glaring mistakes umpires had made during the 2009 playoffs. "Obviously, our objective is to get everything right," Davis said. In the fifth inning of the first game, he had to show that he meant what he said.

With the New York Yankees' Hideki Matsui on first base and nobody out, Robinson Cano popped a flare to Philadelphia Phillie shortstop Jimmy Rollins, who fielded the ball inches from the ground. Had Rollins caught it or trapped it? Rollins contributed to the confusion by treating it like a trap, stepping on second to force Matsui and throwing to first in hopes of a double play, but then instructing Phillie first baseman Ryan Howard to tag Matsui for leaving the bag too early on a pop-out. Rather than rule on the spot, Davis convened his crew for a two-minute conference. The result? The umps got the call right: They ruled that Rollins caught the ball (which replays showed he had), meaning Cano was automatically out and Matsui was out when Howard tagged him. Davis's leadership didn't stem the flood of criticism umpires received for their 2009 postseason performance, but it did publicly reaffirm the umpires' commitment to get calls right.

Probably the oddest play of Davis's career occurred on July 1, 1998, in an interleague contest between the Chicago White Sox and Houston Astros. In the top of the seventh, Astro pitcher Doug Henry threw a wild pitch that somehow wound up in Davis's shirt pocket. Astro catcher Brad Ausmus couldn't find the ball, allowing the Chicago runner on third, Ray Durham, to score.

Source

Ehret, Scott. "Plate Stance Specifics — the Davis Stance." Northwest Umpires.com, undated. (October 19, 2010.) http://www.nwumpires.com/home/index.php?option=com_content&view=article&id=179:the-davis-stance&catid=27:amateur&Itemid=4.

Dana DeMuth

BORN: May 30, 1956
FIRST MAJOR LEAGUE GAME: June 3, 1983
FAVORS: Hitters, slightly
THEY HATE HIM IN: The Secret Service

	2007	2008	2009	2010	Totals
Games	34	33	34	34	135
Innings	307.17	295.5	297	298.67	1,198.33
R/9	10.43	8.68	10.09	9.04	9.57
BB/9	6.97	5.51	7.12	5.45	6.27
K/9	12.57	13.64	14.03	15.04	13.81
K/BB	1.80	2.48	1.97	2.76	2.20

Doctor Jekyll and Mister Hyde! DeMuth's 2007 numbers overwhelmingly favor hitters. His 2008 numbers overwhelmingly favor pitchers. His 2009 numbers careen back toward hitters. And in 2010, despite a slightly above average R/9, his numbers again favor pitchers. Although he may not be consistent, when his numbers are blended together he looks middle-of-the-road. DeMuth's R/9 ranks 17th, which is high, but his BB/9 is 34th, his K/9 38th (exactly the average K/9 for the period under study), and his K/BB 46th. His four-year strike zone rates as average. The only reason he's listed as a hitters' umpire is because of that high R/9, which can't be an accident over nearly 1,200 innings.

Were DeMuth asked about his yin-yanging annual numbers, he almost certainly wouldn't answer. He takes seriously the umpire's adage about avoiding the spotlight. Go to his page at MLB.com. There's no photo and a grand total of 22 words about his personal life. There are no chatty articles about him in his college or hometown newspaper. About the only time he will speak publicly is to take the blame for a crewmate's mistake, as he did on May 19, 2010, after Doug Eddings missed a home run by Josh Hamilton of the Texas Rangers. Eddings was certain the ball bounced off the top of the fence and that Hamilton had only doubled. Crew chief DeMuth supported Eddings and declined to look at a video replay, as he was entitled to do on a home run call. After the game he saw that Hamilton had indeed homered. "I didn't see any doubt in [Eddings] on that and I didn't think the replay was necessary. Obviously I'm wrong. It should have been a home run," he said after the game. "It's bad judgment by me but I have to have trust in the crew."

As that statement shows, DeMuth is hardly the my-way-or-the-highway type. In nearly 3,500 regular season games he has compiled an ejection rate of just over one percent, less than half the major league norm. On July 25, 2003, a haughty Pedro Martinez taunted DeMuth from the mound after DeMuth called a Martinez pitch ball four. Martinez outlined the strike zone for DeMuth, then held out his glove and gestured for DeMuth to try pitching himself. DeMuth had three words for Martinez. No, not "You're outta here!"

but "That's enough, Pedro." On September 1, 2010, DeMuth threw out the Yankees' Jorge Posada for vociferously arguing a called strike three. DeMuth reviewed the call after the game, realized it was wrong, and apologized to Posada the next day. "He's a class act. I apologized to him too," said Posada.

DeMuth's impressive game management skills undoubtedly factored into the decision to put him on the 2009 World Series umpiring crew. The umpires had been buffeted by criticism during the 2009 playoffs, and DeMuth could be depended on not to draw attention to himself. He called balls and strikes in the fifth game of the Series, and in keeping with his regular season performance, more runs scored in that game than in any other. Philadelphia's Cliff Lee, who didn't walk a single batter in game one, was dinged for three walks by DeMuth. New York's A.J. Burnett, who walked just two in seven innings in game two, yielded four free passes in just two innings under DeMuth.

DeMuth was named chief of the 2009 All-Star game umpiring crew. Before the game, President Obama spent ten minutes in the umpires' dressing room chatting amiably with five of them. DeMuth was nowhere to be found. "Where's Dana? Where's the chief?" Obama had to ask. Just another instance of DeMuth fleeing from the spotlight.

SOURCE

Borden, Sam. "Bombers Wonder on Pedro." *New York Daily News,* July 27, 2003. (October 19, 2010.) http://www.nydailynews.com/archives/sports/2003/07/27/2003-07-27_bombers_wonder_on_pedro.html.

Laz Diaz

BORN: March 29, 1963
FIRST MAJOR LEAGUE GAME: June 23, 1995
FAVORS: Pitchers
THEY HATE HIM IN: English Comp class

	2007	2008	2009	2010	Totals
Games	36	34	33	34	137
Innings	324.33	302.33	293	303	1,222.67
R/9	8.27	9.62	10.20	8.52	9.13
BB/9	5.44	5.42	6.02	6.36	5.80
K/9	14.46	14.32	14.04	13.99	14.21
K/BB	2.66	2.64	2.33	2.20	2.45

Go to the ballpark and you're likely to hear all manner of abuse shouted at umpires. Not nice, not clever, not original, but harmless — except on those very rare occasions when somebody actually has it in for an umpire, as one fan did for Laz Diaz on April 15, 2003. Diaz was working first base during a game between the Kansas City Royals and

Chicago White Sox at U.S. Cellular Field. Carlos Lee of the White Sox hit a fly ball to right field to end the eighth inning. Seconds later, a drunken fan attacked Diaz from behind.

What the inebriate didn't know was that Diaz had spent years in the Marine Corps Reserve. "I just turned around and got him off me," an unharmed Diaz shrugged modestly. "The good hand-to-hand combat [the Marines] taught me worked." He later told the *Military Times Edge*, "The Marine Corps—boot camp especially—helped me through my umpiring. Discipline, being able to adjust to the situation, being able to endure the comments from the fans and from the players. I heard words from A to Z in boot camp. You have to take it, not being able to respond or lash out. It gives you a tough skin."

Of all umpires to assault, Diaz would seem the least likely, and not just because of his combat training. A web search reveals the usual number of complaints from cranky bloggers about a call he made against their team and hence "blew," but there are no egregious incidents whole cities hold against him. And Diaz may well be the most cheerful, outgoing umpire in baseball. He even has his own Facebook fan club, for which he has graciously answered irrelevant, intrusive questions like "Who was the first person you kissed?" (He said he couldn't remember.) But some of the questions are on point. Asked whether he gets to know the players and managers well, Diaz wrote, "As far as getting to know the players in a personal way, I really don't know any of them." When asked for funny or interesting stories, he told about a time in Seattle he was working third base. "There was a line drive hit right at me. Trying to get out of the way and not get hit, I got off balance and fell on my behind. I seen [*sic*] the ball go foul, so on my butt, I called the ball foul. Everyone in the stands on my side was laughing."

Asked by his Facebook fans whether he enjoyed ejecting someone, Diaz wrote, "It doesn't feel good ejecting players or managers because afterward I have to right [*sic*] a report. It takes time away from me going to have a drink or two. But if they get out of line I will eject them in a New York minute." The numbers show that Diaz is indeed reluctant to let anything get in the way of his postgame quaff. He has just 23 ejections in over 1,600 games, a rate less than two-thirds the average. He tallied a mere six ejections from 2007 through 2010.

"I like being behind the plate. I feel like I'm in charge of the entire game and no one can mess with me," Diaz told his Facebook fans. Pitchers are happy to have Diaz in charge too. His overall 2.45 K/BB ratio is tenth highest. He is in the lowest fifth for overall walk rate and in the highest fifth for overall strikeout rate. There is no question that Diaz has one of the largest strike zones among major league umpires. But pitchers shouldn't get too confident. Over the last four years Diaz's walk rate has been rising and his strikeout rate falling. His 2010 results were nearly a full walk higher and half a strikeout lower than his 2007 results. And despite his large strike zone, Diaz has saved pitchers just 25 runs over the last four years.

Growing up in Miami, Florida, Diaz played outfield. He signed with the Minnesota Twins in 1984 and played for minor league teams in Elizabethton, Tennessee; Kenosha, Wisconsin; and Visalia, California. His favorite player was Pete Rose.

Mike DiMuro

BORN: October 12, 1967
FIRST MAJOR LEAGUE GAME: July 31, 1997
FAVORS: Pitchers
THEY HATE HIM IN: Japan

	2007	2008	2009	2010	Totals
Games	9	33	34	34	110
Innings	79	286.83	309.17	310.17	985.17
R/9	8.54	9.54	8.82	8.68	8.96
BB/9	5.13	6.21	6.32	5.95	6.08
K/9	15.72	13.24	14.09	14.57	14.12
K/BB	3.06	2.13	2.23	2.45	2.32

DiMuro's father, Lou, was an American League umpire from 1963 to 1982. He was best known for reversing a call during the 1969 World Series between the Baltimore Orioles and Miracle Mets. Oriole starter Dave McNally began the sixth inning of game five with a pitch at the feet of New York's Cleon Jones. The elder DiMuro ruled it a ball, but Met manager Gil Hodges argued that the pitch hit Jones in the foot. DiMuro stuck to his call until Hodges produced the ball, which had shoe polish on it. DiMuro awarded Jones first base. Donn Clendenon followed with a homer and the Mets went on to win, clinching the Series. Sadly, Lou DiMuro was killed crossing a busy street in Arlington, Texas, on June 7, 1982, after working a game between the Rangers and Chicago White Sox.

Son Mike DiMuro missed the first two-thirds of 2007 with an unspecified health problem, but since then hasn't missed any time. He is a pitchers' umpire, with an overall BB/9 two percent lower than average and an overall K/9 two percent above average. This has resulted in an overall R/9 four percent below average. In 2008, however, DiMuro was a bit more charitable to hitters, calling a league-average BB/9 and three percent fewer strikeouts than average. He is not an extreme pitchers' umpire, ranking 28th in K/BB for the period under study, but as his abbreviated 2007 season suggests, when he's out of practice his natural inclination is to call a large strike zone.

DiMuro was in no way out of practice on May 29, 2010, when he worked home plate for a game between the Philadelphia Phillies and Florida Marlins. But right from the first inning the Marlins were unhappy with the breadth of his strike zone. DiMuro's plate judgment seemed to help Florida too, as Josh Johnson and two relievers gave up just one run on seven hits, with no unintended walks. But the Marlin hitters were facing Roy Halladay, a challenge under any circumstances. When leadoff hitter Chris Coghlan took a 3–2 pitch in the bottom of the first, he thought it was ball four and began trotting to first base, only to hear DiMuro call it strike three. All three strikes on Coghlan had been called. "I thought they were balls, that's why I took them," he said. Halladay got into six more three-ball counts, but worked his way out of each. Twenty-four consecutive outs after Coghlan's whiff, Halladay struck out Wes Helms looking, his 11th of the night and the sixth called by DiMuro. When Ronny Paulino followed with a groundout, Halladay had the 20th perfect game in major league history. "I don't want to talk about the strike zone because that's discrediting what [Halladay] did," said Coghlan. Said Helms, "I'm not going to say what I thought [the strike zone] was in the paper." Asked his own opinion of DiMuro's strike zone, Halladay jokingly said, "thanks."

In 1997 DiMuro made a different sort of history by becoming the first American umpire to work in the Japanese major leagues. "It was one of the best experiences of my life. Japanese baseball is amazing," he told his alma mater, the University of San Diego, in October 2009. Time had made DiMuro's heart grow fonder. The Japanese Central League had hired DiMuro in hopes he would help professionalize the Japanese umpiring corps. He didn't expect much trouble. "The arguments will be very short. I won't know what they're saying and they won't know what I'm saying. We'll probably just look at each other and then walk away." But Japanese players and managers were accustomed to deferential umpires, which DiMuro emphatically wasn't. (His career ejection rate is nearly twice the major league norm. From 2007 through 2010 his ejection rate was 2.7 percent, 35 percent above average.) When DiMuro called strike three on a Chunichi Dragon, the player not only argued, but shoved DiMuro, nearly knocking him down. DiMuro was appalled when the player wasn't disciplined. He resigned just three months after arriving.

DiMuro writes the blog for Umps Care, the umpires' charity. In August 2010 he wrote a nostalgic entry about driving to the intersection of Michigan and Trumbull Streets in Detroit, where Tiger Stadium once stood. A month later, while waiting out a three-hour rain delay, he wrote about subjects ranging from the Umpire Media Guide to former player/umpire Bill Kunkel to his misadventures in Japan. Other entries wax eloquent about visits with former umpires like Bill Haller and Doug Harvey and the charitable work the current umpires do.

DiMuro's twin brother Ray was a major league umpire from 1996 through 1998.

SOURCE

Sullivan, Kevin. "American Ump Shakes Up Japan's Major Leagues." *Washington Post,* April 10, 1997. (October 19, 2010.) http://www.washingtonpost.com/wp-srv/inatl/longterm/mia/sports041097.htm.

Rob Drake

BORN: May 24, 1969
FIRST MAJOR LEAGUE GAME: September 3, 1999
FAVORS: Pitchers
THEY HATE HIM IN: Washington

	2007	2008	2009	2010	Totals
Games	35	38	38	34	145
Innings	317.83	341.83	339.83	298.33	1,297.83
R/9	8.83	8.95	9.00	9.62	9.09
BB/9	6.17	5.98	5.93	6.70	6.18
K/9	14.07	14.16	15.33	14.63	14.56
K/BB	2.28	2.37	2.59	2.18	2.36

Drake was officially named a major league umpire on March 31, 2010. It was long overdue. His employers had been exploiting his second-class status as a Triple-A call-up for a decade, denying him the vacation and other perks granted the 68 major league umpires. Between 2007 and 2009, no umpire worked more major league games than Drake (466). Only James Hoye (named a major league umpire on the same day) worked more innings behind the plate over that three-year stretch. At the time his promotion was announced, Drake had worked more major league games than Mike DiMuro, who became a major league umpire in 1999. It's good that the Lords of Baseball rewarded Drake's patience and loyalty, but outrageous that it took so long.

In the three years prior to his promotion, Drake produced consistent numbers that strongly favored pitchers. His BB/9 was four percent below average and his K/9 was six percent above average, giving him a large strike zone. That contributed to an R/9 five percent lower than average. In 2010, however, that changed. Although his K/9 remained at his established level, his BB/9 shot up and his R/9 followed, making Drake an umpire who zagged while most of his colleagues zigged. Most likely Drake's 2010 was an aberration. He averaged 6.12 called strikes per inning, a very high rate (only Wally Bell, Bill Miller, Mike Winters, and Paul Emmel were higher), and if he keeps that up he will probably tilt toward pitchers again in 2011. And despite 2010, Drake's four-year totals still lean the pitchers' way. In fact, his K/9 ranks second highest among the 77 umpires who called 500 or more innings from 2007 through 2010.

Early in his career Drake was tested by players and managers, hardly unusual for a new umpire. He responded strongly — perhaps too strongly. In 2001 he tallied 13 ejections in 103 games, which not only led the majors but constituted a nuclear response to backtalk. Since 2001 he's relied less on his power to banish, bumping along at 2.5 percent clip, slightly higher than average. He alternates good years with bad years. He had a good year in 2007, ejecting just one man in 159 games. In 2008 he went up to four ejections. In 2009 his disposition turned sunny again, and he threw out just one arguer. In 2010 he received the standard four weeks of in-season vacation, which should have relaxed him, but he wound up with five ejections, more than all but six other umpires. In fairness, two of the ejections shouldn't have been his. On August 28 he came to the aid of Triple-A call-up Dan Bellino, who called out Washington's Ian Desmond for running outside the three-foot lane to first base on a sacrifice attempt. First base umpire Drake handled the argument with Washington manager Jim Riggleman and pitcher Scott Olsen, and wound up ejecting them both. After the game, which the Nationals won 14–5, Riggleman was apologetic. "The umpires probably got it right, but it's a terrible rule. It has got to be changed."

Drake is active in Calling for Christ, a ministry headed by fellow umpire Ted Barrett. "Seeing yourself fail on ESPN is humbling! You desire understanding when mistakes are made, but you receive unforgiveness. That's why a personal relationship with Jesus Christ is meaningful," he wrote on the web site of the Arizona Umpiring Academy, closely associated with Calling for Christ. "Every time I walk on the baseball field I want to be perfect. Every morning when I wake up, I pray that He will give me the strength to live a sin-free life. The problem is that both are impossible."

Drake was the home plate umpire on June 27, 2010, when Vernon Wells of the Toronto Blue Jays hit the 506th home run off Jamie Moyer of the Philadelphia Phillies, the most ever yielded by a pitcher. Moyer, 47 years old, won the game handily.

Source

Drake, Rob. "Calling for Christ First Annual Retreat." ArizonaUmpiringAcademy.com, undated. (October 19, 2010.) http://www.arizonaumpiringacademy.com/Instructors/Testimonies_of_Umpires.html.

Bruce Dreckman

Born: August 7, 1970
First Major League Game: April 5, 1996
Favors: Pitchers, slightly
They hate him in: New York and Cincinnati

	2007	2008	2009	2010	Totals
Games	30	34	26	31	121
Innings	269.17	312.67	232.83	279.5	1,094.17
R/9	9.86	8.03	10.09	8.37	9.01
BB/9	6.15	5.90	6.03	6.50	6.14
K/9	13.27	13.61	12.14	14.52	13.45
K/BB	2.16	2.31	2.01	2.23	2.19

From the *Saint Paul Pioneer Press*, July 30, 2005: "[Minnesota Twin pitcher Kyle] Lohse fought Bruce Dreckman's strike zone and the veteran Boston lineup."

From the *Columbus Dispatch*, April 26, 2006: "Sauerbeck, Westbrook, and [Cleveland Indian] manager Eric Wedge all said home plate umpire Bruce Dreckman had a tight strike zone last night, which forced Westbrook and Red Sox starter Curt Schilling to work harder than normal."

From the *Tacoma News Tribune*, June 8, 2006: "[Seattle catcher Kenji] Johjima set up on the outer part of the plate — and [Seattle pitcher Rafael] Soriano hit his glove. Both pitcher and catcher started off the field, thinking they'd teamed for a strikeout. Plate umpire Bruce Dreckman disagreed."

For years Dreckman has had a reputation as a hitters' umpire, a guy with a tight strike zone. It's true that at times he's reluctant to call strike three. His 2009 K/9 was by far the lowest of all umpires working 150 or more innings behind the plate. But he's not a base on balls guy. His aggregate BB/9 of 6.14 is actually one percent below average, putting him 45th out of 77. And when it comes to the bottom line — his R/9 — his aggregate is three percent below average, despite a run-crazy 2009. So Dreckman's reputation is undeserved. Pitchers get a fair shake from him, as evidenced by the sharp rise in his 2010 K/9.

Dreckman also has a reputation in some circles as a hothead. This may stem from his calamitous 1999 season, in which he issued five ejections in 104 games, then had his resignation accepted by the Lords of Baseball after he obeyed his union's order to join a collective job abandonment. Dreckman didn't return to the majors until 2002, and except for a contentious 2004 he's been a model of restraint since, with just three ejections in 496 games from 2007 through 2010. His sole ejection of 2010 came at the expense of New York Yankee manager Joe Girardi, who took the fall for Nick Swisher, called out on strikes by Dreckman after checking his swing on a pitch from Toronto's Jason Frasor. "I thought the strike zone at times was generous, and I didn't think that [Swisher] swung," said Girardi. He had taken his hat off to get in Dreckman's face. After he was ejected he followed Dreckman around the infield, continuing to argue. But Dreckman never lost his cool.

Dreckman was behind home plate on April 13, 2009, for the first regular season game the New York Mets played at Citi Field. He contributed to the inaugural game's lore in the top of the sixth by calling a balk on Met pitcher Pedro Feliciano with a runner on third base, enabling the decisive run to score in a 6–5 Met loss. Feliciano conceded that he momentarily rose from the stretch position, then stopped, and Dreckman had been correct to call the balk. But he was steamed that Dreckman didn't make the call until San Diego batter David Eckstein complained. "I don't think the umpire saw it, but Eckstein started saying, 'balk, balk, balk,' and that's when he called it. To lose by a balk, it's hard."

Dreckman was on shakier ground during the 2010 National League Division Series between the Cincinnati Reds and Philadelphia Phillies. The Reds had a one-run lead in the second game and asked fireballing rookie Aroldis Chapman to protect it. Chapman's third pitch buzzed batter Chase Utley's arm. "I felt like it hit me, so I put my head down and ran to first," said Utley. Dreckman declared Utley a hit batsman, even though it wasn't clear that the ball struck him at all. (Wouldn't someone hit by a 101 mile-an-hour fastball flinch just a little bit?) Utley's trip to first ignited a three-run rally that gave the Phils game two, and they went on to sweep the series. Cincinnati manager Dusty Baker readily forgave Dreckman. "It's a tough play. I couldn't tell myself if he was hit or not. It's easy after the fact when you have slow motion."

Dreckman wears umpire uniform number one.

SOURCE

Krasovic, Tom. "Dusty Baker Defends Umpires Amid Calls for Expanded Instant Replay." MLB Fanhouse.com, October 9, 2010. (October 19, 2010.) http://mlb.fanhouse.com/2010/10/09/dusty-baker-defends-umpires-amid-calls-for-expanded-instant-repl/.

Doug Eddings

BORN: September 14, 1968
FIRST MAJOR LEAGUE GAME: August 16, 1998
FAVORS: Pitchers, very strongly
THEY HATE HIM IN: Orange County

	2007	2008	2009	2010	Totals
Games	34	34	35	34	137
Innings	309.17	306.33	311.17	305.83	1,232.5
R/9	8.67	9.55	9.31	7.47	8.76
BB/9	4.63	5.52	5.67	5.47	5.32
K/9	14.99	14.19	14.09	14.13	14.35
K/BB	3.24	2.57	2.49	2.58	2.70

Do you think walks are annoying? Then Doug Eddings should be your favorite umpire. He granted a whopping 122 fewer walks than an average umpire in the games he called from 2007 through 2010. Only Brian O'Nora had as low a BB/9 over that four-year stretch. What's more, Eddings likes strikeouts. He ranks ninth highest in K/9 for the period under study. His 2.70 K/BB is the highest of any umpire. All of which is the long way of saying that Doug Eddings has the biggest strike zone of any major league umpire.

His 2007 was over-the-top pitcher friendly, that 3.24 K/BB nearly half again the average. Since then he's been incredibly consistent. His annual BB/9s came within 20 points of each other from 2008 to 2010. His K/9 was even more uniform, varying by just ten points from 2008 to 2010. So Doug Eddings is the answer to two questions: Which umpire has the biggest strike zone, and which umpire has the most consistent strike zone?

Eddings's R/9 only fitfully corresponds with his strike zone. It corresponded in 2007, as even the most aggressive hitters found it hard to defend so much territory. His R/9 was a full run below average that year. But in 2008 his R/9 was slightly above average, and in 2009 it was right at the league average. Only in 2010 did Eddings's R/9 go back to reflecting his barn door strike zone, as his 7.47 was lower than that of all but three of his colleagues. Thanks to the 2007 and 2010 results, his overall R/9 ranks fifth lowest out of 77 umpires.

Eddings's most controversial moment behind the plate had nothing to do with his ball-and-strike judgment. The Anaheim Angels were playing the Chicago White Sox on October 12, 2005 in the second game of the American League Championship Series. The score was tied at one apiece in the bottom of the ninth. The Sox had two down and no one on when their catcher, A.J. Pierzynski, came to bat. Angel reliever Kelvim Escobar quickly got two strikes on him. Escobar's next pitch dived into the dirt. Pierzynski swung and missed. Eddings raised his fist in the air to indicate strike three. As Angel catcher Josh Paul rolled the ball back to the mound on the presumption that the inning was over, Pierzynski ran to first base and stood there, as if Paul had dropped strike three. "I didn't hear him [Eddings] call me out, so I ran," he explained.

After consulting with his fellow umpires, Eddings awarded Pierzynski first base. Pablo Ozuna pinch ran for Pierzynski, stole second, and scored on Joe Crede's double to win the game. "It was a swing, our catcher caught it, Doug Eddings called him out, and somewhere along the line, because the guy ran to first base, [Eddings] altered the call," Anaheim manager Mike Scioscia seethed afterwards. He had reason. The Pierzynski gambit swung momentum to the White Sox, who won the next three games to clinch a World Series berth.

Asked for an explanation, Eddings stuck to his guns. "We saw a couple different angles [on replay], and if you watch it, the ball changes direction, so I don't see how you can say it's a clearly caught ball." But what about the strike three call? Crew chief Jerry Crawford tackled that one. "He [Eddings] didn't call him out. He only called the pitch a strike."

When the series moved to Anaheim, Angel fans let Eddings have it. The Angels had to post 15 security guards and a police officer near him. "If I was an Angels fan, I probably wouldn't have liked it. But if I was a White Sox fan, I'm sure I would have said, 'great call.' That's the beauty of being a fan," Eddings mused. He had been through worse in the winter leagues. "In the Dominican, I ejected this one player in four straight games. So, after the game, we're at a taco stand, and the player I'd ejected drove up in a car with some buddies. Then, he pulled up his shirt and had a pistol in his belt. But nothing ever came of it. I've never been scared or intimidated on the field. And I didn't pick this job to be well-liked or popular."

Indeed. Eddings has a fast thumb. His 3.8 percent career ejection rate is well above the major league average of 2.2 percent. "One of the misconceptions is that we take a lot of abuse. I don't take a lot of abuse. I'll get rid of the problem," he told his local paper, the *Albuquerque Journal,* in 2003. However, he was quick to add that "Most of the time, it's discussion. A lot of times, batters will ask after a pitch, 'Is that the lowest you'll go [on a called strike]?' or 'That caught the plate [if he swung]?'"

Very early in his umpiring career, Eddings worked college games with fellow New Mexican Mike Everitt.

Source

Harrison, Randy. "Los Lunas' Eddings Loves His Life in Blue as Big League Umpire." *Albuquerque Journal* via AccessMyLibrary.com, February 7, 2003. (October 20, 2010.) http://www.accessmylibrary.com/coms2/summary_0286-2760989_ITM.

Paul Emmel

BORN: May 2, 1968
FIRST MAJOR LEAGUE GAME: July 31, 1999
FAVORS: Pitchers, strongly
THEY HATE HIM IN: Baltimore

	2007	2008	2009	2010	Totals
Games	29	34	33	34	130
Innings	256.33	300	299.67	300.17	1,156.17
R/9	9.59	8.01	9.22	8.52	8.80
BB/9	5.69	5.46	6.04	5.46	5.66
K/9	13.69	13.86	14.75	14.93	14.33
K/BB	2.41	2.54	2.44	2.74	2.53

Paul Emmel is a solid pitchers' umpire. In all four seasons under study his BB/9 was below the norm and his K/9 was above the norm. Only two things separate Emmel from Doug Eddings, the umpire most favorable to pitchers: His walk ratio is higher, and he's not as consistent (although no one is as consistent as Eddings). Emmel's R/9 and K/9 are virtually the same as Eddings's.

Despite his pro-pitcher leanings, once or twice a year Emmel gets finicky about the strike zone. On August 1, 2007, he called 14 bases on balls in a game involving the Philadelphia Phillies and Chicago Cubs. On April 8, 2008, Emmel flustered starting pitchers Franklin Morales of the Colorado Rockies and Matt Cain of the San Francisco Giants, calling five walks on each over a combined nine and two-thirds innings. Despite issuing 13 passes for the game, Emmel watched only four runs score as Cain and three relievers somehow shut out Colorado. The Rockies saw Emmel's fussy side again on June 13, 2009, during an interleague contest with the Seattle Mariners. Emmel called 11 walks that game. On his very next home plate assignment, a match between the Atlanta Braves and Boston Red Sox, Emmel called another ten. And then on May 11, 2010, Emmel called 16 walks in a game between the San Diego Padres and San Francisco Giants, the two best pitching staffs in the majors that year.

Emmel had an average ejection rate until six tosses in both 2007 and 2008, plus another eight in 2010, pushed him into the totalitarian column. His ejection rate of 4.3 percent over the last four years is more than twice as high as the average umpire. The most colorful ejection of Emmel's career occurred on September 12, 2007, when he ran Baltimore Oriole manager Dave Trembley. The Orioles were hosting the Los Angeles Angels and getting hammered, falling behind 8–0 early. But in the bottom of the fourth the Orioles rallied. With four runs in, two men on, and only one out, Jay Payton hit a grounder into the hole. Angel shortstop Orlando Cabrera backhanded the ball and made a nifty throw to Howie Kendrick at second. Emmel, the second base umpire, called the runner out on the force. But as replays showed, Kendrick was nowhere near the bag when he caught the ball. Trembley argued until Emmel ejected him, and then the fireworks began. Trembley extended his arms to indicate how much his runner was safe by, pursued the retreating Emmel, repeatedly drew a line in the dirt to indicate where he thought Kendrick caught the ball, pointed to his eyes as if to say "try using yours!" and then with a flourish *ejected Emmel.* Unamused, the Lords of Baseball suspended Trembley for three games.

But that was hardly the biggest controversy of Emmel's career. For that you need to go back to a game-ending call on August 6, 2004. The Tampa Bay Devil Rays had a runner on third with one out in the tenth when their designated hitter, Tino Martinez, hit a fly ball to Seattle Mariner left fielder Raul Ibanez. As Ibanez made the catch, Seattle third baseman Willie Bloomquist moved to cut-off position and shortstop Jose Lopez covered third. Tampa Bay runner Carl Crawford tagged up and raced three steps down the line, then retreated—for good reason, as the ball wasn't hit very deep and Ibanez threw a strike to the catcher. But Emmel, the third base umpire, ruled that Lopez had obstructed Crawford's view of the catch. He awarded Crawford home plate on fielder's interference and gave the Devil Rays the win.

"That was the worst call I've ever seen. Emmel's a good umpire. But it was a horrible call," Mariner manager Bob Melvin said. Devil Ray manager Lou Piniella reportedly told team broadcaster Dewayne Staats that he had seen such a call only once before in his long career. True to umpire protocol, Emmel let his crew chief respond. "In this case both the shortstop and the third baseman attempted to impede the runner tagging from third from seeing when the ball was caught, by screening him from the play," contended Joe West, complicating the situation by bringing Bloomquist into it. "What they did was intentional, you can tell. I can listen to Melvin tell me they didn't do that. I have to believe my umpire. That's what I did. The rule makes him score, we didn't make him score."

West's defense of Emmel did not placate Mariner manager Melvin. When Melvin took his lineup card to home plate the next night, he gave the umpires such an earful that West ejected him ten minutes before game time.

Source
Sherwin, Bob. "Obstructed View? Mariners Don't See It That Way." *Seattle Times*, August 7, 2004. (October 20, 2010.) http://seattletimes.nwsource.com/html/mariners/2001999194_mari07.html.

Mike Estabrook

BORN: July 28, 1976
FIRST MAJOR LEAGUE GAME: May 7, 2006
FAVORS: Pitchers, strongly
THEY HATE HIM IN: Cincinnati and Kansas City

	2007	2008	2009	2010	Totals
Games	3	23	23	33	82
Innings	29	199	209.33	291.5	728.83
R/9	5.59	8.23	8.51	8.03	8.13
BB/9	3.41	5.97	5.63	5.22	5.47
K/9	14.28	13.07	13.41	14.70	13.87
K/BB	4.19	2.19	2.38	2.82	2.53

The above chart includes all of Triple-A call-up Estabrook's major league plate appearances through 2010. He first came to the major leagues in 2006, but all of his nine games were in the field. He made his pitch-calling debut in a contest between Texas and Toronto on August 5, 2007.

Estabrook is a pitchers' umpire. His BB/9s have been below the norm every season, and his overall rate of 5.47 is fourth lowest among the 77 umpires who called more than 500 innings from 2007 through 2010. In his first three seasons he was reticent about third strikes, compiling a K/9 two percent below the norm. But he warmed up to punchouts in 2010 and as a result his four-year K/9 is slightly above the major league norm. His R/9s have faithfully reflected his large strike zone, coming in significantly below average each year. In fact, his 8.13 overall rate is the lowest of all current umpires. Want to see a pitchers' duel? Your best chance is to find out when Mike Estabrook is calling balls and strikes and go to that game.

New umpires are often tested, but Estabrook managed to get 128 games into his big league career before ejecting anyone. When the moment arrived, he took a two-fer. He was behind the plate on April 25, 2009, for a game between Atlanta and Cincinnati. The teams had nearly brawled the day before, so when a Derek Lowe pitch hit Cincinnati slugger Joey Votto, Estabrook issued a warning to both sides. That irked the Reds. They felt the Braves had overreacted to an accidental hit batsman the day before, and had intentionally gone after Votto. Red center fielder Jerry Hairston snapped after Estabrook called him out on strikes two innings later. "Jerry told him it was a terrible call. I guess he didn't like how [Estabrook] gestured," said Red manager Dusty Baker. Estabrook ejected Hairston, prompting a visit from Baker. "I came out and asked him what Jerry said, and when I agreed it was a terrible call, he threw me out," said Baker. Replays indicated that Hairston and Baker had good reason to question the call.

Estabrook didn't waste any time racking up his first ejection of 2010. In an April 9 contest between Boston and Kansas City, his first home plate assignment of the season, he tossed Boston designated hitter David Ortiz for questioning a strikeout call on a checked swing. "[Ortiz] obviously said something. It was kind of cut and dried," Red Sox manager Terry Francona conceded. Estabrook's only other ejection of 2010 occurred on June 3, when he was once again questioned about his plate judgment. Catcher Jason Kendall of the Royals thought an 0–2 pitch to the Los Angeles Angels' Torii Hunter should have been strike three. Without leaving his crouch he harangued Estabrook, who crossed to the front of the plate, leaned down to Kendall, and harangued back. Kansas City manager Ned Yost rescued Kendall and was ejected for his trouble, but he got into a finger-pointing, nose-to-nose scream-off with Estabrook before leaving. Replays showed that Kendall was right — and that Estabrook, despite a well below average ejection rate, may need more tutoring in the art of walking away if he wishes to remain on the short list of Triple-A call-ups contending for a major league job.

Although he is one of the youngest umpires working major league games and is presumably in great health, Estabrook had two heart valves replaced when he was a teenager.

Source

Paylor, Terez A. "Yost Protects Kendall, Gets Ejected." *Kansas City Star*, June 3, 2010. (October 20, 2010.) http://www.kansascity.com/2010/06/03/1991466/yost-protects-kendall-and-draws.html.

Mike Everitt

BORN: August 22, 1964
FIRST MAJOR LEAGUE GAME: June 20, 1996
FAVORS: Pitchers
THEY HATE HIM IN: Wrigley Field (although it's not his fault)

	2007	2008	2009	2010	Totals
Games	34	35	34	36	139
Innings	301.67	320	310	321	1,252.67
R/9	8.47	9.45	9.78	8.89	9.15
BB/9	5.31	5.82	6.53	6.28	5.99
K/9	13.54	13.92	14.28	14.19	13.99
K/BB	2.55	2.39	2.19	2.26	2.33

Everitt's R/9, BB/9, and K/9 had all been rising since 2007, but in 2010 they went down. In the case of his R/9 and BB/9, he was just joining the larger trend toward fewer runs and walks. But the drop in K/9 bucked the trend. His 2010 K/9 wasn't much lower than his 2009 K/9, but because the league as a whole saw an increase of .29 strikeouts per nine innings, it was a bigger drop than it looked, and Everitt's rate fell below the norm for the first time during the period under study. Even so, his reputation as a pitchers' umpire remains secure. According to the Toronto Blue Jays' report on umpires, Everitt "gives multiple inches on [the] outside corner," especially against left-handed hitters, which helps explain why his overall R/9 ranks 51st, his BB/9 59th, his K/9 27th, and his K/BB 27th. That said, he had an exceptionally strong pitchers' year in 2007, and if this study had begun in 2008, his R/9 and BB/9 would score above average and he would be ranked a mildly pro-hitter ump.

Everitt was a Triple-A call-up in 1999, when the Major League Umpires Association told its members to resign as a collective bargaining tactic and had its bluff called by the Lords of Baseball, who let 22 umpires go. Everitt was offered one of the newly vacant positions, and since technically he wasn't breaking the union — the umpires had *resigned*— he accepted. "There was hesitation, yet I knew what the right thing to do was. As far as crossing a picket line and being a strike replacement or taking someone's job in that fashion, it's not anything like that," he told the *New York Times*.

Everitt had a couple of noteworthy moments in 2003. On April 27 he called a no-hitter by Kevin Millwood of the Philadelphia Phillies against the San Francisco Giants, the only no-no of the season. Everitt called Barry Bonds out on strikes to end the Giant seventh, which helped Millwood. "I've had a couple of other shots that I've lost in the seventh inning and today I got through that and made it," Millwood told reporters afterward.

The other big moment of 2003 came during the National League Championship Series. The Chicago Cubs were leading the series 3–2 and led the Florida Marlins 3–0 in the eighth inning of game six. They were within five outs of their first World Series appearance since 1945. Luis Castillo of the Marlins pulled a fly ball toward the left field corner. It looked catchable for Cub left fielder Moises Alou. He ran toward the stands, reached up for the ball, and seemingly had it. Except Cub fan Steve Bartman got to it first, depriving Alou of the opportunity to record the second out. Along with every Cub partisan in the world, Alou wanted the left field umpire — Mike Everitt — to call fan interference. Everitt refused. It was an unpopular call, but the correct one. Bartman did not reach onto the field for the ball, and fans are entitled to compete with players for possession of balls hit in the stands. Castillo subsequently walked, the Marlins scored eight runs that inning to win the game, and then the Cubs lost game seven to crush the Wrigley Nation's spirits yet again.

Everitt kept his composure that night, but he's not a turn-the-other-cheek type. While establishing himself in 2000, he led the major leagues with 13 ejections. He hasn't had a year like that since, but his ejection rate remains higher than average. From 2007 through 2010 he was responsible for 14 ejections, a rate of 2.6 percent. But not all the ejections were about a call. On June 16, 2007, Everitt collected four ejections at (where else?) Wrigley Field after San Diego pitcher Chris Young hit Cub slugger Derrek Lee on the hand with a pitch. On the way to first, Lee traded insults with Young, then ran at the 6'10" pitcher. The benches emptied. In the course of restoring order, Everitt thumbed Lee and Young (who were suspended five games each), Padre pitcher Jake Peavy, and Cub hitting coach Gerald Perry. Take away that one incident, and Everitt's ejection rate from 2007 through 2010 aligns with the major league average.

Everitt's integrity led to an unusual and embarrassing moment for his crew on June 17, 2010. The Kansas City Royals were batting in the bottom of the fifth against Houston. They had a man on second and one out. Yuniesky Betancourt hit a soft liner to Astro shortstop Geoff Blum, who seemed to catch the ball off his shoetops. That's what Everitt ruled. Blum stepped on second to double up the runner and the inning was over. The Astros jogged off the field. But then Everitt went to crew chief Tim McClelland with an admission: He'd gotten the call wrong, Blum had trapped the ball. McClelland convened the crew. They decided to give the Astros credit for a 6–3 putout, even though Blum never threw to first, and they advanced the Kansas City runner from second to third. Then they ordered the Astros back on the field so the Royals could send another batter to the plate. In the end, it didn't matter. The Royals failed to score, although they later rallied to win the game.

Source

Kaegel, Dick. "Umpires Reverse Call in Kansas City." MLB.com, June 18, 2010. (October 20, 2010.) http://mlb.mlb.com/news/article.jsp?ymd=20100617&content_id=11304398&vkey=news_mlb&fext=.jsp&c_id=mlb.

Chad Fairchild

BORN: December 30, 1970
FIRST MAJOR LEAGUE GAME: September 30, 2004
FAVORS: Hitters (but that could change)
THEY HATE HIM IN: the Glavine family

	2007	2008	2009	2010	Totals
Games	29	36	34	32	131
Innings	255.5	318.17	315.67	288.5	1,177.83
R/9	10.43	11.17	8.38	9.05	9.74
BB/9	6.20	7.30	5.59	5.96	6.27
K/9	14.90	13.29	13.31	15.16	14.11
K/BB	2.40	1.82	2.38	2.54	2.25

Fairchild appeared in 144 big league games from 2004 to 2006. Only 28 were behind home plate, and these are the numbers he compiled:

Innings	*R/9*	*BB/9*	*K/9*	*K/BB*
245	9.00	6.17	12.97	2.10

Considered together, those first 28 games indicate that Fairchild came up a pitchers' umpire despite a low strikeout rate. In 2007 he turned friendly to hitters (although again the strikeout rate didn't align). The trend toward hitters increased in 2008 as he amassed the third highest R/9 among big league umpires, fueled by a BB/9 17 percent higher than average. But just when it looked like he had established himself as a dependable ally of hitters, look what happened in 2009. Those nosedives in R/9 and BB/9 are remarkable. They moderated somewhat in 2010, but his K/9 shot up by nearly two per nine innings. So what kind of strike zone can hitters and pitchers expect when Chad Fairchild dons the mask?

A fluctuating one, evidently, and not just from season to season, but within seasons as well. In 2010 he made 32 starts behind home plate. Over his first eight starts his K/9 was 15.86. Had he kept that up for the entire year he would have finished with the second highest K/9 in the majors. But over his next eight starts his K/9 dropped to 14.33, very close to the season average. In his next eight starts his K/9 rose to 14.83, and in his last eight starts (it's the home stretch!) his K/9 shot back up again, to 15.64.

Fairchild's fluctuating strike zone is nothing new. It was an issue back in 2007. On June 23 of that year, in a game between Atlanta and Detroit, he called Tiger fireballer Justin Verlander's first five pitches strikes, and didn't stop calling strikes until Verlander racked up 11 strikeouts. The game featured 22 strikeouts overall, nine called. Atlanta catcher Brian McCann was so upset by Fairchild's strike zone that he argued about it, earning an ejection. Manager Bobby Cox chimed in and got tossed for the 131st time of his career, tying the record set by John McGraw. But just five weeks later, in a July 31 game between the New York Mets and Milwaukee Brewers, veteran Met hurler Tom Glavine objected to how tight Fairchild's strike zone was! Fairchild called five walks on Glavine in six innings. For the game, which went 13 innings, Fairchild called 12 ball fours but not a single strike three (there were nine swinging strikeouts). It bothered Glavine all the more because it was his first attempt at his 300th win, and 30 family members were in town. "I didn't give in to the hitter or the strike zone," he said quietly but pointedly.

So it goes across Fairchild's ouvre. How could his R/9 plummet three runs per game from 2008 to 2009? How could his BB/9 go from 6.20 to 7.30 to 5.59? The best guess is that he is a work in progress. It's hard to conclude whether he favors pitchers or hitters or is neutral because his four-year totals are all over the map. He ranks 13th in R/9, which is high and puts him squarely in the hitters' corner; 32nd in BB/9, slightly favorable to hitters; 23rd in K/9, among the top third favoring pitchers; and 38th in K/BB, in the middle of the pack. On the basis of his high R/9, he's rated a hitters' umpire. But his strike zone could change, and there's not necessarily a correlation between strike zone and runs scored anyway, so watch for more twists and turns in the Fairchild story.

And he will be around next year. Prior to the 2010 season, the Lords of Baseball named him a major league umpire. It took him 13 years to reach the summit of his profession. He told his hometown paper, the *Norwalk* (Ohio) *Reflector,* that after working 151 major league games in 2008 and another 144 in 2009, four weeks of in-season vacation would be a relief. "You are on the move a lot as the more recent integrated staff scheduling system has all umpire crews working all 30 major league cities," he said. Still, becoming a major league umpire is "like hitting a lottery ticket, but still loving to go to work."

Fairchild has a two percent career ejection rate, which is average for the years he's been in the major leagues. The in-season vacation must have agreed with him, as he had no ejections in 2010.

SOURCE

Hohler, Don. "Fairchild Officially Becomes a Member of MLB Umpire Crew." *Norwalk* (Ohio) *Reflector*, April 3, 2010. (October 20, 2010.) http://www.allbusiness.com/sports-recreation/referees-umpires/14231101-1.html.

Andy Fletcher

BORN: November 17, 1966
FIRST MAJOR LEAGUE GAME: August 24, 1999
FAVORS: Pitchers, strongly
THEY HATE HIM IN: Hitting coach conventions

	2007	2008	2009	2010	Totals
Games	18	33	34	31	126
Innings	161.67	305.83	298.17	276.17	1,041.83
R/9	7.18	7.89	8.54	9.09	8.28
BB/9	4.79	6.27	6.82	6.19	6.18
K/9	15.20	13.92	14.79	14.76	14.59
K/BB	3.17	2.22	2.17	2.38	2.36

If you believe the best measure of an umpire is his R/9, then you believe Andy Fletcher is among the very best pitchers' umpires. His 8.28 R/9 since 2007 is the lowest of any umpire except Mike Estabrook, a Triple-A call-up. Just having Fletcher call pitches reduces offense by 11 percent. An average umpire would have seen 119 more runs score in Fletcher's 1,041.83 innings.

How does he do it? In 2007, the answer was obvious. His BB/9 was 22 percent below average and his K/9 was 14 percent above average. He was calling so many more strike threes and so many fewer ball fours that it seriously retarded offensive production. But starting in 2008 things got murkier. Although his 7.89 R/9 was 16 percent below average and ranked third lowest in the majors, his BB/9 rose to one percent *above* average, and his K/9 of 13.92 was only a couple of percent above average, not enough to inhibit offense. In 2009 his BB/9 rose to *six* percent above average, yet his R/9 remained eight percent below average. In 2010 his BB/9 came way down and his K/9 stayed high, but his R/9 actually rose. Clearly Fletcher's R/9 had come untethered from strike threes and ball fours.

Which doesn't mean his low R/9 is a fluke. In 2008, batters hit only .233 when Fletcher was behind the plate, with a .307 on-base percentage and a .378 slugging percentage. The major league norms were significantly higher: .264/.333/.416. In 2009 hitters compiled a .259 average for Fletcher, with a .332 on-base percentage and a .387 slugging percentage. Better than 2008, but again well below average. In 2010 Fletcher's slash stats were .263/.326/.404; the on-base percentage and slugging percentage were each one point higher than the major league norm, not enough to account for an R/9 three percent above average. Something in the way Fletcher calls a game makes life hard on hitters. The Toronto Blue Jays might have found the answer. They noted in their umpire report that Fletcher "will reward pitchers for making their pitch."

You would expect a high ejection rate from Fletcher, driven by unhappy hitters and their protective managers. At 2.6 percent his ejection rate is higher than average, but not outrageously so. For the most part Fletcher keeps things low-key, perhaps because of the embarrassment from one of his first ejections, on August 5, 2001. A foul tip eight days earlier had swelled the knuckles of his throwing hand to the point where he couldn't wear his wedding ring. As he called the game between the Philadelphia Phillies and San Francisco Giants, the pain grew, and it became harder for him to throw. When Giant pitcher Livan Hernandez requested a new ball in the fourth inning, Fletcher asked Giant catcher Benito Santiago to throw it. Santiago had been steaming about Fletcher's plate judgment, and refused. Fletcher flung the ball in the dirt in front of Santiago and demanded he throw it to Hernandez. When Santiago refused again, Fletcher ran him. After the game, crew chief Larry Young acknowledged that he had never seen an ejection like that. "We just talked to Andy. We told him about alternate methods that he could have used." Added Young dryly, "I believe he was very receptive to that."

In 2008 Fletcher led the majors in ejections with eight. He was involved in six disputes, two of which resulted in double ejections. Of the six, three involved whether a ball was foul or something else (infield hit, hit batsman, or strikeout) and one involved a close play at second base. Only two concerned his ball-and-strike judgment, not bad for a guy who puts hitters so much on the defensive. In 2009 Fletcher recorded no ejections at all. In 2010 he had four ejections and only one was about his ball-and-strike judgment; another stemmed from his ruling a checked swing strike three, but he was working first base and was not calling balls and strikes.

Fletcher missed half the 2007 season recovering from knee surgery. He had also suffered a concussion and taken numerous balls in the mask, so he became the first umpire to wear a mouth guard when working home plate. Mark Letendre, director of umpire medical services, supported Fletcher's decision. The primary purpose of the mouth guard is to reduce damage to teeth and jaws, but there is speculation that it also reduces the likelihood of concussions. When he needs to be understood, Fletcher removes the mouth guard and either holds it in his hand or sticks it in a pocket.

Source

Kirk, Jim. "MLB Umpire Andy Fletcher Uses Mouthguard to Prevent Concussions." UmpAttire.com, August 17, 2009. (October 20, 2010.) http://umpattire.blogspot.com/2009_08_01_archive.html.

Marty Foster

BORN: November 25, 1963
FIRST MAJOR LEAGUE GAME: September 10, 1996
FAVORS: Pitchers
THEY HATE HIM IN: The Bronx and Detroit

	2007	2008	2009	2010	Totals
Games	31	34	32	25	122
Innings	281.67	300.33	285.5	220.67	1,088.17
R/9	9.84	8.51	8.67	9.79	9.16
BB/9	5.43	6.23	6.65	5.63	6.01
K/9	13.87	14.20	14.15	15.25	14.32
K/BB	2.55	2.28	2.13	2.71	2.38

Is Marty Foster too old-school?

That question raged for days after Foster made a controversial call at third base in a July 6, 2009 game between the Toronto Blue Jays and New York Yankees. Derek Jeter was at second and tried to steal third. The throw beat him by so much that Blue Jay third baseman Scott Rolen had time to place his glove in front of the bag and await Jeter's arrival. Jeter came in head first, arms outstretched, left hand going for the base. Rolen reached to intercept the hand, but in one quick motion the canny Jeter pulled it back and slipped his right hand onto the bag. Safe!

Foster called him out.

"No way!" cried Jeter, leaping to his feet. Yankee third base coach Rob Thomson yanked him away, preserving Jeter's record of more than 2,000 games without an ejection. Instead, Yankee manager Joe Girardi took up the argument and received the dismissal. After the game, Jeter went public about his exchange with Foster. "I was told I was out because the ball beat me and he [Rolen] didn't have to tag me. I was unaware of that change in the rules."

Crew chief John Hirschbeck responded for Foster. He did not deny that Foster said a tag was unnecessary, and seemed troubled by the remark. "You can't just say, 'The ball beats you, you're out.' It's not a reason to call someone out because the ball beats you. It used to be that way. It's not true anymore." Hirschbeck explained that in the old days (he began his career in 1983, 13 years before Foster) if a play looked obvious to the fans in the park, umpires avoided a contrary call for fear they'd be criticized. In this case, the ball cleanly beat Jeter, Rolen applied the tag, and Rolen held onto the ball. The old school says Jeter is out. But the new school, which lives in the age of slow-motion replays from multiple angles, recognizes that a much larger audience is watching on television, and even if the umpire makes the contrary call and gets roundly booed, if *Baseball Tonight* shows he was right, the controversy disappears.

You can imagine how Hirschbeck's candor must have gone down in the umpire's dressing room. So Hirschbeck talked to the media again the next day, saying that what Foster actually told Jeter was, "The ball beat you, and I had him tagging you." Hirschbeck pronounced himself satisfied with this version of events, which probably restored harmony within his crew. But Jeter and Thomson didn't buy it. "He knows exactly what he said and he didn't say that," Jeter responded, and Thomson echoed, "I didn't hear him say that."

Another way Foster is old school is his Nineties-style short fuse. His lifetime ejection rate is twice the average, and he led the majors in ejections in 2004 and 2005. On July 26, 2010, Foster may have pushed Major League Baseball's tolerance for arbitrary dismissals too far. In the third inning of a scoreless game between Detroit and Tampa Bay, he called the Rays' B.J. Upton safe on a steal. Tiger manager Jim Leyland argued the call — for good reason, as Upton was out by a foot. As Leyland grew more animated, some of the sunflower seeds he'd been chewing flew out of his mouth and landed on Foster's uniform. Not only did Foster eject Leyland, but he told Leyland he would write in his postgame report that Leyland had spit on him intentionally. "I said, 'You mean to tell me that you're going to write up that I deliberately spit on you?' He said, 'Yes.' I said, 'Well that's a blatant lie.'"

The Lords of Baseball suspended and fined Leyland. They did not make any announcement about Foster, but he missed the next three weeks of the season. Most likely they didn't suspend him. He could have been injured, on extended vacation, or on personal leave. The union issued no statement, which it would have done if it felt Foster had been unfairly treated. And reporters didn't inquire, in part because they don't consider umpires newsworthy, in part because research has become a lost art for most daily journalists, and in part because the Foster-Leyland incident was overshadowed by Tampa Bay pitcher Matt Garza going on to hurl the first no-hitter in Rays' history. So we may never know why Foster disappeared after his argument with Leyland.

Foster's aggregate numbers reveal he has a larger than average strike zone, calling three percent fewer walks and affirming four percent more strikeouts than the typical umpire. Hitters had good years with him behind the plate in 2007 and 2010 (paradoxically, given the size of his K/BB ratio), but in 2008 and 2009 they struggled, even though he was much more generous with bases on balls. Overall Foster ranks 50th in R/9, 56th in BB/9, 11th in K/9, and 15th in K/BB, all consistent with a pitchers' umpire.

Source
King, George A. III. "Jeter Calls Out Umpire." *New York Post*, July 9, 2009. (October 21, 2010.) http://www.nypost.com/p/sports/yankees/item_tRzPAjUkZXhQVJihBPZENJ.

Greg Gibson

BORN: October 2, 1968
FIRST MAJOR LEAGUE GAME: June 14, 1997
FAVORS: Hitters
THEY HATE HIM IN: WEEI Radioland

	2007	2008	2009	2010	Totals
Games	34	36	28	35	133
Innings	302.67	333.83	248.67	322.83	1,208
R/9	10.65	9.25	10.17	7.00	9.19
BB/9	6.99	6.58	5.97	6.22	6.46
K/9	12.76	12.91	12.70	14.27	13.19
K/BB	1.83	1.96	2.13	2.30	2.04

What a difference a year can make. Had this study covered 2007 through 2009 only, Gibson would be described as one of the best hitters' umpires in the game. His R/9 for the three-year period was 9.99, his BB/9 was 6.55, and his K/9 was just 12.80. Had his 2010 record been comparable to the previous three years, he'd have the sixth highest R/9, the 16th highest BB/9, the second lowest K/9, and the seventh lowest K/BB, all of which would place him far on the hitters' end of the umpiring spectrum. But in 2010 he saw a lot more strikeouts and dramatically fewer runs; only James Hoye had a lower R/9 for the year. As a result, his overall R/9 now tilts the pitchers' way, ranking just 46th out of 77. He has fallen to 19th in BB/9, risen from second lowest to eighth lowest in K/9, and risen from seventh lowest to 15th lowest in K/BB. Gibson still calls a hitter-friendly strike zone, and his R/9 will almost certainly rise from its 2010 abyss. But try consoling the hitters whose slash stats amounted to just .236/.308/.373 in front of him in 2010.

Gibson had an eventful 2008. In January, a neighbor informed him that someone purporting to be a friend was roaming the block asking intrusive questions about him. The so-called friend inquired "if Greg was a member of any clubs or groups, anything like the KKK [Ku Klux Klan]." Gibson contacted union president John Hirschbeck and learned that at least three other umpires — Sam Holbrook, Ron Kulpa, and Hirschbeck himself — had similar experiences. Turned out the "friend" was an investigator hired by the Lords of Baseball to conduct background checks on umpires in the wake of a National Basketball Association scandal in which a referee admitted to betting on games he worked. "We're not against background checks. But this should have been done uniformly and in a more respectful way," said Hirschbeck on behalf of Gibson and the others.

On April 26, just a few weeks into the season, Gibson was working third base when crewmate Kerwin Danley was hit on the jaw by a Brad Penny fastball. Danley was taken to the hospital. As soon as the game ended, Gibson went to check on him and support Danley's family (some of whom were at the game and witnessed the beaning). Gibson stayed with Danley into the night and spoke with the media shortly after Danley's release. "Typical K.D., he's worried about his chest protector. That's kind of the way we're geared and the way we think. But he was fine, and he'll be back." Gibson's behavior quietly refuted insinuations that he might have racist tendencies — Kerwin Danley is African-American.

On September 3, 2008, Gibson was the first umpire consulted when a manager (in this case Joe Maddon of the Tampa Bay Rays) wanted an instant replay review of a home run call, an option the Lords of Baseball had instituted just a week before. Gibson, the home plate umpire, deferred to third base umpire Brian Runge, who made the call. Runge in turn deferred to crew chief Charlie Reliford, who reviewed footage of the home run and ruled Runge's call correct.

Gibson made news of a less flattering kind in late 2009. Before the start of the American League Division Series between the Boston Red Sox and Los Angeles Angels, former Red Sox ace Curt Schilling was asked by WEEI radio what he thought of the umpires assigned to the games, one of whom was Gibson. "The thing I have with Greg Gibson was that he was having an argument with Tito [Red Sox manager Terry Francona] and he said, 'Tito, do you realize you are arguing with the best young ump in baseball right now?' Dead serious." At the time Schilling told the story, some 30 umpires younger than Gibson had worked behind the plate in a major league game. And if you accept ejection rate as a valid reflection of an umpire's temperament, Gibson's career 3.3 percent rate, 50 percent higher than the norm, doesn't bring the word "best" to mind.

On May 18, 2004, Gibson called balls and strikes for the 17th perfect game in major league history, thrown by Randy Johnson of the Arizona Diamondbacks against the Atlanta Braves.

Source

"Curt Schilling Makes the Call on Series Umps." *USA Today*, October 9, 2009. (October 21, 2010.) http://content.usatoday.com/communities/gameon/post/2009/10/68500682/1?loc=interstitialskip.

Manuel Gonzalez

BORN: December 4, 1979
FIRST MAJOR LEAGUE GAME: May 17, 2010
FAVORS: Way too early to tell
THEY HATE HIM IN: Also way too early to tell

	2007	2008	2009	2010	Totals
Games	0	0	0	2	2
Innings	0	0	0	18	18
R/9	0.00	0.00	0.00	7.50	7.50
BB/9	0.00	0.00	0.00	5.00	5.00
K/9	0.00	0.00	0.00	13.00	13.00
K/BB	0.00	0.00	0.00	2.60	2.60

Gonzalez made his major league debut working third base in a game between the Arizona Diamondbacks and Florida Marlins. A Triple-A call-up assigned to the International League, he was substituting for John Hirschbeck. His appearance became a widely, if briefly, acknowledged footnote to the game, in which the Diamondbacks triumphed 5–1. For on the night of May 17, 2010, Gonzalez became the first Venezuelan to umpire a major league game. "It's been amazing. It's one of those things you think about and think about and then when it happens, it's a great part of your life," he said. "It's a special occasion especially being in Miami. There are a lot of Venezuelans around here." His father and wife were in the stands for his debut.

Two months later Gonzalez got his first opportunity to call a major league game, working Milwaukee's July 19 visit to Pittsburgh. Brewer pitcher Chris Capuano won his first game in three years as Milwaukee prevailed, 3–1. Gonzalez saw only 247 pitches and the game went just 2:35, not including a 50-minute rain delay. In the second inning, Garrett Jones of the Pirates became Gonzalez's first big league victim of a called strike three. In the fifth, Pedro Alvarez of the Pirates became the first batter to receive a walk from Gonzalez. The first run of Gonzalez's big league career scored when Prince Fielder of the Brewers hit an opposite-field homer.

On August 18, 2010, Gonzalez got a second chance to call a big league game, working a contest between non-contenders Seattle and Baltimore. The results were similar to his first performance: five walks, 12 strikeouts as opposed to 14. But this time 11 runs scored instead of just four.

Gonzalez first gained umpiring experience as a teenager in the Miami area. Among his colleagues: Laz Diaz.

Source

Associated Press. "Gonzalez Works 3rd During Marlins Game." *ESPN.com*, May 17, 2010. (October 21, 2010.) http://sports.espn.go.com/mlb/news/story?id=5196677.

Brian Gorman

BORN: June 11, 1959
FIRST MAJOR LEAGUE GAME: April 24, 1991
FAVORS: R/9 says hitters, everything else says pitchers
THEY HATE HIM IN: Fine dining establishments north of Los Angeles

	2007	2008	2009	2010	Totals
Games	34	33	33	33	133
Innings	302.17	288.33	293.67	297.5	1,181.67
R/9	10.96	9.74	8.40	9.11	9.56
BB/9	6.17	5.34	5.61	6.08	5.80
K/9	13.22	13.89	13.88	14.22	13.80
K/BB	2.14	2.60	2.47	2.34	2.38

Brian Gorman's father Tom pitched four games in relief for the 1939 New York Giants, all in the span of five days. Tom Gorman did well in three appearances against the Cincinnati Reds, but then got lit up for four runs in two innings against the St. Louis

Cardinals and never pitched in the majors again. Rather than accept those five days as the apex of his professional career, Tom Gorman switched to umpiring and returned to the big leagues as an arbiter in September 1951. He is best known for working home plate during the first game of the 1968 World Series, when Bob Gibson of the Cardinals struck out 17 Detroit Tigers, still a Series record. Gorman the elder retired in 1976. Today, Brian Gorman wears the same uniform number as his dad (9).

In 2007 Brian Gorman was a hitters' umpire, but since then his R/9s have come down and his strike zone has expanded. His 2010 strike zone was exactly one whiff per nine innings larger than it was in 2007, with little change in his walk rate (although his BB/9 took quite a tumble in 2008 and stayed low in 2009). His overall BB/9 is low (63rd) and his K/9 is average (39th), making his K/BB the 16th most friendly to pitchers. And his R/9 has come way down from its 2007 peak (fourth in the majors that year).But it would be wrong to conclude that Gorman is a pitchers' umpire. His overall R/9 still favors hitters, ranking 19th among the 77 umpires who called more than 500 innings during the years under study.

Tom Gorman, the father, felt the need to eject just 23 men in the 3,802 regular season games he worked as an umpire. Brian has been busier, ejecting 40 in more than 2,400 games. Although he may not be as patient as his dad (or perhaps he is, but is living in different times), Brian's career ejection rate is lower than that of most contemporaries, and since 2007 has plummeted to below one percent. As his sister told the *Los Angeles Times* in 1995, "He has the classic umpire temperament. He's real calm. You need a nuclear attack to get him angry." Bruce Froemming, whose long career overlapped both Gormans, was even more complimentary. "I liked his dad but I think I like Brian's umpiring better. Brian is more serious and has a very flexible mind."

The Gormans' filial connection became part of the wave of nostalgia around the last regular season game at New York's Shea Stadium on September 28, 2008. Both Gormans were native New Yorkers, Tom from the storied Irish neighborhood of Hell's Kitchen and Brian from Whitestone, Queens, just up the road from Shea. Tom worked home plate for the first regular season game at Shea, a 4–3 Met loss to the Pittsburgh Pirates on April 17, 1964. "I think I was there," Brian said, "but this is going to sound silly, I can't be sure. I was only five years old at the time." Now Brian was on hand to work the last regular season game at Shea. There was talk of him handling the plate, but Brian didn't push it, deferring to crew chief Gerry Davis and taking his regular turn at first base.

Since 1999 Brian Gorman has missed only one postseason (2005), a sign that he is well-regarded within Major League Baseball's bureaucracy. In 2009 he was assigned to both the American League Division Series and the World Series. He was unable to escape the general embarrassment umpires suffered that postseason. Working first base in game two of the World Series, Gorman made a pair of calls that looked wrong on the replays. He admitted that he erred on one, but stuck to his guns on the other, a shoe-level line drive by the New York Yankees' Johnny Damon that Gorman ruled Philadelphia first baseman Ryan Howard caught for an out, although replays suggested the ball hit the ground first. Howard himself believed the ball hit the ground, because he threw to second to get the lead runner rather than step on first for a double play. "We can't base a decision on that," Gorman said. Whether or not he got the call wrong, Gorman demonstrated an ability to discuss it forthrightly, and perhaps for that reason was promoted to crew chief in 2010.

Gorman moved to Los Angeles in the 1990s. Although he describes himself as a meat-and-potatoes guy, in 2007 he became a prominent investor in a new, upscale restaurant in Ventura County. Neighbor Vin Scully heard about the restaurant and plugged it on Dodger broadcasts. "I'm told he went on the air and called me a restaurateur. That guy gets a free dinner when he walks in here," beamed Gorman.

Source

Lynch, John. "Umpire Answers Calling: Gorman Follows Legendary Dad." *Los Angeles Times*, March 11, 1995. (October 21, 2010.) http://articles.latimes.com/1995-03-11/sports/sp-41580_1_tom-gorman.

Chris Guccione

BORN: June 24, 1974
FIRST MAJOR LEAGUE GAME: April 25, 2000
FAVORS: Pitchers, slightly
THEY HATE HIM IN: Chicago's North Side

	2007	2008	2009	2010	Totals
Games	40	37	33	35	145
Innings	356.17	324.33	296.33	312	1,288.83
R/9	9.02	10.10	8.23	8.13	8.90
BB/9	6.52	6.38	6.44	5.63	6.25
K/9	13.32	13.13	15.19	13.67	13.78
K/BB	2.04	2.06	2.36	2.43	2.21

Guccione worked 1,255 big league games before the Lords of Baseball finally granted him status as a major league umpire in 2009. No umpire has toiled longer as a temp worker. For eight full seasons and parts of a ninth he was classified as a Triple-A call-up, although he worked as hard as any major league umpire. Harder, in fact, working more than 150 games in four of those seasons while his fully-initiated brethren typically worked 135 or less. For this nose-grinding effort he earned the per diem minimum wage for umpires.

Baseball executive Mike Port tried to spin this as a positive in a 2009 interview with the *Cleveland Plain Dealer*. Asked how much experience umpires typically have before they're hired, Port said, "They probably average ten to 12 years of minor league experience, in addition to their service at the major league level as a call-up umpire. The last umpire added to the staff, Chris Guccione [note: four more were added in 2010] had worked more than 1,200 major league games as a vacation or injury replacement." Whether you're a boss or an employee, do you really think it takes more than eight years of full-time work to decide whether someone is right for his job? Long waits like Guccione's are more about exploitation than training and development.

Derived from the third highest number of innings behind the plate for the period under study, Guccione's statistics prove that R/9 is dependent on many more factors than BB/9 and K/9. His overall BB/9 and K/9 are very close to the norm. If the number of runs scored strictly corresponded with the size of an umpire's strike zone, Guccione would have an overall R/9 in the low 9.30s. Instead, he's down at 8.90. This may indicate that while the *size* of Guccione's strike zone is average, its *location* is an inch or two away from the hitters' power; hitters are looking high and inside and Guccione is looking low and outside. There's support for this theory in the slugging percentages hitters compile when he works home plate. Only in 2008 did they have a good year, powering the ball at a .442 clip. No surprise that his R/9 reached its zenith that season. But in 2007 the hitters' slugging percentage was .390, fourth lowest for any umpire with 150 or more innings called. In 2009 it was a paltry .383, third lowest in the majors. The slugging percentage in front of Guccione rose somewhat in 2010, to .407, but his R/9 sank to 8.13, 11th lowest in the majors.

Over a career spanning more than 1,500 games, the sunflower seed-munching Guccione has 47 ejections, a 3.1 percent rate, which is well above average. He had three ejections in 2010, bouncing Texas Ranger manager Ron Washington for debating a caught stealing call on June 4, then thumbing Los Angeles Dodgers Garret Anderson and Russell Martin over separate ball-and-strike disputes on June 27. In all three cases, replays proved Guccione correct.

But in his very first postseason game, Guccione got one wrong. He was assigned to right field for the opening game of the American League Division Series between the New York Yankees and Minnesota Twins on October 6, 2010. The Yankees had a 6–4 lead and Mariano Rivera on the mound with two outs and nobody on in the bottom of the ninth. The Twins' Delmon Young slapped a soft liner to right. On the run, the Yankees' Greg Golson stuck his glove down and snagged the ball an inch from the ground for the game-ending out. But Guccione called it a trap, which put a man on first and the tying run at the plate in the person of Jim Thome, one of the great home run hitters of all time. At the Yankees' insistence, the umpire crew discussed the call, but they did not overturn it. Luckily for Guccione and the umpires in general, Thome popped out on Rivera's first pitch and the flub did not affect the game's outcome.

Colorado native Guccione is one of the shortest umpires in the ranks, topping out at 5'9".

Source
Morona, Joey. "MLB Umpires Seemingly Always Safe." *Cleveland Plain Dealer,* May 20, 2009. (October 21, 2010.) http://www.cleveland.com/dman/index.ssf/2009/05/mlb_umpires_seemingly_always_s.html.

Tom Hallion

BORN: September 5, 1956
FIRST MAJOR LEAGUE GAME: June 10, 1985
FAVORS: Pitchers
THEY HATE HIM IN: Colorado

	2007	2008	2009	2010	Totals
Games	33	34	35	34	136
Innings	291.5	303.33	296	302.67	1,193.5
R/9	9.97	9.26	8.94	8.71	9.21
BB/9	5.71	5.70	6.29	6.30	6.00
K/9	15.28	13.59	13.80	14.21	14.21
K/BB	2.68	2.38	2.19	2.25	2.37

Hallion was one of the umpires who submitted his resignation as part of a negotiating tactic in 1999. The Lords of Baseball called the union's bluff and accepted 22 of the resignations, including Hallion's. He was out of the game until 2003, when he was allowed to return to the minors. After two years of a second apprenticeship, he returned to the big leagues in 2005. Like several other umpires let go and eventually rehired, Hallion proved a model employee on his return. He earned assignments to the All-Star game, National League Division Series, and World Series in 2008. "He has shown strong leadership and we are very proud of him," said baseball executive Jimmie Lee Solomon.

Much as Hallion longed to return to umpiring after the 1999 fiasco, he didn't wait for an invitation. A native of upstate New York, he had studied business at the State University of New York–Buffalo, but had since moved to Kentucky. An acquaintance there suggested he become a financial advisor. Hallion followed through, and hired on at PaineWebber in Louisville. "If I can't have baseball, I'm going to have the next best thing," he said of the career switch. In 2005 he moved to Morgan Keegan, and at last word was a vice president in Regions Financial Corporation's brokerage unit. He administers a $50 million portfolio, which includes investments from 25 major league umpires. When he's not working games, he's in his hotel room with his laptop and cell phone, following the stock market, talking to clients, and placing trades. He makes about $50,000 a year as a financial advisor, a lot less than he makes as an umpire, but way more than most people make from their second job.

Behind the plate, Hallion is a pitchers' umpire, though not a fanatic about it. He had an odd year in 2007, posting a high 9.97 R/9 despite giving pitchers plenty of strike zone; his K/BB ranked fourth that year. Since then his R/9 has gone down every year, faithfully reflecting the larger trend in major league baseball. Meanwhile, his strike zone has shrunk somewhat, although not so much that hitters feel secure with him handling the plate. Overall Hallion's numbers put him 44th in R/9, one percent below average; 57th in BB/9, three percent below average; 14th in K/9, three percent above average; and 17th in K/BB, seven percent above average. In each case, the results favor pitchers.

Hallion brings a moderate temper to the ballpark. His 2.1 percent ejection rate since returning to the majors in 2005 puts him right at the major league average. In his first go-round he was more cantankerous, compiling an ejection rate over three percent. In 1989 he led the National League with 11 ejections. The low point of his on-field behavior — and perhaps the incident that prompted the Lords of Baseball to accept his resignation — was a June 26, 1999 argument with practically everyone in the Colorado dugout. After getting the third out, Colorado pitcher Mike DeJean complained to third base umpire Terry Tata about a checked swing call Hallion made. Overhearing, Hallion ordered DeJean into the dugout. That angered Rockie manager Jim Leyland. Hallion ejected DeJean and Leyland, then bumped Rockie catcher Jeff Reed and pitching coach Milt May. His bellicosity prompted National League president Leonard Coleman to suspend him for three days without pay. The incident underscored the growing tensions between labor and management that soon led to the umpires' disastrous mass resignation.

Nine years later, and 23 years after he reached the major leagues, Hallion was assigned to his first World Series. He was emotional about it, telling Bloomberg.com, "It's the pinnacle of umpiring. It's your ultimate goal." Unfortunately, Hallion suffered a moment of national embarrassment in game three. The Tampa Bay Rays were trailing the Philadelphia Phillies 4–1 going into the seventh inning. Their leadoff hitter, Carl Crawford, tried to ignite a rally by bunting for a hit. Phillie pitcher Jamie Moyer flipped the ball from his glove to first baseman Ryan Howard, who caught it with his bare hand. Hallion, working first base, was relying on standard umpiring technique, which is not only to see the play, but to *hear* it. Ball hitting glove and foot hitting bag make different sounds, and whichever one you hear first determines safe or out. Hallion called Crawford safe, but replays showed Crawford was clearly out. Hallion owned up to his error forthrightly. "Bang-bang play, and I tried to get the best angle on it. I really didn't get a sound to be able to judge."

A blip on an otherwise stellar comeback, as it turned out. After the 2009 season Hallion received two honors: His colleagues appointed him to the committee that successfully negotiated a new five-year contract with the Lords of Baseball, and then the Lords of Baseball named him a crew chief.

SOURCE

Sessa, Danielle. "Hallion Decides Who's Safe or Out in World Series, Stock Market." Bloomberg.com, October 24, 2008. (October 21, 2010.) http://www.bloomberg.com/apps/news?pid=20601079&refer=home&sid=auUP_SGljPuc.

Angel Hernandez

BORN: August 26, 1961
FIRST MAJOR LEAGUE GAME: May 23, 1991
FAVORS: R/9 says pitchers slightly, K/BB says hitters slightly
THEY HATE HIM IN: Tampa Bay and Toronto

	2007	2008	2009	2010	Totals
Games	36	34	35	35	140
Innings	314.5	299.33	307.67	312.5	1,234
R/9	10.36	8.72	9.48	8.04	9.15
BB/9	7.04	5.71	6.61	5.79	6.29
K/9	12.68	13.02	13.49	14.52	13.43
K/BB	1.80	2.28	2.04	2.51	2.13

Born in Havana, Hernandez grew up in greater Miami's Cuban expatriate community. Laz Diaz, then a hitting prospect but today a fellow umpire, recalled the teenage Hernandez working one of his games. "He was a no-nonsense kind of guy. And he's still a no-nonsense kind of guy."

Outside the umpiring fraternity there is considerable debate about whether Angel Hernandez is a no-nonsense kind of guy. He is among the most vilified umpires in the major leagues. Google the phrase "Angel Hernandez Worst Umpire" and you get more than 16,000 hits. Even the players complain about Hernandez. In 2006 *Sports Illustrated* conducted a poll of 470 current major leaguers, and they voted Hernandez the third-worst umpire in baseball, behind only C.B. Bucknor and Bruce Froemming (since retired). In 2010, *ESPN The Magazine* conducted a poll of 100 players, and 22 of them named Hernandez the worst umpire in baseball, behind only Bucknor and Hernandez's 2010 crew chief, Joe West.

Based on a cursory review of the countless blog entries about Hernandez, fan criticisms fall into three categories. The first is run-of-the-mill whining: He blew a call that hurt my team. The second is somewhat less common: His strike zone changes dramatically within a game. The third is downright damning: He wants to be noticed. A basic tenet of the profession is that if you *haven't* been noticed, you've had a good game. This type of accusation is tantamount to saying that Hernandez isn't merely incompetent, he's bad *on purpose.*

To prove their argument, the aggrieved hordes point to one of the oddest ejections in recent annals. On August 7, 2001, the Chicago Cubs brought former Chicago Bear football player Steve "Mongo" McMichael to Wrigley Field to lead the crowd in "Take Me Out to the Ballgame" during the seventh inning stretch. Hernandez worked home plate that day. In the bottom of the sixth, with Chicago trailing 2–1, the Cubs' Ron Coomer tried to score from third on a wild pitch. To the huge displeasure of the capacity crowd, Hernandez called Coomer out even though it looked like (and replays confirmed) he was safe. The boos persisted through a one-two-three top of the seventh, and then McMichael was cued to sing. "Don't worry about that call at the plate. Mongo will talk to the ump after the game," the 330-pound former defensive lineman promised, to delirious cheers. Hernandez stared daggers at the press box, and after McMichael finished singing, Hernandez ejected him. McMichael laughed and left the park a few minutes later. "The anger in his eyes. His mama didn't give him enough attention," he taunted. The Cubs publicly apologized to Hernandez and his crewmates.

Hernandez does have a higher than average ejection rate, and what's worse, it has risen to 3.4 percent since 2007, 70 percent higher than the average for the period. He was doing fine in 2010 until June 1, when he scored two ejections in half an inning. The host Toronto Blue Jays were leading the Tampa Bay Rays 5–3 in the ninth, but closer Kevin Gregg got into a one-out jam, walking two batters to bring slugger Carlos Pena to the plate. Pena watched four pitches go by: ball, strike, strike, ball, for a 2–2 count. He asked home plate umpire Hernandez for time and stepped back. Hernandez, citing pressure from the Lords of Baseball to keep games moving, said no. Gregg took advantage, throwing strike three before Pena was ready. Tampa manager Joe Maddon came out to argue and was ejected. "I'm all for supporting league policy but when it comes to speed-up rules in those situations I think they can basically be thrown in the trash can," Maddon said. He wasn't as angry as he could have been, because after he left, Hernandez squeezed Gregg's strike zone. Gregg walked two more batters to force in a run, then gave up a three-run double. As he left the field, Gregg had words with Hernandez and received Hernandez's second ejection of the inning. "All we ask is that [the strike zone] is consistent throughout the game and consistent in the ninth inning," Gregg said afterward.

Looking at his annual plate calling numbers, it's easy to see why critics contend that Hernandez has an inconsistent strike zone. His BB/9 yo-yoed from 7.04 in 2007 (15 percent above average and fourth highest among his peers) to 5.71 a year later (eight percent below average) to 6.61 in 2009 (three percent above average) to 5.79 in 2010 (four percent below average). His K/9 was consistently below average in the first three years of this study, but then shot up in 2010. Hernandez's R/9 has also jumped around. But when you total his numbers, they're reasonably close to average. His R/9 is low, favoring pitchers, and his K/BB is also low, favoring hitters.

Just as in the Tampa Bay-Toronto game, he gives both sides heartache, and in equal measure.

SOURCE

Chastain, Bill. "Rays Use Wild Ninth to Seal Win Over Jays." MLB.com, June 2, 2010. (October 21, 2010.) http://tampabay.rays.mlb.com/news/article.jsp?ymd=20100601&content_id=10692474&vkey=recap&fext=.jsp&c_id=tb.

Ed Hickox

BORN: July 31, 1962
FIRST MAJOR LEAGUE GAME: May 16, 1990
FAVORS: Hitters, slightly
THEY HATE HIM IN: Volusia County Jail

	2007	2008	2009	2010	Totals
Games	34	32	3	35	104
Innings	304	285.33	24	309	922.33
R/9	9.00	9.68	15.38	9.44	9.52
BB/9	6.07	6.21	10.88	6.20	6.28
K/9	13.20	14.51	11.63	14.16	13.89
K/BB	2.17	2.34	1.07	2.28	2.21

On April 18, 2009, Hickox was working his third game of the season behind home plate. The Cleveland Indians had made a mockery of the contest by running up a 20–2 lead against the New York Yankees. But the Yankees weren't forfeiting, so the teams continued playing—very much to Hickox's detriment. The Indians' Ben Francisco fouled a pitch straight back. The ball hit Hickox in the mask so hard that the mask cracked. Hickox wobbled for a moment, steadied, then borrowed a mask from the Yankees and ordered play to resume. Two innings later he was still seeing stars, however, so he went to the hospital, where he was diagnosed with a concussion. Published reports said he would be out for a week. Instead, he was out for the season.

It could have been worse. In 1999, Hickox cost himself five seasons by following his union's advice to resign as part of a negotiating tactic. Major League Baseball accepted his resignation. He was not rehired until 2005. Like so many of the rehired umps, he came back a changed man. Pre–1999 Hickox had a higher than average ejection rate, inflated by nine dismissals in just 56 games during his rookie 1990 season. Post-2005 Hickox has racked up only four ejections for a rate less than one-third the average. In 2006 he worked 148 games without throwing anyone out. He also went all of 2008 and 2009 without an ejection (although of course he spent most of 2009 on medical leave). When he ejected Jose Bautista of the Toronto Blue Jays for arguing a called third strike on September 4, 2010, it was his first ejection in nearly three years. The last had come on September 29, 2007, and it had nothing to do with his umpiring. In a rancorous game the New York Mets needed to win to remain in playoff contention, Florida Marlin catcher Miguel Olivo threw punches at Met shortstop Jose Reyes, and Hickox sent Olivo to the showers.

Not only is Hickox peaceable, he is also among the most neutral ball and strike callers in the game. When you combine his results for all four seasons under study you find that his BB/9, K/9, and K/BB are *all* within one percent of average. That could be a fluke, but if it is, it's a pretty big one. More likely Hickox calls the prototypical modern strike zone. The hitters seem to like that. His R/9 ranks 22nd among the 77 umpires who called 500 or more innings from 2007 through 2010. On that basis, Hickox grades out as slightly pro-hitter.

Hickox dealt with the loss of his occupation by becoming a police officer. "There are a lot of similarities between a police officer and an umpire," he told the *Florida Times-Union* in 2008. "You have to deal with hostile situations, you have to make split-second decisions, you have to go by the rules, you have to handle people and personalities, you have to defuse situations." During the off-season he continues to work as a part-time detective for the Daytona Beach Shores police department in Florida.

When he returned to umpiring, it was with a condition: "My wife supported me to come back to umpiring, but it was with the promise that I would never put our family through this again. I'm certainly a union man, and I'll back my partners. But I put peer pressure and I put my partners ahead of my family before, and that will never happen again." Whenever he's working a series on the East Coast and gets a day off, he flies to Florida to visit his family, something he can do more easily than most because he is a licensed pilot.

On July 26, 2010, Hickox called a no-hitter by Matt Garza of the Tampa Bay Rays against the Detroit Tigers. Prior to that, his most memorable moments on the field occurred while working third base. He was at third on June 14, 1996, when Hall-of-Famer Cal Ripken broke the global record for consecutive games played held by Sachi Kinugasa. Who? Kinugasa, third baseman for the Hiroshima Carp from 1965 through 1987, participated in 2,216 straight Japanese League games, 86 more than Lou Gehrig compiled for the Yankees. Hickox was also at third on September 22, 1993, when Hall-of-Famer Nolan Ryan took the field for the last time. The infamous detail about that one: Ryan started the game but failed to get a single out. And Hickox was on third on September 4, 1993, when one-armed Jim Abbott of the New York Yankees threw a no-hitter against the Cleveland Indians. "As I was walking off the field, I picked up the rosin bag," Hickox recalled.

SOURCE

Elliott, Jeff. "Umpire Enjoying Return to the Majors." *Florida Times-Union,* February 7, 2008. (October 22, 2010.) http://www.jacksonville.com/tu-online/stories/020708/spm_244863023.shtml.

John Hirschbeck

BORN: September 7, 1954
FIRST MAJOR LEAGUE GAME: May 6, 1983
FAVORS: Pitchers, slightly
THEY HATE HIM IN: Old-school union halls

	2007	2008	2009	2010	Totals
Games	26	0	23	30	79
Innings	233.17	0	193.33	264.83	691.33
R/9	10.54	0.00	8.61	9.04	9.43
BB/9	5.71	0.00	6.38	5.68	5.88
K/9	13.36	0.00	14.57	13.97	13.93
K/BB	2.34	0.00	2.28	2.46	2.37

Although John Hirschbeck has been in the major leagues since 1983 and has appeared in more than 3,000 games, the average fan has no idea he is the most important umpire of his generation.

If you don't remember what umpires were like in the 1990s, ask someone who does. Chances are you will hear of confrontation, arrogance, and obesity. You will be told that instead of walking away from arguments, umpires demanded complete submission, pointing to the chip on their shoulder and daring anyone to knock it off; that their union leader, an over-the-top lawyer named Richie Phillips, continued to foment their sense of grievance long after the many inequities they suffered had been addressed; and that umpires regarded themselves as the lone guardians of the game's integrity, even though many were too out of shape to keep up with the action.

The real story is more nuanced, of course, but it is true that the umpires alienated players, management, and fans. By the late 1990s veterans like Hirschbeck could acknowledge that the new militancy had brought tremendous benefit, but also tremendous harm. Privately they may even have conceded that some of their individual and collective behavior was excessive. But to a man they remained silent, an old-school brotherhood putting solidarity ahead of individual concerns.

Like his fellow umpires, Hirschbeck could have continued that way for years. But in 1999, Richie Phillips proposed that all union members submit their resignation as a way of wringing further concessions from the Lords of Baseball. Hirschbeck correctly saw it as a suicidal move. Forced to choose between personal conviction and group loyalty, he went with his conscience, refusing to go along with the mass resignation and urging his colleagues to do the same. To the union diehards, that made him a traitor. To most of his fellow umpires, that made him a liberator.

After the mass resignation led to the bloodbath Hirschbeck predicted (22 umpires let go), the umpires voted to decertify the old union and create a new one, the World Umpires Association. They made Hirschbeck their first president, and he headed the union until April 2009. During that period the umpires shed much (though not all) of their arrogance, hostility, and fat, and began moving toward a place in the game where they get the respect they deserve without resorting to heavy-handedness. Not all of them will thank John Hirschbeck for that, but they should.

What made Hirschbeck's break from the union especially painful was that on September 27, 1996, he was at the center of one of the biggest umpire controversies in recent times, and the union aggressively supported him. Hirschbeck called strike three on Roberto Alomar of the playoff-bound Baltimore Orioles, then ejected Alomar for arguing — whereupon Alomar spat in Hirschbeck's face. After the game, Alomar compounded the insult by claiming Hirschbeck had changed for the worse after his eight-year-old son's death from adrenoleukodystrophy (ALD), a rare genetic disorder. When Hirschbeck heard that he made a beeline for the Oriole clubhouse, intending to fight Alomar. He was stopped within 20 feet of Alomar by a colleague. "Our umpires are the best in the world and should never be subject to the kind of insolent behavior that was accorded to John Hirschbeck," acknowledged acting commissioner Bud Selig. But after Alomar apologized and donated $50,000 to ALD research, the Lords of Baseball suspended him for just five games — in 1997, allowing him to participate in the 1996 playoffs. The umpires voted to boycott the playoffs unless Alomar was punished more harshly. The Lords of Baseball got a court order forcing the umpires to work. So the umpires settled for delaying by 17 minutes the first playoff game involving Baltimore.

Hirschbeck has since forgiven Alomar, and the two have become friends. When Alomar became eligible for election to the Hall of Fame in 2010, Hirschbeck told the *Baltimore Sun*, "If I could vote, I would vote for him."

In 2003 Hirschbeck's younger brother Mark, also an umpire, had to give up the profession. John and Mark Hirschbeck were the first brothers to umpire in the major leagues. Mark participated in 1,766 games from 1987 to 2003. The physical demands of the job wore down his right hip, and when cortisone shots stopped helping, he opted for a hip replacement. Several surgeries and serious infections later, Mark still can't sit or stand in one place for long, and any chance that he might return to the big leagues has vanished.

Hirschbeck himself has endured some serious health problems, and hasn't put in a full season since 2005. He missed all of 2008 due to back surgery. He returned in 2009, but then lost two months to testicular cancer. Fortunately he caught the malignancy early and recovered in time for 2010. "Thousands of people find out they have cancer every day. I look at myself as one of the luckiest ones I've ever heard of." Still, after that experience he told the *New Haven Register* that "I'm 55, and I don't plan on working a whole lot longer." On May 20, 2010, he was hit by a warmup pitch during a game between the Milwaukee Brewers and Pittsburgh Pirates and left the game half an inning later due to what the Pirate medical staff called "concussion-like symptoms." "I felt so bad. He's a nice guy," said Milwaukee catcher Gregg Zaun, who lost the ball in the twilight glare.

A crew chief since 2000, Hirschbeck has shown a capacity for honesty his colleagues would do well to emulate. (See Marty Foster's profile for a great example.) He recognizes that increased television coverage has raised the pressure on his profession, and it has made him wistful. "When I first started, you had the Saturday game of the week, and that was it. Then came ESPN. Now, I can get ESPN on my cell phone. I'm glad I umped when I umped. It's much more stressful [now]. We used to have fun back then. You had fun doing your job."

Hirschbeck gives pitchers a larger than average strike zone — his four-year K/BB ranks 18th overall — but the hitters compile a slightly higher than average R/9 nonetheless. He can be grumpy, and has been getting more so. His lifetime ejection rate is 2.8 percent, higher than the 2.2 percent average since 1990, and since 2007 he's been tossing dissidents at a 3.9 percent clip, nearly twice the norm.

Hirschbeck was behind home plate when Barry Bonds broke Henry Aaron's all-time home run record on August 7, 2007. He was also behind home plate on October 6, 2010, when Roy Halladay of the Philadelphia Phillies tossed the second no-hitter in postseason history, a 104-pitch gem over the Cincinnati Reds in game one of the National League Division Series.

SOURCE

Borges, David. "Hirschbeck Ready to Return Following Big League Scare." *New Haven Register,* November 3, 2009. (October 22, 2010.) http://www.nhregister.com/articles/2009/11/03/sports/3_hirschbeck_feature.txt.

Bill Hohn

BORN: June 29, 1955
FIRST MAJOR LEAGUE GAME: May 29, 1987
FAVORS: Pitchers, despite having a hitters' strike zone
THEY HATE HIM IN: Atlanta

	2007	2008	2009	2010	Totals
Games	3	26	24	34	87
Innings	26.17	235.5	210.83	298.5	771
R/9	9.97	7.41	8.88	8.71	8.40
BB/9	7.57	6.57	5.93	6.30	6.33
K/9	12.04	13.91	13.28	12.30	13.05
K/BB	1.59	2.12	2.24	1.95	2.06

Which umpire has the worst temper? A lot of fans would guess Joe West, since he's widely portrayed as the most confrontational ump in the game. And a good guess that would be. Bob Davidson would be another good guess. But they are both runners-up to Bill Hohn.

Hohn led the majors in ejections in 2008 and 2009, even though he missed 30 games in 2008 and 40 games in 2009. He relaxed a bit in 2010, but still had four ejections. His rate since 2007 is an appalling 5.7 percent, nearly three times the major league norm for the period. His career ejection rate is 3.9 percent, nearly double the major league average.

Perhaps it's due to pain. Hohn began having problems with his lower back during the 2005 playoffs. He was diagnosed with herniated discs and an inflamed left sciatic nerve. Three surgeries cost him the entire 2006 season. He tried to come back in 2007, but lasted just 13 games before needing three and a half months off. He returned to the field on August 31, worked three games, and shut down for the year. Wisely, Hohn waited until May to start his 2008 season, and that allowed him to work without interruption through the end of September. In 2009 he was ready when the bell rang, but got in trouble by mid–August and required six weeks of leave before returning for the last two weeks of the season. Not until 2010 did Hohn put in a full year's work.

But is pain really an excuse for having so high an ejection rate? Hohn himself doesn't think so. He told the *Arizona Daily Star* that plenty of umpires are in pain. "Many umpires have hurt their discs in their neck and back and had knee surgeries, concussions, broken hands and thumbs from foul tips." And pain cannot explain Hohn's fist bump with catcher

John Baker of the Florida Marlins on July 29, 2009, one of the most inexplicable moments in recent umpiring history.

The fist bump may have grown out of a confrontation Hohn had with the Atlanta Braves five weeks earlier in a game against the Boston Red Sox. Atlanta reliever Eric O'Flaherty had an 0–2 count on Boston's J.D. Drew with a runner on second and one out in the seventh inning. The Braves trailed by a run. O'Flaherty's next pitch was over the plate for strike three, but Hohn called it ball one. Drew singled on the next pitch to give the Red Sox an insurance run. As Atlanta manager Bobby Cox trundled to the mound to replace O'Flaherty, he told Hohn the bad call had cost the Braves a run. By the time everyone was finished shouting, Hohn had tossed Cox, O'Flaherty, and Chipper Jones.

So now, on July 29, Hohn was working another Atlanta game, this time against Florida. The Braves were trailing by three in the eighth but had Jones on first with no out and Brian McCann batting. The first pitch from Florida's Dan Meyer was outside. Hohn called it strike one. McCann took the next two pitches for balls, but swung at the 2–1 and hit into a double play. Knowing McCann never would have swung at the double play pitch if the count had been 3–0, the Braves barked at Hohn from the dugout. Hohn strode over and told Cox he was going to eject someone, but didn't know who. Cox volunteered himself and got his wish. After the Braves' turn at bat ended, McCann calmly asked Hohn to at least admit he blew the call. Instead, Hohn tossed him. Shortly thereafter the game ended and Hohn bumped fists with the Marlin catcher, a blatant breach of neutrality. "As a player, it makes you not want to play when that stuff happens. Because you don't have a chance," said Jones. Afterward, Hohn had no explanation other than to say "The league reviewed it." Crew chief Gary Darling told the media "There's nothing there" and refused to answer questions.

Fittingly, Hohn became the last umpire to eject Bobby Cox from a regular season game. Cox, the most ejected individual of all time, incited Hohn, the most ornery umpire in recent memory, by arguing a pitch call on September 17, 2010. Cox didn't even have to leave the dugout. But after Hohn ran him, he came out on the field for one last chat, and also had a few words with Hohn's supervisor, Gary Darling.

Hohn's four-year totals behind the plate place him third lowest out of 77 umpires for R/9, which would ordinarily earn him a strongly pro-pitcher rating. But his strike zone is small. His K/9 for the period under study is fourth lowest of all umpires. His walk rate is high, coming in at 28th, and his K/BB ranks 59th, solidly on the hitters' side of the ledger. The most likely explanation for the discrepancy between run production and strike zone is that his strike zone is small in the wrong places, i.e. he's still giving pitchers the calls down and away. But ultimately, as with much else about him, Hohn's plate numbers are inexplicable.

Source

Trotto, Sarah. "Back in Baseball's Empire: MLB Ump Calls Winders Games While on Rehab." *Arizona Daily Star,* May 13, 2008. (October 22, 2010.) http://azstarnet.com/sports/baseball/professional/minor/article_b204764a-49c9-5412-a573-b90e0a84ed0e.html.

Sam Holbrook

BORN: July 7, 1965
FIRST MAJOR LEAGUE GAME: June 26, 1996
FAVORS: Hitters, strongly
THEY HATE HIM IN: St. Louis

	2007	2008	2009	2010	Totals
Games	34	35	35	28	132
Innings	307.5	307.5	313	245.17	1,173.17
R/9	10.77	10.83	8.40	9.76	9.94
BB/9	6.61	6.32	6.27	6.28	6.38
K/9	13.23	13.38	14.03	13.88	13.62
K/BB	2.00	2.12	2.24	2.21	2.14

Remember 1998, the year Mark McGwire and Sammy Sosa chased Roger Maris's single season home run record? Go back to August 29 of that year. McGwire had 54 home runs, the most by a National Leaguer since Ralph Kiner hit that many in 1949. A crowd of 47,627 fans came to Busch Stadium to see the Cardinals take on the Atlanta Braves — and to see McGwire take another step toward Maris. He batted in the bottom of the first to thunderous applause. The Braves' Tom Glavine, notorious for nibbling at the outside corner, ran the count to 3-2. His payoff pitch was a surprise, on the *inside* corner and down at the knees. McGwire laid off, dropped his bat, and started for first. But the umpire, a young man in only his first full season, called McGwire out on strikes. McGwire went crazy. He had to be restrained by third base coach Rene Lachemann. The umpire — Sam Holbrook — ejected him.

It may sound like a young umpire making his mark (pun intended). The crowd certainly saw it that way, booing without cease and delaying the game by throwing garbage on the field. Warnings from the public address announcer that the game might be forfeited were met with jeers. Alarmed, the Cardinals brought in extra police to stand on the field, and they cut off beer sales early. After the game, they spirited the umpires out a side exit.

What the crowd couldn't see was that Holbrook had done everything in his power to keep McGwire in the game. "I said, 'Tony, please get him out of here.' I feel I bent over backwards. I have nothing against Mark McGwire. I'd like to see him get the record as much as anybody else," Holbrook explained afterward. But his plea to Cardinal manager Tony LaRussa went unheeded and McGwire refused three separate requests to stop arguing, so Holbrook had no choice. McGwire acknowledged that after the game: "I said things to the umpire you can't say on TV. Did I cross the line? Yeah, I probably crossed the line. I own up to it. He had a right to throw me out."

Were McGwire still playing, he'd jump at the chance to bat with Holbrook behind the plate. Aside from an anomalous R/9 in 2009, a year in which he also got strikeout-happy, Holbrook has solidly favored hitters in both run production and strike zone. His

R/9 was in the top ten in 2007, 2008, and 2010, and his overall rate ranks sixth among the 77 umpires who called 500 or more innings from 2007 through 2010. Take out 2009 and his three-year R/9 soars to 10.50, higher than the R/9 for any major league season in the Steroid Era. Part of the reason for Holbrook's generosity to hitters is his small strike zone. His BB/9 ranks 22nd and is three percent above average. His K/9 ranks 51st and is one percent below average. His K/BB ratio also ranks 51st and is four percent below average.

Although Holbrook led the majors in ejections with 11 back in 2006, for the period under study his ejection rate is only slightly above average. In 2010 he had three ejections. Two of them came in the span of four days. On June 19 he ejected Washington manager Jim Riggleman for disputing a pitch call that went against the Nationals. On June 22 he tossed Philadelphia manager Charlie Manuel for disagreeing with an interference call on Phillie baserunner Raul Ibanez, whose attempt to take out the pivot man on a double play took him well beyond reach of second base. Holbrook capped his ejection tally for 2010 on August 17 by thumbing Washington's Ivan Rodriguez for overreacting to a ruling that his foul tip with two strikes had been held long enough by Atlanta catcher David Ross, so even though Ross dropped the ball, Rodriguez had struck out.

Holbrook was another of the 22 umpires whose resignation was accepted by the Lords of Baseball in 1999. He missed all of the 2000 and 2001 seasons before returning in late 2002. The time working as a meter reader, welder, and stockbroker gave him a chance to reflect on his vocation. "Let's face it, you need to have self-confidence to do this," he told *ESPN Insider* in 2006. "Everybody always thinks they can do it better than you. Everyone is looking to find error. And we are human, so we're gonna make mistakes. We have to deal with that, learn from it and go on trying to be the best we can."

Holbrook started the 2010 season late to help his wife through a serious illness.

Source

Berkow, Ira. "It's Going, Going, Gone for McGwire." *New York Times,* August 30, 1998. (October 22, 2010.) http://www.nytimes.com/1998/08/30/sports/baseball-it-s-going-going-gone-for-mcgwire.html?scp=3&sq=sam%20holbrook&st=cse.

James Hoye

BORN: February 8, 1971
FIRST MAJOR LEAGUE GAME: June 8, 2003
FAVORS: Pitchers, slightly
THEY HATE HIM IN: The Ohio State computer science department (he coulda been a programmer)

	2007	2008	2009	2010	Totals
Games	36	37	41	34	148
Innings	315	343	369	306.5	1,333.5
R/9	11.00	9.81	8.80	6.78	9.12
BB/9	6.14	6.17	6.02	6.61	6.22
K/9	14.03	14.22	13.15	14.09	13.85
K/BB	2.29	2.30	2.18	2.13	2.23

Between 2007 and 2010, no umpire worked more innings behind the plate than James Hoye. That's because for the first three years of the period under study he was a Triple-A call-up, so he lacked union protection and could be worked to death. Hoye appeared in 457 major league games over those three seasons, second only to fellow indentured servant Rob Drake. At one point (May 18–27, 2008) he worked four games behind the plate in ten days. Hoye was rewarded for his hard work in 2010, when the Lords of Baseball promoted him to big league status. Never again is he likely to call 41 games in a season.

From 2007 through 2009 Hoye showed a slightly enlarged strike zone that had no impact on run production. In fact, hitters did well when Hoye wore the mask, bringing in 9.82 runs for every nine innings he called. In 2010 Hoye tightened up his strike zone. His walk rate was nine percent above average at 6.61. His strikeout rate was slightly below average at 14.09. In a logical universe hitters would have produced an R/9 somewhere over 10.00 for him. Instead, they did worse for him than for any other umpire. His 6.78 R/9 for the season was the only one under 7.00, and Hoye came very close to having a higher BB/9 than R/9. His R/9 from July 2 through September 14, a stretch of 14 starts, was a microscopic 5.03, and it's not as if he saw only weak-hitting teams. He had Cincinnati, Philadelphia, and Tampa Bay twice each, and he had Boston three times.

Hoye's 2010 results changed him from an umpire with a pitchers' strike zone and hitters' run production to an umpire with a neutral strike zone and pitchers' run production. It's unlikely his R/9 over the next few years will be as low as it was in 2010, so the more interesting question will be whether his strike zone continues to contract. If it does, he will be bucking the larger major league trend. Whichever way he goes, it will be easy to discern, because he's starting from neutral: Over the four-year period under study he ranks 40th in BB/9, 36th in K/9, and 40th in K/BB, placing him firmly in the middle of the umpiring pack.

When it comes to game management, Hoye is a smooth operator, with a career ejection rate of 1.3 percent. He didn't eject anyone in 2010. In 2009 he worked in 156 games but had only one ejection, during a May 6 game between Tampa Bay and New York. The Yankees trailed 3–0 when Hoye called strike three on Nick Swisher to end the seventh inning. Swisher pointed with his bat to show Hoye how far outside the pitch was. "It's not like I was trying to completely show him up. I just think my emotions got the best of me," Swisher admitted. Replays show that Swisher did have the better eye on that pitch: The breaking ball from the Rays' Andy Sonnanstine cleanly missed the outside corner.

Hoye was born and raised in the Cleveland area, but has shown no special favor to the Indians, at least when he's worked the plate. During the period under study he called 11 games involving the Tribe. They won five and lost six. Hoye began umpiring in high school as a way to make extra cash. He didn't think of it as a potential profession until he went to Ohio State University, where he majored in computer science. He met some umpires working Triple-A games in Columbus, and that kindled his ambition. "I graduated in December of '94, and I went to umpiring school in January." A little more than eight years later he made his major league debut at Shea Stadium, working first base for an interleague contest between the Seattle Mariners and New York Mets. Ichiro Suzuki got four hits and stole two bases to lead the Mariners to a 13–1 win.

SOURCE

Strunsky, Steve. "One Eye on the Ball, the Other on the Majors." *New York Times,* August 22, 1999. (October 22, 2010.) http://www.nytimes.com/1999/08/22/nyregion/one-eye-on-the-ball-the-other-on-the-majors.html?scp=2&sq=james%20hoye&st=cse&pagewanted=1.

Marvin Hudson

BORN: March 3, 1964
FIRST MAJOR LEAGUE GAME: July 29, 1998
FAVORS: Hitters, slightly
THEY HATE HIM IN: Cleveland

	2007	2008	2009	2010	Totals
Games	32	34	36	34	136
Innings	296.5	305	320	302.67	1,224.17
R/9	8.74	10.12	8.41	9.84	9.27
BB/9	6.34	7.35	6.64	5.77	6.53
K/9	13.42	13.66	14.77	13.80	13.92
K/BB	2.12	1.86	2.22	2.13	2.13

Since becoming a full-time major league umpire, Hudson has been amazingly durable. In a profession where concussions, bad backs, and aching knees are endemic, he's barely missed a day, working at least 133 games in all 11 of his full-time seasons. In 2009 he finished fifth in innings behind home plate. The secret of his success is his plate stance. "You want to get in the slot and get as low as you can. I like to try to get my head down next to the catcher's ear," he told Jim Kirk — not the *Star Trek* captain, but a sporting goods store owner and blogger who closely follows umpires. The slot is the space between the hitter and catcher, and by getting as low as possible, Hudson lets the catcher shield him, minimizing exposure to foul tips.

Pitchers might argue that Hudson's plate stance puts them at a disadvantage. Umpires usually align their eyes with the top of the strike zone, so if Hudson is squatting lower, he's taking away the high strike. And with more of the catcher's body between him and the outside corner, there's some question about how well Hudson sees pitches away. Hudson was indeed generous with bases on balls from 2007 through 2009, lending credence to suspicions about his stance. But in 2010 his walk rate plunged below average. And Hudson's overall strikeout rate slightly favors pitchers, ranking 30th of the 77 umpires with 500 or more innings called from 2007 through 2010. One more piece of contrary evidence for pitchers to consider: Hudson's four-year R/9 is neutral. Still, in the last analysis, those three years of high walk rates do make Hudson a hitters' umpire.

Unusual things can happen when Hudson calls balls and strikes. On June 20, 2008, he called an interleague game between the Arizona Diamondbacks and Minnesota Twins. Randy Johnson, second on the all-time strikeout list, pitched for Arizona. Johnson went eight innings and got just *one* strikeout (a swing and miss). On July 19, 2009, Hudson didn't credit pitchers for the New York Mets with a single strikeout against the Atlanta Braves, who averaged more than 6.5 strikeouts a game that season. But Hudson's presence can also create pro-pitcher magic. On June 2, 2007, he called the kind of classic you hardly ever see anymore, a 1–0 contest in which both pitchers threw complete games. The winner was Joe Blanton of the Oakland Athletics and the tough-luck loser was Carlos Silva of the Minnesota Twins. Exactly three years later, Hudson called one of the oddest games for a pitcher ever, as Armando Galarraga of the Detroit Tigers threw a perfect game, only to lose it when Hudson's crewmate at first base, Jim Joyce, incorrectly credited the Cleveland Indians' 27th batter with an infield single. Overlooked in the ensuing brouhaha was that under Hudson's beneficent eye, Indian pitcher Fausto Carmona also pitched a complete, no-walk game.

When it comes to game management, Hudson's career ejection rate of 1.9 percent is slightly below the norm. After just one ejection in 2007 and none in 2008, he tossed four backtalkers in 2009, but replays showed all three calls in dispute (one resulted in a double ejection) were correct. In 2010 he had six ejections, but five were due to the fight between the Florida Marlins and Washington Nationals described in the early pages of this book to illustrate how a high ejection rate may not be the umpire's fault. Prior to that evening, Hudson had a season ejection rate under one percent and a career ejection rate of 1.7 percent, both well below average. The brawl raised his season ejection rate to 4.4 percent, which would be alarming without context, and raised his career rate by ten percent.

The most unusual situation of Hudson's career was not the Galarraga game, but a score change made three innings after the fact on April 28, 2007. The Baltimore Orioles were playing the Cleveland Indians and had runners on first and third and one out in the top of the third. Ramon Hernandez flied to Indian center fielder Grady Sizemore, who made a spectacular diving catch. The runner on third (Nick Markakis) tagged up, but the runner on first (Miguel Tejada) took off before the ball was caught, thinking it would drop for a hit. Sizemore threw to first to double up Tejada and end the inning.

Hudson, the home plate ump, shocked the Orioles by disallowing Markakis's run. Oriole bench coach Tom Trebelhorn argued the run should count, citing an approved ruling in the comments section of Rule 4.09 of the *Major League Rule Book*. Rather than tell Trebelhorn to get lost, Hudson consulted with crew chief Ed Montague. They discussed the matter off and on into the sixth inning. Montague had crewmate Bill Miller review the obscure section of the *Rule Book*, and when Miller affirmed that it was on point, Montague dialed the press box and informed the official scorer that Markakis's run counted. "I can't take away a run on our screw-up. What's right is right. We have to score the run," Montague said. The Indians protested, saying the umpires could not change a decision three innings after making it. But the run stood.

SOURCE

Fordin, Spencer. "O's Win Contested Game to Snap Skid." MLB.com, April 28, 2007. (October 22, 2010.) http://baltimore.orioles.mlb.com/news/article.jsp?ymd=20070428&content_id=1934992&vkey =recap&fext=.jsp&c_id=bal.

Dan Iassogna

BORN: May 3, 1969
FIRST MAJOR LEAGUE GAME: August 20, 1999
FAVORS: Hitters in odd-numbered years, pitchers in even-numbered years
THEY HATE HIM IN: Philadelphia

	2007	2008	2009	2010	Totals
Games	34	33	34	34	135
Innings	294.5	293	308.5	297	1,193
R/9	10.21	8.75	10.47	8.33	9.45
BB/9	6.51	5.90	6.88	6.12	6.36
K/9	13.11	15.42	13.83	15.09	14.36
K/BB	2.01	2.61	2.01	2.47	2.26

Umpiring was University of Connecticut graduate Iassogna's answer to the question "What are you going to do with a degree in English?"

His plate numbers support the argument that R/9 tends to follow strike zone size. They also support the argument that Iassogna is inconsistent. In 2007 his strike zone was small and his R/9 was correspondingly large. In 2008 his strike zone was large and his R/9 was correspondingly small. In 2009 he went back to his pattern of 2007. In 2010 he went back to his pattern of 2008. Will the real Dan Iassogna please stand up? Given the bipolar nature of his annual results, it would come as no shock if he tacked strongly in the hitters' direction in 2011.

Iassogna's career ejection rate stands at three percent, well above average. But of late he has improved. From 2007 through 2010 his ejection rate fell to 1.8 percent, ten percent below average for the period. He had a bad year in 2002, when he led the majors in ejections with ten. The 2005 campaign was brutal too, as he thumbed seven in 134 games, a 5.2 percent ejection rate. He had his best year in 2009, when he chalked up just one dismissal in 136 games. He appears to focus more on managers than players. His sole victim in 2009 was Philadelphia manager Charlie Manuel for arguing over a foul tip. In 2010 Iassogna's two ejections were manager Ozzie Guillen of the Chicago White Sox and manager Jerry Manuel of the New York Mets. Although no manager baited umpires more than Atlanta's Bobby Cox, Iassogna had kind words for him. "He's one of the best managers I've ever worked with because you know where he stands at all times on the field. You will never be surprised by one of his actions, ever. The most difficult managers to work with are the guys that pat you on the back, and they've got the knife in the other hand."

Iassogna probably believes the Philadelphia Phillies get their managers from a cutlery plant. The 2009 confrontation with Charlie Manuel was the latest in a series of battles Iassogna has had over the years with Phillie managers. On July 14, 2001, the Phillies' notoriously hotheaded skipper, Larry Bowa, argued a 2–0 pitch that Iassogna called a strike in the seventh inning of a game the Phils were losing. "That pitch was so bad, you'd have to have your eyes shut to call that a strike," Bowa said the next day, adding, "He missed about 20 pitches that I didn't say anything about. I screwed up. I should have said something in the third inning. That was my fault." But Bowa was just warming up. "Every other umpire says 'that's enough' when you argue a pitch. This guy jerks his mask off and walks all the way over to the dugout. Everybody talks about players being rushed to the big leagues, well, there are some umpires being rushed to the big leagues, too."

Five weeks later, on August 22, 2001, Bowa jumped on Iassogna again. This time Iassogna was at second base and called Philadelphia's Bobby Abreu out on a stolen base attempt. "How many plays are you going to fuck up?" Bowa shouted on his way to second base. Iassogna threw him out before he arrived. "He ran me and he gets another notch in his belt, I guess," Bowa moped afterward. Iassogna's response? "I don't want to get into what he said, but he said enough for me to eject him immediately."

Iassogna and Bowa continued to feud until the Phillies fired Bowa after the 2004 season. In came Charlie Manuel. On April 24, 2006, with two out and nobody on in the bottom of the first, the Phils' Chase Utley hit a grounder to Florida Marlin shortstop Hanley Ramirez. Racing to his left, Ramirez snagged the ball on the outfield grass behind second base and threw a one-hopper to first in time to get Utley, ruled Iassogna. A furious Utley threw down his batting helmet, earning the first ejection of his career. Then Manuel argued, and he got tossed too.

For all that, from 2007 through 2010 the Philadelphia Phillies went 14–3 in games where Iassogna called balls and strikes.

Source

O'Brien, David. "First Person Cox Tribute: Umpire Dan Iassogna." AJC.com, September 22, 2010. (October 23, 2010.) http://blogs.ajc.com/atlanta-braves-blog/2010/09/22/first-person-cox-tribute-umpire-dan-iassogna/.

Adrian Johnson

BORN: May 25, 1975
FIRST MAJOR LEAGUE GAME: April 19, 2006
FAVORS: Hitters, strongly
THEY HATE HIM IN: Los Angeles

	2007	2008	2009	2010	Totals
Games	16	35	36	34	121
Innings	141.83	322	316.67	297.83	1,078.33
R/9	9.14	9.36	9.92	9.28	9.47
BB/9	5.77	7.04	7.33	6.98	6.94
K/9	13.26	13.86	13.39	14.41	13.80
K/BB	2.30	1.97	1.83	2.06	1.99

The above chart includes just about every game Johnson has called in the majors. His only other appearance behind home plate came on May 21, 2006. It must have been a thrill for the Houston native to draw an interleague contest between the Texas Rangers and Houston Astros for his pitch-calling debut. Taylor Buchholz hurled a shutout and was backed by home runs from Morgan Ensberg and Jason Lane as the Astros beat the Rangers, 5–0. Johnson called his first major league strike three on the Rangers' Hank Blalock.

In 2010 Johnson joined the trend toward fewer runs and walks. But that did not make him a pitchers' umpire. His R/9 stayed five percent above average and his walk rate a whopping 15 percent above average, the sixth most generous to hitters for the year. Johnson's 2.06 K/BB gave him the tenth most hitter-friendly strike zone of 2010. His four-year R/9 ranks 25th, putting him in the top third for generosity to hitters. His walk rate for the period under study is fourth highest, and his strikeout rate is average, giving him a strongly pro-hitter K/BB of 1.99, tenth lowest of the 77 umpires who called 500 or more innings from 2007 through 2010. There is no question that Johnson's plate work benefits hitters more than pitchers.

Through 2009 Johnson displayed an easygoing temperament, posting a 1.6 percent ejection rate, 20 percent below average. But in 2010 he became more assertive, notching five ejections, one less than he had registered in his prior big league career. Only six umpires had more ejections in 2010. Three of Johnson's thumbings occurred during a July 20 game between the Los Angeles Dodgers and San Francisco Giants. Two-time Cy Young Award winner Tim Lincecum struggled early and the Dodgers surged to a 5–1 lead. In the fifth, Lincecum buzzed the Dodgers' Matt Kemp with one pitch, then hit Kemp with the next. As batter and pitcher took steps toward each other, home plate umpire Johnson intervened. He also warned both benches. Lincecum soon departed. The Giants' next pitcher, Denny Bautista, threw a pair of inside pitches to Russell Martin. Johnson decided both pitches were legitimate. Bench jockeys in the Dodger dugout disagreed. They demanded an ejection, so Johnson gave them one: He threw Dodger coach Bob Schaefer out of the game. When the Dodgers' hard-throwing Clayton Kershaw hit Aaron Rowand in the seventh, Johnson decided it was deliberate, and ejected both Kershaw and Dodger manager Joe Torre.

That wasn't the end of the Dodgers' frustration with Johnson. In the ninth, acting manager Don Mattingly sent out Jonathan Broxton to save what had become a one-run game. Broxton loaded the bases, so Mattingly went to the mound for a pep talk. After he left the mound, first baseman James Loney asked him a question, and Mattingly returned to the mound to answer. Giant manager Bruce Bochy claimed that under Section 8.06(d) of the *Major League Rule Book*, Mattingly's return constituted a second visit and Broxton had to be removed. Johnson, who had shouted, "No, no, no!" at Mattingly as he returned to the mound, was not going to require Broxton's removal, but had no choice when Bochy insisted, citing the correct rule. With the Dodgers' closer out of the game, the Giants went on to win, 7–5.

Just before the 2010 season, the Lords of Baseball promoted Johnson from a Triple-A call-up to a full-fledged major league umpire. Johnson had considerably less experience (371 big league games) than the other three members of the Class of 2010, Rob Drake (1,218), James Hoye (734), and Chad Fairchild (561). He was also considerably younger, just 34 compared to 40 for Drake and 39 for Hoye and Fairchild. However, the only Triple-A call-up older than him and with more experience was Brian Knight, so it's not as if he leaped past a legion of more senior candidates to get the job.

On June 25, 2010, Johnson called a no-hitter by Edwin Jackson of the Arizona Diamondbacks. Given Johnson's small strike zone, it was something of a surprise that he presided over a no-hit game. But it wasn't surprising that with Johnson calling balls and strikes, Jackson walked eight and needed 149 pitches, the most thrown in a big league game by any pitcher since 2005, to complete his masterpiece.

Source

Schulman, Henry. "Giants Use Coach's Gaffe to Beat L.A." *San Francisco Chronicle*, July 21, 2010. (October 23, 2010.) http://articles.sfgate.com/2010-07-21/sports/21991441_1_matt-kemp-mound-tim-lincecum.

Jim Joyce

BORN: October 3, 1955
FIRST MAJOR LEAGUE GAME: May 23, 1987
FAVORS: Hitters, slightly
THEY HATE HIM IN: Detroit

	2007	2008	2009	2010	Totals
Games	34	35	33	28	130
Innings	298.17	307.17	305.17	251.67	1,162.17
R/9	9.78	9.84	8.97	8.30	9.26
BB/9	6.58	5.86	6.99	5.90	6.35
K/9	12.35	12.77	13.06	14.23	13.06
K/BB	1.88	2.18	1.87	2.41	2.06

Have you read John Hirschbeck's profile? If so, you will recall that ugly moment in 1996 when Roberto Alomar spat in Hirschbeck's face. Alomar later said Hirschbeck's loss of a son to a rare disease had made Hirschbeck bitter. When Hirschbeck learned what Alomar said, he ran into the Baltimore Oriole clubhouse intending to fight Alomar. But within 20 feet of his target someone overtook him, put him in a bear hug, and dragged him back to the umpires' dressing room. That someone was Jim Joyce.

Joyce had Hirschbeck's back again on August 20, 1997, when New York Yankee third baseman Charlie Hayes alleged that Hirschbeck uttered an ethnic slur at the Yankees' starting pitcher, Hideki Irabu. Joyce agreed that Hirschbeck cursed, but denied that Hirschbeck made any racial remarks. And then during those watershed weeks in 1999 when Hirschbeck led an insurrection against the umpires' union and its advice to resign, Joyce rescinded his resignation and joined Hirschbeck in the struggle over the umpires' collective destiny. No surprise, then, that when Major League Baseball pressured Joyce and a couple of other umpires in 2001 to call more strikes, the new umpires' union, headed by Hirschbeck, filed a grievance and got the Lords of Baseball to back off.

"Why so many pitches in this game? And why did it take so long? Hunt for strikes HIGH, LOW and IN," demanded baseball executive Sandy Alderson in an email to Joyce. In their effort to apply business school principles to the pace of baseball games, Alderson and his claque had decided to measure an umpire's skill by the pitchers' work product. Joyce said, "[Hunt] was not a real good word to choose. It's a hard word to use, to tell an umpire to hunt for strikes. It almost makes it sound like you should make it up. We're not in that business." He added, "I'm not really responsible for pitch counts. It's the pitcher's count, not my count. They call it a pitch count for a reason. They don't call it an ump's count."

A decade later, Jim Joyce is still a reluctant strike caller. For the period under study he has the fifth lowest aggregate K/9 of all umpires. Although his K/9 has gone up steadily since 2007 and matched the big league average in 2010, it was seven percent below average in 2007, six percent below average in 2008, and six percent below average again in 2009. Joyce was stingy with walks in 2008 and 2010, but more than made up for it in 2007 and 2009, so it's no surprise that his aggregate K/BB is eight percent lower than average, putting him 60th for the period under study. The only good news for pitchers when he's behind the plate is that his R/9 is neutral. Hitters may have less plate to defend when Joyce is calling balls and strikes, but they're not capitalizing on it.

Joyce's career ejection rate is slightly higher than average, but since 2005 his ejection rate has been below one percent. On June 2, 2010, however, he faced a test of equanimity that went way beyond a manager shouting insults. Detroit's Armando Galarraga was within one out of pitching a perfect game when Jason Donald of the Cleveland Indians hit a grounder to first. Galarraga raced to the bag, took the throw from first baseman Miguel Cabrera for the out, and showed first base umpire Joyce the ball. Joyce astonished everyone in Comerica Park by calling Donald safe. Within minutes the entire nation heard about Joyce's missed call, and it became a topic of popular conversation. Not since Don Denkinger blew a game-changing call in the 1985 World Series had an umpire found himself in so bright and unforgiving a spotlight.

Joyce could have stuck to the standard script: "I had Donald beating the throw, we umpires are expected to get everything right and then improve, everyone get off my back." Instead he chose the truth. "I was convinced [Donald] beat the throw, until I saw the replay," he said afterward. "It was the biggest call of my career, and I kicked the shit out of it. I just cost that kid a perfect game." He apologized to Galarraga that night. The next day, when Galarraga brought the Tigers' lineup card to home plate, Joyce openly wept. In a heartwarming moment of good sportsmanship and forgiveness, Galarraga patted him on the back, and Joyce returned the gesture. "You don't see an umpire after the game come out and say, 'Hey, let me tell you I'm sorry,'" said Galarraga.

Joyce is one of the very few umpires who commands broad respect. When *Sports Illustrated* conducted polls of the players in 2003 and 2006, the players both times voted him the second best umpire in the majors, behind only Tim McClelland. Soon after his blown call, *ESPN The Magazine* conducted a poll of 100 players, 50 in each league, and 53 of them named Joyce the best umpire in the game.

Sources

Associated Press. "Umpire: 'I Just Cost That Kid a Perfect Game.'" ESPN.com, June 2, 2010. (October 23, 2010.) http://sports.espn.go.com/mlb/recap?gameId=300602106.

Chass, Murray. "Mixed Messages in the Pitch Count Controversy." *New York Times*, July 26, 2001. (October 23, 2010.) http://www.nytimes.com/2001/07/26/sports/baseball-mixed-messages-in-the-pitch-count-controversy.html.

Jeff Kellogg

BORN: August 29, 1961
FIRST MAJOR LEAGUE GAME: June 12, 1991
FAVORS: Hitters
THEY HATE HIM IN: Arizona

	2007	2008	2009	2010	Totals
Games	35	34	33	34	137
Innings	306.67	301.17	300.83	302	1,210.67
R/9	9.51	10.07	7.75	8.94	9.07

	2007	2008	2009	2010	Totals
BB/9	6.25	6.42	7.21	6.02	6.41
K/9	12.41	12.79	13.76	14.13	13.27
K/BB	1.99	1.99	1.91	2.35	2.05

Kellogg has called two no-hitters. On September 6, 2006, he was behind the plate when Anibal Sanchez of the Florida Marlins, making his 14th major league appearance, shut down the Arizona Diamondbacks. It had been 6,365 games since Randy Johnson's perfect game of May 18, 2004, the longest stretch between no-hitters in major league history. (Measured by time rather than games, the longest period between no-hitters was August 8, 1931, to September 21, 1934.) "Everything was working for him: fastball, changeup, breaking ball. For a game it was as good as any I've seen," lauded Kellogg.

Then on April 17, 2010, Kellogg called a no-hitter by Ubaldo Jimenez of the Colorado Rockies against the Atlanta Braves. It was the first no-hitter in Rockie history. Jimenez struggled early with Kellogg's strike zone, walking five batters in the first four innings. When he started the fifth inning with another walk, Colorado pitching coach Bob Apodaca suggested Jimenez pitch exclusively from the stretch. Jimenez's location firmed up, and he didn't yield another baserunner the rest of the way. His catcher was Miguel Olivo, who had also caught Anibal Sanchez's no-hitter. When Olivo and Kellogg are behind the plate together, watch for magic.

Of all the unusual circumstances around the two no-hitters, Kellogg's role as plate umpire ranks among the more remarkable, because he solidly favors hitters, even though in 2010 he joined the major league trend toward pitchers. His BB/9 was above average from 2007 through 2009, then matched average in 2010. And though his K/9 has been going up each year, it remains consistently *below* average, with a cumulative score four percent below the norm. This gives him one of the smallest strike zones in the major leagues. Kellogg's four-year 2.05 K/BB is eight percent lower than average and is smaller than the K/BB of all but 16 other umpires. Kellogg's overall R/9 is below average, but that's due to an aberrant 2009, when his R/9 was lowest in the majors. Omit 2009 and his three-year R/9 is 9.51, 44 points higher than his four-year tally and 21 points higher than the average for those seasons. That number is much more reflective of his small strike zone.

Kellogg is hard to provoke. His lifetime ejection rate is just 1.4 percent, around two-thirds the norm. Since 2004 he's had only two seasons with more than a single ejection. In 2008 it wasn't his fault. One ejection came over a disputed home run that he called correctly, but the other three stemmed from a fight. On June 5 the Tampa Bay Rays were angry about Boston center fielder Coco Crisp's hard slide into second base on a steal attempt the day before, so the first time Crisp came to bat, Tampa's James Shields, who had hit Dustin Pedroia with a pitch an inning earlier, hit Crisp. The ensuing fracas lasted 15 minutes. When it was over, home plate umpire Kellogg ejected Crisp, Shields, and Tampa Bay designated hitter Jonny Gomes. In 2010 both of Kellogg's ejections grew out of one incident, and again the Red Sox were involved. Kellogg ejected Mike Cameron and manager Terry Francona for contesting a called strike three. Replays showed Kellogg got the call right. Kellogg's cool comportment around the Red Sox and everyone else undoubtedly factored into his promotion to crew chief in 2010.

Kellogg had a Hollywood moment in 2001, when he played himself in a universally-panned movie called *Summer Catch*. Set in Cape Cod and starring Jessica Biel and Freddie Prinze, Jr., it was ostensibly about a troubled pitcher getting the hot girl and a shot at the majors, but was really a hackneyed chick flick set against a sports-lite backdrop. Appearing as themselves with Kellogg were players Henry Aaron, Ken Griffey, Jr., Pat Burrell, Dave Collins, Doug Glanville, and Mike Lieberthal. Former slugger Dick Allen made a cameo as a scout. A small role for Carlton Fisk was left on the cutting room floor, no doubt to Fisk's relief.

SOURCE

Gilbert, Steve. "Umpiring Is Not a Simple Life." MLB.com, August 28, 2007. (October 23, 2010.) http://mlb.mlb.com/news/article.jsp?ymd=20070828&content_id=2174931&vkey=news_mlb&fext=.jsp&c_id=mlb.

Brian Knight

BORN: October 2, 1974
FIRST MAJOR LEAGUE GAME: May 7, 2001
FAVORS: Hitters, strongly
THEY HATE HIM IN: Baltimore

	2007	2008	2009	2010	Totals
Games	28	34	35	30	127
Innings	247.83	298.17	310.17	263	1,119.17
R/9	10.13	9.03	10.18	9.65	9.74
BB/9	6.46	6.43	6.30	6.47	6.41
K/9	12.67	13.13	13.84	13.69	13.36
K/BB	1.96	2.04	2.20	2.12	2.08

"Helenan umpires major league game" blared the headline in Montana's *Helena Independent Record*. The story celebrated the May 7, 2001, debut of Brian Knight, whose father had been a popular local umpire for decades. The younger Knight worked third base in a game between the Chicago White Sox and Texas Rangers. "It was awesome. It was unbelievable. It was the experience of my life so far," he told his hometown paper. His grandmother happened to be in Arlington when he received the call, and she witnessed his initial major league performance. Crewmate Wally Bell gave her a game ball.

Knight remained a Triple-A call-up for nearly a decade. He worked just five more major league games in 2001, none behind home plate. He got into one game in 2002 and

15 in 2003 before reaching the next level, working a quarter of the season in the majors in 2004, 2005, and 2006. In 2007 he participated in 123 games, almost as many as a typical major league umpire. In 2008 and 2009 he worked full time in the majors, without the designation of full-fledged major league ump. He was widely expected to receive a promotion to major league status in 2011.

No one was happier to see Knight get steady work in the majors than pitcher Jon Lester of the Boston Red Sox. With Knight behind the plate, Lester hurled a no-hitter on May 19, 2008, against the Kansas City Royals. Not that Knight was a huge help. Of Lester's nine strikeouts, Knight called just one, and the rest were swinging. Knight also called two walks on Lester, the only at-bats separating the young Boston pitcher from a perfect game. A month later, Knight called yet another Lester effort, this time against the Philadelphia Phillies, and though Lester was touched for six hits, Knight called only one walk against him and Lester went seven innings without giving up a run to earn the victory.

Beyond Jon Lester, there probably aren't many pitchers happy to see Knight. His remarkably consistent BB/9 is three percent higher than average. And though his K/9 has increased over the years, his overall score of 13.36 is three percent lower than average. The tight strike zone has contributed to an overall R/9 five percent above the average umpire's. Knight's R/9 would have been even higher if not for a dip in 2008. Knight's BB/9 was high and his K/9 low that year, and hitters compiled a .262 batting average and .332 on-base percentage for him, right around average. Only the hitters' .398 slugging percentage was below normal, so that probably accounts for the 12 or more runs that should have scored and didn't in Knight's 34 plate assignments.

Although Knight gets his share of grief from fan blogs, his ejection rate is below average at 1.6 percent. He is willing to own up to mistakes, as he did on July 6, 2007, after working home plate in a ten-inning game between the Baltimore Orioles and Texas Rangers. Down 3–1 in the seventh, the Orioles loaded the bases. Ranger reliever C.J. Wilson threw a wild pitch that shot past catcher Adam Melhuse, enticing Chris Gomez, the Oriole on third, to try to score. The ball bounced off the wall and came right back to Melhuse, who put the tag on Gomez for the out, ruled Knight. But it appeared to the Orioles and many others that Knight missed the call. A moment later Nick Markakis doubled in the other two runners, so either Gomez or Knight had cost the O's a run, which proved crucial because the Rangers won in the tenth. After the game, Knight came clean. "I've seen the replay, and I see that I missed the call. I was fighting to get the best position I could get and I called what I saw at the moment. That's pretty much all I can say about it. I just saw the tag beating him." Said Gomez, "It's pretty frustrating. That was a big run."

Statistical oddity: Over a 13-game stretch from August 20, 2008 through May 6, 2009, the home team won every game Knight called. From 2007 through 2009, the home team went 59–38 (.608) in games where Knight handled ball and strike duties. In 2010 the good times between Knight and the home teams ended, as the hosts finished 15–15.

SOURCE

Cotton, Tom. "Helenan Umpires Major League Game." *Helena Independent Record,* May 7, 2001. (October 23, 2010.) http://helenair.com/sports/article_4a87ba0f-da22-5441-8d09-fbc8b6bcf2cl.html.

Ron Kulpa

BORN: October 5, 1968
FIRST MAJOR LEAGUE GAME: July 23, 1998
FAVORS: Pitchers
THEY HATE HIM IN: San Francisco

	2007	2008	2009	2010	Totals
Games	35	32	23	36	126
Innings	309.67	294.67	200.33	316.67	1,121.33
R/9	9.79	7.61	9.08	8.73	8.79
BB/9	6.07	5.56	6.60	6.79	6.24
K/9	13.49	14.75	14.20	14.24	14.16
K/BB	2.22	2.65	2.15	2.10	2.27

Proud St. Louis native Kulpa worked home plate for the last regular season game at the old Busch Stadium (October 2, 2005) and the first regular season game at the new Busch Stadium (April 10, 2006). "That was my ballpark. That's where I went to all my games," Kulpa said of the old yard. "But this is a thrill. This is an honor," he said of working the first game at the new yard. To get that honor he had to pull a few strings. First he talked Paul Emmel into switching crews. Then he persuaded crew chief Bruce Froemming to let him call the initial game. "This is his town. He deserves it," Froemming said. Kulpa's family had purchased a sidewalk brick outside the new stadium and dedicated it to Kulpa's father. "It says, 'Joe Kulpa, fan of the game, fan of the umpires,'" Kulpa *fils* revealed.

Kulpa was a huge fan of pitchers in 2008, posting the second lowest R/9 of any umpire and the fifth highest K/9. His BB/9 also strongly favored hurlers, ranking 11 percent below average. In 2009 and 2010 his numbers stabilized in a contrarian manner: His BB/9 and K/BB favored hitters, but his R/9 continued to favor pitchers. Overall Kulpa is very tough on runs, sixth lowest of all umpires who worked 500 or more innings from 2007 through 2010. His strike zone moderately favors pitchers, as despite the high walk counts in 2009 and 2010 his BB/9 is average and his K/9 is well above average, 16th highest among his colleagues. This gives him a four-year K/BB that is slightly pitcher-friendly. When both run production and strike zone size favor pitchers over a four-year stretch, it's safe to conclude that the umpire in question, in this case Kulpa, is pro-pitcher.

Kulpa's career ejection rate is right at the major league average, but he's had some high-profile dismissals. He was the last umpire to eject Barry Bonds. That occurred on August 4, 2006. Bonds was batting in the bottom of the ninth against Brian Fuentes of the Colorado Rockies. Earlier in the game Bonds had hit the 723rd home run of his career, and he had a runner on base in a game the Giants trailed by three. Fuentes's 2–1 offering was a sidearm fastball down and away — for a strike, said Kulpa. The normally undemonstrative Bonds had words with Kulpa, who dusted home plate in an apparent attempt to defuse the situation. But the two continued to jaw, and Kulpa tossed Bonds. Giant fans went crazy. They caused an 11 minute delay by throwing debris on the field and shouting "Barry! Barry!" Bonds refused to depart, sitting in the dugout with his arms folded. The umpires needed an escort from the field as fans continued throwing objects after the Giants lost. "It was a good pitch and I'd been calling that pitch all night," Kulpa explained. "I gave him every opportunity to stay in the ballgame, and he crossed the line. When you cross the line, I have a job to do." Said Bonds, "There were two unprofessional people out there at that moment. He was very unprofessional and so was I."

More serious was a July 15, 2000, confrontation with Carl Everett, then the center fielder for the Boston Red Sox. Kulpa, in his first full season as an umpire, warned the notorious plate-crowder and hothead to stay within the confines of the batter's box. Four pitches into the at-bat, Kulpa warned Everett again, drawing a line where the chalk had been kicked away by previous hitters. Everett went nuts. He threw down his helmet, then struck Kulpa, apparently with a head butt, so that Kulpa reeled. Red Sox manager Jimy Williams and two coaches pulled Everett into the dugout, where his violent outburst continued. As crew chief Randy Marsh explained, "Our interpretation is his foot cannot be closer than six inches to the plate. I think Ronald handled himself appropriately. He basically warned him a few times." Everett was suspended ten games and assessed a $5,000 fine for assaulting Kulpa. The following spring training, an unrepentant Everett said, "I'll never apologize to that guy. He did some acting. I never head-butted him." Kulpa refused to comment.

On a more positive note, Kulpa was behind the plate on June 7, 2007, when Curt Schilling of the Red Sox came within one out of throwing a no-hitter against the Oakland Athletics. "I told my crewmates and my dad that I didn't think I'd ever come that close again to working a no-hitter," Kulpa told the *Philadelphia Daily News*. In his very next start behind home plate, Kulpa called a no-hitter by Justin Verlander of the Detroit Tigers.

Source

Hummel, Rick. "Another Homecoming for Kulpa." *St. Louis Post-Dispatch,* April 11, 2006. (October 23, 2010.) http://www.stltoday.com/stltoday/sports/columnists.nsf/rickhummel/story/3DD4E78D287EFF888625729E000C5015?OpenDocument.

Jerry Layne

BORN: September 28, 1958
FIRST MAJOR LEAGUE GAME: April 19, 1989

FAVORS: Pitchers if you go by R/9, hitters if you go by everything else
THEY HATE HIM IN: Orange County

	2007	2008	2009	2010	Totals
Games	19	32	33	32	116
Innings	180.5	276.5	296	278	1,031
R/9	9.37	9.18	7.97	8.55	8.69
BB/9	7.23	7.55	6.05	6.93	6.90
K/9	12.32	13.35	14.29	13.73	13.54
K/BB	1.70	1.77	2.36	1.98	1.96

"Seems very influenced by a catcher's receiving," was one team's appraisal of Layne's work behind the plate. The operative word is *seems,* for Jerry Layne is a puzzle. In 2007, 2008, and 2010 his strike zone was as small as he is big—and he is very big, the second heaviest umpire in the majors at 255 pounds (only Joe West weighs more) and at 6'4" one of the tallest. In 2007 he called 18 percent more walks than the average umpire, the season's third highest walk rate. In 2008 he called 21 percent more walks than the average umpire, the fourth highest walk rate. In 2010 he called 15 percent more walks than the average umpire, the eighth highest walk rate. In all three years his K/9 was below average. But in spite of that postage stamp strike zone, his R/9 was lower than the norm in all three seasons.

If that was the only inconsistency, we could submit it as Exhibit A in the case against a relationship between R/9 and the size of an umpire's strike zone. But then in 2009, Layne radically expanded his strike zone, reducing the number of walks allowed by 1.5 per game (a full 20 percent) while increasing the number of strikeouts by nearly one per game. And that *did* have an effect on his R/9, reducing it by well over a run. So now you have an umpire who shifts from a tiny strike zone to a big strike zone, and whose R/9 goes from completely contrary to overly consistent. What's up with that?

Well, maybe he *is* influenced by a catcher's receiving. On October 20, 2009, during the fourth game of the American League Championship Series between the New York Yankees and Los Angeles Angels, manager Mike Scioscia of the Angels was concerned that Layne was missing inside pitches. Layne was miked for Fox Sports's "Sounds of the Game" feature, and since his conversation with Scioscia was cordial and curseless, Fox aired it. Said Layne of Angel catcher Mike Napoli, "I told him, I said I needed to look inside. He butts way inside though, I got to go over his head, and I got hands and everything else in front of me. I just asked him to give me a peek, is what I asked. He said, 'I can get lower.' I said you don't have to get so far inside." Scioscia offered to help, but at first Layne demurred. "He does whatever he's gotta do," he said of Napoli. Scioscia persisted: "If he gets lower to give you a better look?" "Well he hasn't done that yet," Layne replied. Next inning, Napoli squatted lower. It didn't help. The Angels lost 10–1. But if Layne's concerns in that one game can be generalized, it could be that if more catchers give him a clear view of the inside pitch, the size of his strike zone will increase and his R/9 will diminish.

Layne was already *persona non grata* among Angel fans over a call he made two games earlier, while working second base. The Yankees had a runner on first and none out in the bottom of the tenth. New York's Jorge Posada hit a double play grounder to second baseman Maicer Izturis, who flipped to shortstop Erick Aybar, who threw to first to nail Posada. But Layne ruled that Aybar never touched second base, and the runner was safe. Replays showed Layne was correct, but in an odd twist to a postseason in which umpires were lambasted for errant calls, he was criticized for being *right*. The so-called neighborhood play, where the pivot man takes the ball in the neighborhood of second base (rather than on it) before throwing to first, was customarily called an out. Why was Layne suddenly going by the book? Scioscia, for one, realized the Angels were making a faulty argument and backed off.

Layne is an old National League umpire who came up in the confrontational days of the late 1980s and early 1990s, so you might expect him to have a higher than average ejection rate. There, at least, he follows expectations. Layne's career ejection rate is 2.7 percent, some 20 percent higher than average. But since the good old days of 1996 (11) and 1997 (eight), his annual ejection totals have plummeted. In fact, since 1998 his rate stands at 1.9 percent, slightly below average. He didn't eject anybody in the 127 games he worked in 2008. So Layne has clearly mellowed. No doubt that was one of the factors considered when the Lords of Baseball made him a crew chief in 2010.

For undisclosed reasons, Layne missed half the 2007 season. His woes were likely unrelated to a frightening incident on August 18, 2006, when he was hit in the head by a broken bat and had to be carried off the field. He was diagnosed with a bruised jaw and returned to action the next day. He wasn't so lucky on June 7, 2008, when a foul tip caught him in the mask and caused a concussion. That put the big man out of action for six days.

Layne volunteers for Disabled American Veterans, regularly visiting VA hospitals. "I want to bring smiles and brighter days to those veterans who have given so much to our country," he told the U.S. Department of Veterans Affairs in 2008.

SOURCE

Waldstein, David. "The Biggest Secret of Baseball's Unwritten Rules: They Don't Exist." *New York Times,* October 19, 2009. (October 24, 2010.) http://www.nytimes.com/2009/10/19/sports/baseball/19umpire.html.

Alfonso Marquez

BORN: April 12, 1972
FIRST MAJOR LEAGUE GAME: August 13, 1999
FAVORS: Hitters, strongly
THEY HATE HIM IN: The Arizona state legislature

	2007	2008	2009	2010	Totals
Games	31	34	2	35	102
Innings	276.5	319.17	17.83	308.5	922
R/9	8.98	9.98	10.10	9.16	9.41
BB/9	5.86	7.22	7.07	6.80	6.67
K/9	12.50	13.37	14.64	12.98	13.00
K/BB	2.13	1.85	2.07	1.91	1.95

Affectionately known as Fonzie, Marquez is the only major league umpire born in Mexico. When he was seven years old his mother smuggled him into the United States. They settled in Fullerton, California, where his father had a gardening business. His family was among the millions of illegal immigrants granted amnesty under the Reagan Administration's Immigration Reform and Control Act of 1986.

Marquez was so good at umpiring local games that friends lent him the money to attend the Joe Brinkman Umpire School. Considered a natural, he made it to the major leagues at 27. "He's hilarious. He's a fun guy. There's not many people that don't like him," said his colleague Rob Drake. Marquez is active in Ted Barrett's Calling for Christ ministry and has his own charity, Fonzie's Kids, dedicated to providing clothing and athletic gear to poor Mexican children. He is widely admired in his native land, as Barrett learned when he accompanied Marquez on a trip there. "For them to look and say, 'Hey, this is one of our people. This is one of our countrymen. And he's made it to a high level.' I would say that he's making a difference just as people look at him." Marquez himself said, "I think it's pretty cool to show them that it can be done. It gives people hope to try to do things because it's possible."

Marquez has a significantly smaller than average strike zone. His cumulative BB/9 is seven percent higher than the norm (13th overall) and his cumulative K/9 is six percent lower than the norm (76th overall, second lowest). Going by K/BB, only five umpires have a smaller strike zone: Scott Barry, Tim McClelland, Randy Marsh, Jerry Crawford, and Paul Schrieber—and Marsh and Crawford have retired. So Marquez is one of the very toughest umpires on pitchers. This is reflected in his R/9, which is slightly higher than average. But all five of the umpires with smaller strike zones rank significantly higher than Marquez in R/9, so it's possible that somewhere inside that tiny strike zone, Marquez is giving pitchers breaks.

Among the younger crop of umpires, Marquez ranks among the more feisty. His career ejection rate is 2.7 percent, some 20 percent higher than the norm of 2.2 percent. His rate since 2007 is an even higher 3.1 percent, which means in recent years he's been 50 percent faster with the thumb than the average umpire. Yet on the two occasions Marquez found himself at the center of national attention, he declined to eject anybody.

The first occasion was on October 11, 2003, during the third game of the American League Championship Series between the New York Yankees and Boston Red Sox. This was the infamous game in which Boston's Pedro Martinez pushed 72-year-old Yankee coach Don Zimmer to the ground. Martinez blew a 2–0 lead in the fourth by giving up a double to Hideki Matsui. He hit the next batter, Karim Garcia. A fight nearly broke out, but Marquez, the home plate umpire, quickly restored order. After the side was retired and the Yankees took the field, Roger Clemens threw high and tight to Boston's Manny Ramirez. Marquez kept them apart, but he couldn't stop the hordes from streaming out of the dugouts and bullpens. The ensuing scrum ended with Zimmer's hubris (Boston view) or Martinez's elder abuse (New York view). Marquez and his colleagues needed 13 minutes to restore order, but in a show of tremendous restraint, he refrained from ejecting anyone.

The second occasion also came during the postseason, in Marquez's only World Series plate appearance, the October 22, 2006, game between the St. Louis Cardinals and Detroit Tigers. Kenny Rogers, a crafty left-hander playing for the Tigers, had a brown smudge on his pitching hand. The television cameras focused on it, and someone alerted Cardinal manager Tony LaRussa. He talked to Marquez about it. Rather than inspect and eject, Marquez quietly told Rogers that he needed to wash his hands. Rogers did, and a potential embarrassment was averted. Which is not to say that everyone applauded Marquez's leniency. Many in the media criticized him for failing to eject an apparent cheater.

On April 17, 2008, Marquez called a 22-inning game between the Colorado Rockies and San Diego Padres, the longest major league contest since 1993. Perhaps the 6:16, 659-pitch ordeal aggravated his bad back, because he eventually needed surgery that caused him to miss all but one week of the 2009 season.

SOURCE

Baxter, Kevin. "Answering the Call." *Los Angeles Times,* June 22, 2007. (October 24, 2010.) http://articles.latimes.com/2007/jun/22/sports/sp-marquez22.

Randy Marsh

BORN: April 8, 1949
FIRST MAJOR LEAGUE GAME: May 22, 1981
FAVORED: Hitters, strongly
THEY HATED HIM IN: Detroit and The Bronx

	2007	2008	2009	2010	Totals
Games	36	19	32	0	87
Innings	318.83	168	286.17	0	773
R/9	8.98	10.66	10.00	0.00	9.72
BB/9	6.52	7.13	7.08	0.00	6.86
K/9	11.69	11.95	12.49	0.00	12.04
K/BB	1.79	1.68	1.76	0.00	1.76

After missing half of 2008 due to heart surgery, Marsh put in a full season in 2009, then retired. He worked as a major league umpire for 29 years, appearing in 3,707 games, 936 of them behind the plate.

No umpire was more patient. Over his long career Marsh compiled only 45 ejections, a 1.2 percent rate, little more than half the average. In his last three seasons he didn't eject *anyone*. "I've learned to let them come out and see what they have to say. They might not always get the answer they want, but there is mutual respect. Listen. See what's going on here. Then make your decision," he told *USA Today* in a 2008 interview.

Marsh's listen-and-decide philosophy was never tested more than on October 19, 2004, during the sixth game of the American League Championship Series between the New York Yankees and Boston Red Sox. The Yankees were losing 4–1 in the eighth and facing a tied series when a Derek Jeter single made it 4–2 and brought up Alex Rodriguez as the tying run. Rodriguez swung at a Bronson Arroyo pitch and hit a dribbler along the first base line. Arroyo fielded it and reached to tag Rodriguez, only to lose the ball when Rodriguez slapped it out of his glove. Jeter scored and Rodriguez went to second. Marsh, working first base, had been blocked by first baseman Doug Mientkiewicz, so when Boston manager Terry Francona protested the call, Marsh listened, then brought in the rest of his crew. After consultation, Marsh decided to call Rodriguez out for runner's interference, prompting such abuse from the Yankee Stadium crowd that police in riot gear ringed the field for the rest of the game.

Marsh's retirement hurt hitters more than pitchers. Look at those K/9s. His overall 12.04 is by far the lowest of any umpire from 2007 through 2010, nearly a full whiff lower than the next strike Scrooge over those years, Alfonso Marquez. His BB/9s are highly hitter-friendly too, the 6.86 aggregate amounting to 10 percent above average. Overall, Marsh's K/BB ratio was third lowest among the 77 umpires who worked 500 or more innings during the period under study. The very small strike zone contributed to an R/9 that was 15th highest. Marsh reputedly mollified pitchers by being consistent in his calls; if you got a pitch the first time you threw it, you would get it again the next time you threw it.

One of several umpires from Kentucky, Marsh grew up near Cincinnati and worked his first major league game at Riverfront Stadium. The Reds lost to the Los Angeles Dodgers in 12 innings. Marsh's last game, on October 6, 2009, may not have been as personally meaningful, but mattered more to the world. It was the one-game playoff between the Detroit Tigers and Minnesota Twins for the American League Central title. Marsh worked home plate. The game went 12 innings and the Twins won, 6–5. Sadly, Marsh created controversy by ruling that Detroit's Brandon Inge was not hit by a pitch with the bases loaded in the top of the 12th. Replays showed the ball grazed Inge's billowing shirt. The Tigers failed to score, the Twins won in their next at-bat, and Detroit's season was over. Tiger manager Jim Leyland reported that three weeks after the season ended, Marsh called him to apologize for the mistake.

For Marsh, the toughest calls were not the close ones but the unexpected ones, like that glove-slapping play by A-Rod. Just the same, when asked to define the essence of umpiring, he pointed to the ultimate close one, Jackie Robinson stealing home in the first game of the 1955 World Series, just under the tag of New York Yankee catcher Yogi Berra. "I look at that photo all the time, and you know, there it is, stopped in time forever, and I still can't tell you if he's safe or out. I show people that photo and tell them, 'There, *that's* being an umpire.'"

SOURCE

Borow, Zev. "Law and Order." *ESPN The Magazine,* August 14, 2006. (October 24, 2010.) http://sports.espn.go.com/espn/print?id=3661613&type=story.

Tim McClelland

BORN: December 12, 1951
FIRST MAJOR LEAGUE GAME: September 3, 1981
FAVORS: Hitters, very strongly
THEY HATE HIM IN: Kansas City (still)

	2007	2008	2009	2010	Totals
Games	37	34	36	33	140
Innings	333	298.33	315.67	283.17	1,230.17
R/9	9.41	10.77	11.55	8.77	10.14
BB/9	6.32	7.39	8.44	6.10	7.07
K/9	12.54	12.37	13.71	13.54	13.03
K/BB	1.98	1.67	1.62	2.22	1.84

Pine tar: the two words that put McClelland on the baseball map. If the association escapes you, it's because you either don't remember or never saw the video of George Brett storming from the dugout trying to murder McClelland. The date was July 24, 1983, and McClelland was working home plate. It was his first full season as a big league umpire. Brett's Kansas City Royals trailed the New York Yankees by a run in the ninth. Brett stepped to the plate against the Yankees' closer, Goose Gossage, and hit a two-run homer to put the Royals on top. As Brett counted coup in the dugout, an uncharacteristically calm Yankee manager Billy Martin approached McClelland and quoted Section 1.10(b) of the *Major League Rule Book*, which has since become Section 1.10(c): "The bat handle, for not more than 18 inches from its end, may be covered or treated with any material or substance to improve the grip. Any such material or substance, which extends past the 18 inch limitation, shall cause the bat to be removed from the game."

Martin pointed out that pine tar extended more than 18 inches from the handle of the bat Brett used to hit his homer. Using home plate to measure, McClelland agreed. Under the discretion granted him by Rule 9.01(c), he nullified the home run and called Brett out. Which prompted Brett's crazed charge from the dugout and fueled a controversy that dominated sports pages for weeks. The Royals lodged a protest. One week later, American League president Lee MacPhail overruled McClelland, restored Brett's homer, and ordered the game to resume from the top of the ninth.

More than a quarter-century later, McClelland still gets mileage out of the incident, using Brett as a foil at banquet speeches. "I say George Brett isn't a very smart man because he charged out of the dugout. I'm 6'6", I weigh 260 pounds, I have protective equipment on, and I have a bat in my hand. What George thought he was gonna do, I don't know ... George isn't a very smart man, I'll have to tell you that. When he was being looked at when he was in high school, one of the scouts came up to him and said 'George, what do you run the 40 yard dash in?' George said, 'my gym shorts.'"

As McClelland noted, he's a big man, the tallest umpire in the majors and heavier than all except Ted Barrett, Jerry Layne, and Joe West. He has also emerged as the players' favorite. In 2003 and 2006, *Sports Illustrated* asked the players who the best umpire was. With 68 candidates to choose from, the players (550 in 2003, 470 in 2006) cast roughly a quarter of their ballots for McClelland. The runner-up both years was Jim Joyce, with less than half as many votes. Joyce bested McClelland 53 to 34 percent in a June 2010 poll of 100 players (50 in each league) conducted by *ESPN The Magazine,* but that was shortly after Joyce touched the nation with his class after blowing a call that denied Armando Galarraga of the Detroit Tigers a perfect game. Management respects McClelland too. Since 1999 he has worked every postseason except 2010, and in the course of his career he has participated in nine League Championship Series and four World Series. McClelland ranks as one of the leaders of the umpire corps, up there with John Hirschbeck and Joe West.

In the 2003 poll, *Sports Illustrated* broke down the vote for McClelland by hitters and pitchers. It found that he received 26.4 percent of the hitters' votes to 16.7 percent of the pitchers' votes. Not that 16.7 percent is a bad number. It still exceeds what runner-up Joyce got. But it's considerably lower than what McClelland got from hitters. Take one look at his plate numbers and you can see why: McClelland is a huge hitters' umpire. He had the third lowest K/9 and the third highest BB/9 from 2007 through 2010, meaning he has a tiny strike zone. His K/BB confirms this, the overall 1.84 ratio lower than all but Paul Schrieber's, Jerry Crawford's, and Randy Marsh's. The latter two have retired, so going into 2011, only Schrieber has a smaller strike zone among active umpires. And in McClelland's case the stamp-sized strike zone translates into runs, runs, runs. McClelland's R/9 for the period under study is a fat nine percent above the major league average, and ranks behind only Gerry Davis's as the highest.

But for all the esteem McClelland has earned within the baseball community, fans probably think first of two botched calls during the fourth game of the 2009 American League Championship Series. McClelland was working third base. In the fourth, he called out New York's Nick Swisher for leaving the bag too early on a sacrifice fly. Replays showed the call was incorrect. But that was nothing compared to the travesty an inning later, when Swisher came to bat. The Yankees had runners on second and third with one out when Swisher hit a comebacker to Los Angeles Angel pitcher Darren Oliver, who threw to catcher Mike Napoli in an attempt to nail lead runner Jorge Posada. Posada scampered back to third, chased the whole way by Napoli. When Posada arrived, he found teammate Robinson Cano already there. Both runners knew it was illegal to have two men on a base, so they each stepped off. Napoli tagged them both. They should both have been out. But McClelland ruled that Cano was safe and Posada out. "Obviously, or not obviously, there were two missed calls. I'm just out there trying to do my job and do it the best I can," McClelland said afterwards. Reggie Jackson probably spoke for most of the baseball community when he said, "Today was not a good day for the umpires. But the third base umpire is a great umpire."

Over his long career, McClelland's ejection rate is 1.9 percent, slightly below average. In keeping with his steady demeanor, his ejection rate is also 1.9 percent for the period under study. He was named a crew chief in 2000. As a leader among umpires, his opinion about instant replay is particularly noteworthy. The day after Jim Joyce blew the Galarraga perfect game, McClelland said, "I know I wasn't for [instant replay]. But after watching what I went through in the playoffs last year and then what Jim's going through, I think more and more umpires are coming around to it. Maybe this is not the sentiment of our union or our union leadership, but this is my own opinion."

McClelland called the perfect game pitched by the Yankees' David Wells against the Minnesota Twins on May 17, 1998.

Source

"Tim McClelland, Major League Umpire." YouTube, January 31, 2009. (October 24, 2010.) http://www.youtube.com/watch?v=zMG_xLQp3Jk.

Jerry Meals

Born: October 20, 1961
First Major League Game: September 14, 1992
Favors: Pitchers, but the runs score anyway
They hate him in: Colorado

	2007	2008	2009	2010	Totals
Games	32	34	34	34	134
Innings	281.83	302.5	303.83	302.17	1,190.33
R/9	10.06	9.94	9.83	8.61	9.60
BB/9	6.45	6.10	5.60	6.08	6.05
K/9	13.25	13.39	14.07	13.94	13.67
K/BB	2.05	2.20	2.51	2.29	2.26

Meals is the smallest umpire in the major leagues, standing 5'8" and weighing 168 pounds. But he doesn't have a Napoleon complex. His 1.8 percent career ejection rate is below average, and he has never totaled more than five ejections in a season. Temperamentally, this makes him the mirror image of Bill Hohn, who, like Meals, was born in Butler, Pennsylvania.

Meals has his moments, though. On August 23, 2010, he ejected both Yunel Escobar and manager Cito Gaston of the Toronto Blue Jays on questionable grounds. Escobar didn't like a called strike during his at-bat. He stepped out the box, moped a bit, but didn't say much. After he flied out to end the inning, Escobar headed to his defensive position at shortstop. He must have said something to Meals, because he was abruptly ejected. Gaston ran from the dugout to ask for an explanation, and just as tensions began to escalate, he got the boot as well. "I couldn't get out there quick enough to save my guy. And then I was gone just about as quickly," Gaston complained. Neither Meals nor his crew chief, Gerry Davis, disclosed what prompted the dual ejections, the only ones Meals had in 2010.

In each of the last three years, Meals has called a game without any walks. On May 22, 2008, he didn't grant a single base on balls in a match between the New York Mets and Atlanta Braves. Johan Santana and Tim Hudson threw 15 of the game's 17 pitcher innings, which would ordinarily explain everything, but Santana was having an off day, yielding 12 hits and striking out only one (opposing pitcher Hudson). On August 1, 2009, the pinpoint hurlers were Chris Carpenter of the St. Louis Cardinals and a trio of Houston Astros. And then on May 5, 2010, Meals called the first walkless game of the season as Pittsburgh's Charlie Morton and three relievers bested the Chicago Cubs' Ted Lilly, Carlos Zambrano, and Carlos Marmol.

Overall, Meals calls three percent fewer walks than an average umpire. He sees two percent fewer strikeouts than average, but his K/9 increased substantially in 2009 and stayed there in 2010. His overall K/BB is 2.26, slightly on the pitchers' side. But that doesn't translate into fewer runs when he's behind the plate. His four-year R/9 is 16th among the 77 umpires who called 500 or more innings from 2007 through 2010. Meals's R/9 has trended downward every year since 2007, but 2010 was the first year it came in below average. If his strike zone stays as it was in 2009 and 2010, his R/9 ought to remain where it is. But if his strike zone shrinks to 2007 and 2008 levels, look for his R/9 to rise.

In the 2009 postseason Meals became one of several umpires subjected to public opprobrium. In the third game of the National League Division Series, Philadelphia and Colorado went into the ninth inning tied. They each had won a game in the best-of-five series, so whoever grabbed game three would have a tremendous advantage. The Phillies had Jimmy Rollins on second and one out when Chase Utley came to bat. Colorado closer Huston Street threw a breaking ball low. Utley checked his swing, but the ball hit his bat, then his leg, and trickled onto the field. Utley raced up the line and beat Street's throw to first. A batted ball that touches the hitter in the batter's box is foul, but Meals ruled fair ball. Utley was safe at first and Rollins advanced to third, allowing the next batter, Ryan Howard, to hit a game-winning sacrifice fly. "Yeah, the ball came up and grazed off his leg and continued rolling up the line," Meals conceded afterward. He implied that Utley was responsible for the missed call. "Chase Utley took off like it was nothing. He gave no indication to us that it hit him. Whatever percent of the time, you're going to get a guy that's going to stop if it hits him." A poker-faced Utley, interviewed on national TV, said, "It might have hit me but I've been on the wrong end of that one so I ran it out and it worked out for us." The Phils went on to win the series.

Meals was behind home plate on May 6, 1998, when Kerry Wood of the Chicago Cubs tied Roger Clemens's record of 20 strikeouts in a nine-inning game. Wood gave the Houston Astros just one hit, and Meals didn't ding him for a single walk. Eight of the strikeouts were called. Losing pitcher Shane Reynolds, who also went the distance, struck out ten.

Source

Harding, Thomas, and Adam McCalvy. "Ump Admits Missed Call on Utley Hit." MLB.com, October 12, 2009. (October 24, 2010.) http://mlb.mlb.com/news/article.jsp?ymd=20091012&content_id=7438306&vkey=news_phi&fext=.jsp&c_id=phi.

Chuck Meriwether

BORN: June 30, 1956
FIRST MAJOR LEAGUE GAME: May 23, 1987
FAVORED: It depended on the season
THEY HATED HIM IN: No place in particular, despite many gripes about the quality of his work

	2007	2008	2009	2010	Totals
Games	33	33	34	0	100
Innings	304	295	302.5	0	901.5
R/9	9.41	9.00	10.23	0.00	9.55
BB/9	6.66	5.83	6.10	0.00	6.20
K/9	13.03	14.03	13.98	0.00	13.68
K/BB	1.96	2.41	2.29	0.00	2.21

An undisclosed problem put Meriwether on the disabled list in 2010. In a March 8, 2010, blog entry for Umps Care, the umpires' charity, Mike DiMuro reported that Meriwether would retire after the season. Multiple stories said Meriwether had to retire due to a severe back injury, but another claimed Meriwether's knees were shot. Neither would be a surprise given that Meriwether stands 6'5" and over his career would have crouched behind the catcher some 175,000 times. And it couldn't have helped that he was hit on the shin by a Joba Chamberlain fastball in his last home plate appearance, an 11-inning playoff game between the New York Yankees and Minnesota Twins on October 9, 2009. Prior to 2010, Meriwether had shown outstanding durability, working a full schedule every year since 1992. He participated in 2,594 major league games, including 645 appearances behind home plate.

Meriwether's statistics varied considerably over his final three seasons. In 2007 he favored hitters, shrinking his strike zone so much that pitchers yielded nine percent more walks than average when he worked the plate. In 2008 he favored pitchers, calling seven percent fewer walks than average but three percent more strikeouts. In 2009 his BB/9 again favored pitchers, but it didn't matter as hitters romped to a ten percent above average R/9. When you total up his numbers, however, they come remarkably close to the major league average for 2007–2009. His R/9 of 9.55 was just one percent higher than the norm. His BB/9 of 6.20 was just one percent lower than the norm. And his K/9 of 13.68 *was* the norm. If you believe that in baseball the breaks don't even out over a single season, but do even out over the long haul, you can use Meriwether's game-calling numbers as evidence.

Meriwether had a long fuse. His career ejection rate was just one percent, less than half the norm. In 2002, 2005, 2006, and 2009 he didn't eject anyone at all. The last man Meriwether ordered off the field was LaTroy Hawkins, then pitching for the New York Yankees. On May 20, 2008, Hawkins retaliated against the Baltimore Orioles after Yankee star Derek Jeter was unintentionally hit on the hand by a pitch and had to leave the game. Hawkins zipped one inside to the Orioles' Luke Scott, and on the next pitch threw at Scott's head. As Scott advanced toward the mound, bat in hand, Meriwether ejected Hawkins and restrained Scott. The benches emptied, but there was no fight. Scott homered in his next at-bat, and Jeter returned to action the next day.

Meriwether had some notable moments in his career. He was behind home plate on October 27, 2004, when the Boston Red Sox ended their 86-year World Series curse by beating the St. Louis Cardinals. Three years later, when the Red Sox won the World Series again, Meriwether was again the home plate umpire for the clinching game. Those were the only two World Series games Meriwether ever called. And on September 27, 2008, Meriwether was the home plate umpire for Greg Maddux's last appearance, a 2–1 win over the San Francisco Giants that gave Maddux 355 career victories.

"You have to respect everybody in the game: the custodians, the groundskeepers, the people preparing the concession stands before the games," Meriwether told students at Tennessee's Martin Methodist College in November 2008. He received a degree from the tiny school (enrollment 900) in 1976. "Most of the time, when an official or a referee or an umpire gets in trouble, it's when an athlete has made a mistake. I know you find that hard to believe, but an umpire is going to get into trouble when you have a bad throw to first base, and the first baseman has to reach up, come off the bag, and make the tag. You have a clean throw to first base, and you're not going to have any trouble."

Source
DiMuro, Mike. "Retirements Will Prompt New Hiring." Umps Care Charities, March 8, 2010. (October 24, 2010.) http://umpscareblog.com/03/08/2010/retirements-will-prompt-new-hiring/.

Bill Miller

BORN: May 31, 1967
FIRST MAJOR LEAGUE GAME: July 28, 1997
FAVORS: Pitchers, strongly
THEY HATE HIM IN: Colorado

	2007	2008	2009	2010	Totals
Games	35	36	35	34	140
Innings	313.5	322.17	318	297	1,250.67
R/9	9.85	7.96	8.86	8.67	8.83
BB/9	6.06	5.39	5.60	5.15	5.56
K/9	14.50	13.46	14.58	15.03	14.38
K/BB	2.39	2.50	2.60	2.92	2.59

Bill Miller is no hothead. His career ejection rate is 1.7 percent, well below average. But he will speak up when he perceives a crewmate in trouble, as Colorado Rockie catcher Yorvit Torrealba learned on August 24, 2009. In the heat of an extra-inning game against the San Francisco Giants, Torrealba showed up home plate umpire Angel Campos by visibly disagreeing with ball-and-strike calls. When Torrealba swatted a single in the 13th inning, he got an earful from Miller, who was stationed at second base. The two were still trading barbs when the game ended. Miller desisted from tossing Torrealba, but the Lords of Baseball looked into the incident and fined Miller for starting the dispute — and for allegedly calling Torrealba an undisclosed derogatory name. (Torrealba was fined too.) Miller declined comment.

Torrealba's behavior was surprising, given that Miller has an expansive strike zone that strongly favors pitchers. In 2007, Miller's 14.50 K/9 was nine percent above the major league norm. He had an unusual year in 2008, as his K/9 plunged more than a strikeout per game to just below average, but his already low BB/9 fell too, so he wasn't punishing pitchers. Hitters were going to the plate knowing Miller wouldn't give them any breaks and swinging at the first decent pitch they saw; although Miller ranked sixth in innings called in 2008, he ranked 19th in pitches seen. Not surprisingly, Miller had the third lowest R/9 among his peers, coming in below eight runs per game. In 2009 his BB/9 remained quite low and his K/9 rose, giving him the fourth highest K/BB in the game at 2.60. In 2010 he lowered his BB/9 and raised his K/9 even more, so that his K/BB ballooned to 2.92, 24 percent above average. His four-year K/BB is second only to Doug Eddings in favor of pitchers, and his R/9 for the period under study is ninth lowest, evidence that Miller's large strike zone dampens offense. He's one of the best umpires to have behind the plate if you crave a pitching duel.

Miller is durable and hard-working. He receives four weeks of vacation during the season, yet from 2007 through 2009 he compiled the fourth highest total of innings called, behind three Triple-A call-ups the Lords of Baseball exploited to exhaustion (James Hoye,

Rob Drake, and Chris Guccione, all since promoted to major league status). He eased off a bit in 2010. The only season Miller needed time away was 2002, and then it was just a few days. On July 19 he was working home plate during a game between the New York Mets and Cincinnati Reds when the Mets' Mo Vaughn hit a pop foul over the third base dugout. Miller slipped while pursuing the play and badly sprained an ankle. He added a few sick days to a two-week vacation and returned in early August to finish out the season.

Miller was born in Vallejo, California, near San Francisco and Oakland. He got to call an interleague game between the Giants and Athletics on May 18, 2007. What should have been a pleasant day on his native turf turned ugly. The Athletics jumped to a 5–0 lead after three and kept scoring, eventually winning 15–3. But that wasn't the bad part. In the eighth inning, with the game already lost, Giant pitcher Steve Kline and manager Bruce Bochy harangued Miller over his ball-and-strike judgment until Miller had to eject them. Kline had given up a grand slam after Miller called a ball on a pitch Kline considered strike three. Barry Bonds and pitching coach Dave Righetti had to walk the shouting Kline to the clubhouse, where Kline later admitted, "I wasn't around the plate all night, so that's probably why [Miller] didn't give it to me. I just lost it there."

Miller has a BA in history from UCLA.

SOURCE

Associated Press. "MLB Won't Suspend Torrealba, Umpire." ESPN.com, August 26, 2009. (October 24, 2010.) http://sports.espn.go.com/mlb/news/story?id=4425010.

Ed Montague

BORN: November 3, 1948
FIRST MAJOR LEAGUE GAME: October 1, 1974
FAVORED: Hitters, slightly
THEY HATED HIM IN: Probably some of the old AL umpires still hold a grudge against him

	2007	2008	2009	2010	Totals
Games	31	26	5	0	62
Innings	271	229	45	0	545
R/9	10.20	8.29	11.80	0.00	9.53
BB/9	6.21	6.52	6.60	0.00	6.37
K/9	13.22	13.48	14.40	0.00	13.43
K/BB	2.13	2.07	2.18	0.00	2.11

Although he didn't announce his retirement until February 2010, Montague did not work after May 10, 2009, due to a concussion and neck problems. He was also more than 60 years old. He worked in 4,369 regular season games, four All-Star games, 25 Divisional

Series games, 40 League Championship Series games, and 34 World Series games over a 35-year span.

In a note posted on the World Umpires Association web site to announce his retirement, Montague wrote that "I feel very humbled and blessed that I was born into, and grew up around, this great game that I love. (Thank you Mom & Dad.)" Dad, also named Ed Montague, was a reserve infielder for the Cleveland Indians from 1928 to 1932, and later became a scout for the New York Giants. Montague *pere's* greatest baseball achievement was securing the signature of teenage center fielder Willie Mays on a major league contract in June 1950. Later, when the Giants moved to the Montagues' hometown of San Francisco, Dad took young Eddie to the Giants' clubhouse. "My dad introduced me [to Mays]. [Mays] pulled a brand-new glove with his name embroidered on it, and he gave it to me. I remember holding it out the window [on the way home] saying, 'This is Willie Mays's glove.'"

Montague was widely considered a top-notch umpire, one of the reasons he was named to so many postseason crews. From 2007 through 2009, his BB/9 and K/9 never strayed more than five percent from the norm—even in 2009, when he worked only 45 innings. Overall, Montague's BB/9 was two percent above the norm in his last three seasons, and his K/9 was two percent below the norm. This favoritism toward hitters was faithfully reflected in his R/9, which was one percent above the norm. It's fair to conclude that at the end of his career, Montague was a consistent game caller with a strike zone a bit smaller than average.

He also had a long fuse. His career ejection rate was 1.3 percent, less than two-thirds the norm. Montague's last ejectee was Philadelphia manager Charlie Manuel, who questioned Montague's ball-and-strike judgment in the last inning of the last game Montague ever worked behind home plate—the April 25, 2009, contest between Philadelphia and the Florida Marlins. Montague called ball four on a pitch that replays confirmed was high and inside, but Manuel disagreed. He must have said a magic word, because Montague interrupted play and walked toward the Phillie dugout. Manuel met him halfway, and after a brief exchange, Montague tossed him. The two gray-haired antagonists could be seen (and even heard on one video replay) trading f-bombs. Later, a sheepish Manuel said, "When I looked at it, the umpire had it right."

As you might expect, Montague witnessed several baseball milestones. He worked home plate on August 13, 1979, when Lou Brock of the St. Louis Cardinals smacked his 3,000th hit. He was at first base on September 11, 1985, when Pete Rose broke Ty Cobb's all-time hit record. In game six of the 1986 World Series, he worked the right field line and had an unsurpassed view of the Mookie Wilson ground ball that passed through Bill Buckner's legs to give the New York Mets a fateful extra-inning victory over the Boston Red Sox. In 1991 he was behind home plate for another fateful World Series game six, the one in which Kirby Puckett homered in the 11th to give the Minnesota Twins a win over the Atlanta Braves. On April 11, 2000, Montague worked the first-ever regular season game at the Giants' new stadium (currently known as AT&T Park), a sweet honor for the San Francisco native. And on October 5, 2001, he was the first base umpire when Barry Bonds of the Giants hit his 71st and 72nd home runs of the season to break Mark McGwire's single-season record, and was at third base two days later when Bonds hit his 73rd.

But it hasn't been all peaches for Montague. He sided with the hardcore National League umpires in 1999 when they decided to submit their resignations en masse as a union negotiating tactic. He became a bitter enemy of John Hirschbeck, who led the American League umpires opposed to the stratagem. Major League Baseball called the umpires' bluff and accepted 22 of their resignations, but not Montague's. He was too good to let go. "I'm still bitter about [Hirschbeck's faction] jumping off the ship when it came down to the nuts-and-bolts deal," Montague admitted to the *San Francisco Chronicle* in 2003.

Knowing the end had come, Montague told a Bay Area gathering in November 2009 that "It's been a lot of fun." Then he turned reflective. "Nobody ever feels worse than an umpire when he makes a mistake. I've lived with it. I remember my dad always saying, 'Leave it at the ballpark.' It's very hard to leave it at the ballpark. It kind of eats at you and you remember stuff. But then, there were a lot of good calls."

Source

James, Marty. "Locals Learn from Best at Umpire Clinic." *Weekly Calistogan*, November 18, 2009. (October 24, 2010.) http://napavalleyregister.com/calistogan/sports/article_90938a11-6731-5062-9753-2f17d5726bf9.html.

Casey Moser

BORN: April 18, 1977
FIRST MAJOR LEAGUE GAME: July 7, 2005
FAVORS: Pitchers, so far (the sample size is way too small to be conclusive)
THEY HATE HIM IN: Seattle

	2007	2008	2009	2010	Totals
Games	0	1	4	0	5
Innings	0	9	40.5	0	49.5
R/9	0.00	15.00	3.56	0.00	5.64
BB/9	0.00	9.00	4.22	0.00	5.09
K/9	0.00	6.00	13.11	0.00	11.82
K/BB	0.00	0.67	3.11	0.00	2.32

Moser called one game in 2005. When you add those stats to the totals above, his R/9 rises to 6.98 and his BB/9 rises to 5.90. Those numbers are still low, so based upon an extremely limited sample (58 innings), he looks like a pitchers' umpire, even though his K/9, when the 2005 appearance is included, comes to just 12.72, well below the norm.

In 2009 Moser had four chances to work home plate and compiled an astonishingly low R/9. In his first game, Jason Hammel of the Colorado Rockies faced Barry Zito of the San Francisco Giants and just one run scored. Four days later, seven runs scored in a game started by Robert Ray of the Toronto Blue Jays and Jered Weaver of the Los Angeles Angels. On July 19, Moser called a game between Russ Ortiz of the Houston Astros (ERA for the year: 5.57) and Hiroki Kuroda of the Los Angeles Dodgers; seven runs. In Moser's final 2009 home plate stint, the Chicago White Sox (starter: Mark Buehrle) and Seattle Mariners (Felix Hernandez) went 14 innings before Ken Griffey Jr. singled in the lone run of the game. R/9 for the four games: 3.56!

Through 2009 Moser had appeared in just 35 big league contests. In 2010 he was reappointed to the list of Triple-A call-ups, but his prospects for major league status may be dimming. He didn't work a single game behind the plate in 2010. The other returning Triple-A call-up born in 1977, Mike Muchlinski, received 16 home plate opportunities. Among the aspiring umpires born in 1978, Dan Bellino enjoyed more favor. And in 2010 a pair of first-time Triple-A call-ups, Al Porter and Victor Carapazza, got serious looks from Major League Baseball and almost certainly passed Moser on the prospect list.

Moser has accumulated two ejections in his brief career. On April 24, 2008, in just his 12th game (and second behind home plate), Seattle manager John McLaren challenged his plate judgment and got the thumb. On July 18, 2009, Moser tossed Houston Astro manager Cecil Cooper for arguing a call at first base. Moser was also the subject of some controversy on May 27, 2010, when he ruled in play a ball hit off the top of the wall at San Francisco's AT&T Park by the Washington Nationals' Adam Dunn. The Nationals argued that Dunn had homered, so Moser's crewmates reviewed the instant replay. They upheld Moser's call.

SOURCE

Gurnick, Ken. "Notes: Penny Peeved at Umpire." MLB.com, March 25, 2006. (October 24, 2010.) http://losangeles.dodgers.mlb.com/news/article.jsp?ymd=20060325&content_id=1362460&vkey=spt 2006news&fext=.jsp&c_id=la.

Mike Muchlinski

BORN: February 26, 1977
FIRST MAJOR LEAGUE GAME: April 24, 2006
FAVORS: Hitters, so far (the sample size is small)
THEY HATE HIM IN: Minnesota

	2007	2008	2009	2010	Totals
Games	7	7	11	16	41
Innings	61	60.33	96.17	139.5	357
R/9	7.82	10.44	13.66	8.71	10.18
BB/9	6.05	3.58	8.98	5.74	6.30
K/9	10.03	16.56	16.19	13.87	14.29
K/BB	1.66	4.63	1.80	2.42	2.27

On July 20, 2009, the Minnesota Twins jumped to a 12–2 lead against the Oakland Athletics. What followed was the greatest comeback in Athletics franchise history. But even though the A's led 14–13 in the ninth with two outs, the Twins had a chance to tie. Michael Cuddyer was on second and Carlos Gomez on first. A's pitcher Michael Wuertz threw a pitch that bounced short of the plate, sailed over catcher Kurt Suzuki's head, and dribbled to the backstop. Suzuki didn't know where the ball was. Once he found it, he chased it down while Cuddyer rounded third and tried to score. Suzuki's throw reached Wuertz as Cuddyer slid into home plate. From all appearances, including the replays, Cuddyer was safe. But home plate umpire Mike Muchlinski called him out. Game over, historic story line preserved. "There's no doubt in my mind I was safe," Cuddyer bristled. His manager, Ron Gardenhire, took a longer view: "It's hard to say [Muchlinski] blew it because we did enough blowing it ourselves."

A native of Tacoma, Washington, Muchlinski is a Triple-A call-up who works in the Pacific Coast League when he's not filling in for an injured or vacationing major league umpire. A lot of his big-league games are on the West Coast. His first home plate assignment was an April 26, 2006 contest between the Chicago White Sox and Seattle Mariners. Neither Mark Buehrle (seven innings) nor Bobby Jenks (one inning), Chicago's two pitchers, recorded a walk or strikeout. The first batter Muchlinski called out on strikes was slugger Jim Thome.

If you add Muchlinski's nine plate appearances from 2006, his rookie year, his numbers look more favorable to pitchers. His BB/9 and K/9 both dip, and his K/BB ratio remains about the same (2.29 instead of 2.27), so it's not that his strike zone changes. But his R/9 comes all the way down to 9.69 — still high, but not as high as the 10.18 figure he compiled from 2007 through 2010, which would tie him with Gerry Davis for highest in the majors if he worked enough innings (although you may feel that 436.33 innings, the equivalent of 872.67 pitcher innings, *do* entitle you to draw conclusions about his plate work). Muchlinski's R/9 is especially high considering that nearly one-third of the innings he's called have been in pitchers' havens like the Oakland-Alameda County Coliseum (69 innings), Safeco Field (52 innings), and PetCo Park (18.67 innings). If he'd worked more games in towns with hitters' parks, like Denver, Cincinnati, and Philadelphia, there's no telling how high his R/9 might have gone. The one time he worked in Philadelphia, 15 runs scored. The one time he called a game at Coors Field, 18 runs scored.

Muchlinski has a slow fuse, with a career ejection rate of one percent despite the fact that he's at the beginning of his career and managers and players are testing him. The first ejectee of his big league career was manager Bob Geren of the Athletics, who argued on August 19, 2007 that a collision between his second baseman, Mark Ellis, and Kansas City Royal baserunner Joey Gathright constituted runner's interference. Muchlinski ruled that Ellis hit Gathright. "[Muchlinski] had [Ellis] not in the act of fielding the ball," said crew chief Dana DeMuth, who conceded that the rest of the crew reviewed the play with Muchlinski after the game. Perhaps coincidentally, Muchlinski did not appear in another big league game in 2007. On August 23, 2009, Muchlinski ejected Ryan Braun of the Milwaukee Brewers for throwing his helmet after he was called out on a close play at first.

Muchlinski was the home plate umpire for the 2009 Triple-A All-Star game. Given the steadily increasing number of major league games he has been assigned each season, he appears likely to win a promotion from minor league status in the next few years.

SOURCE

Thesier, Kelly. "Controversial Call Goes Against Twins." MLB.com, July 21, 2009. (October 25, 2010.) http://mlb.mlb.com/news/article.jsp?ymd=20090721&content_id=5972788&vkey=news_mlb&fext=.jsp&c_id=mlb.

Paul Nauert

BORN: July 7, 1963
FIRST MAJOR LEAGUE GAME: May 19, 1995
FAVORS: Pitchers, although hitters don't seem to mind
THEY HATE HIM IN: Tampa Bay

	2007	2008	2009	2010	Totals
Games	35	34	34	32	135
Innings	313.67	307.33	303.67	294.17	1,218.83
R/9	10.30	9.08	9.63	7.25	9.09
BB/9	5.62	5.45	6.08	5.42	5.64
K/9	13.26	13.24	14.79	13.92	13.79
K/BB	2.36	2.43	2.43	2.57	2.45

Nauert's K/BB keeps growing. It went from 2.36 to 2.43 in 2008, held steady in 2009 despite big increases in both walks and strikeouts, and then rose to 2.57 in 2010. Nauert's overall K/BB of 2.45 is ten percent above average and places him 12th among the 77 umpires who worked 500 or more innings during the period under study. He unquestionably has one of the largest strike zones in the majors.

Yet Nauert's R/9 bounces around, and without that tailspin in 2010 (to the third lowest R/9 for the season) it would average out as hitter-friendly. Why the discrepancy? It can't be explained by what hitters do when Nauert is calling balls and strikes. Their slash statistics varied little from 2007 to 2009: .271/.336/.430 in 2007, .270/.327/.440 in 2008, .269/.328/.440 in 2009. The slashes dropped to .246/.309/.372 in 2010 (that anemic .372 slugging percentage ranked third lowest for the year, behind only James Hoye and Bob Davidson), so we at least have an explanation for the tailspin. But the results for the first three years of the study prove that R/9 can move independently not only of BB/9 and K/9, but of hitting performance. Nauert's R/9 discrepancy could be a matter of offensive sequence. A two-out walk followed by a triple, then a third out produces one run; a two-out triple followed by a walk, then a third out produces no runs; the umpire's R/9 is affected, but all his other metrics aren't.

Nauert possesses the virtue of patience. His career ejection rate is only 1.3 percent, less than two-thirds the norm. He's never ejected more than three people in a season, although in 1998 he worked just 89 games, so three was a high number. Nauert is also durable. In his six full seasons (2004 through 2010) he has missed less than one week of work (in 2009) for reasons other than scheduled vacation. Although he is slow to anger, Nauert has a knack for arousing anger in others. The most notable incident involved Carl Crawford of the Tampa Bay Devil Rays, who thought he had beaten out a grounder to shortstop in a September 3, 2007, game between the Devil Rays and Baltimore. When first base umpire Nauert called him out, Crawford went berserk. He believed (correctly) that Oriole first baseman Kevin Millar's foot was off the bag. Coach George Hendrick stepped between Crawford and Nauert, but Crawford literally climbed Hendrick's back, pushing Hendrick into Nauert. For that outburst, Crawford was suspended two games and fined $1,000. "Because we lose a lot of games I understand a lot of calls are not going to go our way, but sometimes you just have to be like, 'C'mon, man.' It's ridiculous sometimes," said a still steaming Crawford two days later. Nauert did not comment.

Nor did Nauert comment after an April 23, 2007, confrontation with batting coach Gerald Perry of the Chicago Cubs. After Nauert called strike three on the Cubs' Mark DeRosa in the bottom of the 12th to end a tense game against the Milwaukee Brewers, Perry found Nauert under the stands and challenged him to a fight. Crew chief Brian Gorman interceded, and Perry escaped discipline. On July 30, 2008, Nauert's antagonist was veteran reliever Arthur Rhodes of the Seattle Mariners. Nauert called three straight walks on Rhodes in the bottom of the eighth, allowing the eventual winning run to score for Texas. Rhodes became Nauert's sole ejection of 2008. "You've got to make your calls out there," Rhodes groused.

Back in 1999, Nauert stood with the hard-line umpires during their union's ill-fated attempt to wring concessions from the Lords of Baseball by submitting mass resignations. He was one of 22 umpires whose resignation was accepted. His response: denial. "I don't accept them accepting my resignation. I plan on being here tomorrow. I'll be here for the game. It's really unfortunate it had to come to this. But you have to stand up for what you believe in. I come from a family of nine kids, and I learned to stand up for what I believe in," he said on September 1, 1999, his last day. He missed the 2000 and 2001 seasons and all but 30 games in 2002 before returning to the bigs.

Nauert is deeply involved in umpire training. Although he has worked at the Wendelstedt Umpire School, one of the two gateways to professional umpiring, he focuses more on amateur umpires and those who prefer to remain at the lower levels. "Ninety percent of American umpires work amateur baseball. Those guys are more important to the development of kids than I am. You need quality officials at those levels just as much as you need us," he told the *Miami Herald* in 2007.

Source
Shea, John. "Rookie Umpire Is Called Out." *San Francisco Chronicle,* September 2, 1999. (October 25, 2010.) http://www.sfgate.com/cgi-bin/article.cgi?f=/e/a/1999/09/02/SPORTS13613.dtl.

Jeff Nelson

BORN: June 1, 1965
FIRST MAJOR LEAGUE GAME: May 9, 1997
FAVORS: Pitchers
THEY HATE HIM IN: Baltimore

	2007	2008	2009	2010	Totals
Games	20	33	34	33	120
Innings	182.33	293.33	294.83	301.5	1,072
R/9	5.82	8.56	11.02	8.66	8.80
BB/9	5.53	5.12	7.39	6.75	6.27
K/9	13.92	14.39	13.28	14.03	13.90
K/BB	2.52	2.81	1.80	2.08	2.22

Nelson went over to the hitters' side in 2009. He had the fourth highest R/9, fourth highest BB/9, 12th lowest K/9, and fourth lowest K/BB, putting him at the extreme end of favoring offense. But in every other year under study he has been a solid pitchers' umpire. Take out his 2009 stats and you get an R/9 of just 7.96, a BB/9 of 5.85, a K/9 of 14.14, and a K/BB of 2.42. Had his 2009 numbers been at all consistent with the other three seasons, his R/9 would be the lowest of all umpires and his strike zone metrics would be in the top quarter favoring pitchers. Nelson's 2007 R/9 was the lowest (by far) of any single-season R/9 for the period under study, and his 5.12 BB/9 in 2008 was the lowest that season.

Nelson has an average fuse, compiling a career ejection rate of two percent. He had a busy August 2010, throwing out four doubters, two of them on August 20. He put Nick Markakis of the Baltimore Orioles through a rough at-bat in the sixth inning, calling a strike on a breaking pitch low and away, then a strike on a ball that appeared to dip below the knees, and then strike three on a pitch slightly outside. Markakis argued after the second called strike, and argued again after the third. Nelson tried to walk away, but when Markakis refused to leave the batter's box and continued to chirp, Nelson ran him. Oriole manager Buck Showalter took up Markakis's cause but was not ejected — until the ninth inning, when Nelson ruled that a close pitch to Elvis Andrus of the Texas Rangers was a ball. "There are so many pitches during the course of a game that can go either way. We understand that completely. We just want our share. That's all," Showalter said. The double ejection followed an August 15 ejection in which Nelson's ball-and-strike calling also came into question, this time by Chicago White Sox pitching coach Don Cooper. Apparently Nelson has a reputation for a low strike zone (which would certainly explain his low R/9), but some managers, coaches, and players haven't heard about it.

On April 12, 2010, Minnesota native Nelson had the honor of working home plate for the first regular season game ever played at Target Field in Minneapolis. His crew for the day consisted of two fellow Minnesotans, Mark Wegner and Tim Tschida, plus Californian Kerwin Danley. Nelson and Tschida had visited the park while it was under construction to help formulate the ground rules. They identified the left field corner as a potential trouble spot, so naturally in the third inning of that first game, Mike Cameron of the Boston Red Sox hit a long fly there. The ball soared over the fence, but fair or foul? Third base ump Danley ruled foul. When Red Sox manager Terry Francona questioned the call, Nelson and crew agreed to check the instant replay. They upheld Danley's judgment, and the Twins went on to win, 5–2.

In 2007 Nelson missed almost three months with testicular cancer. While recovering, he watched local umpires across southern Minnesota. "One night, I am working the plate for an American Legion game in Pine Island and I see Jeff sitting in a lawn chair behind the backstop," reported one old friend. Asked about the busman's holiday, Nelson smiled and said, "I know just about every small town in the area now." He made a remarkably quick return from chemotherapy, culminating in a home plate assignment at the Metrodome on August 31. "This was the perfect place to come back in. My family was here. I had a lot of friends here today." However, he admitted that "I felt pretty good at the start of the game, but I was pretty whipped at the end." Since then, he hasn't missed any time.

Nelson's experience with cancer has made him especially sympathetic to children afflicted by the disease. "I thought it was scary. I can't imagine what it's like when a kid has cancer." He is an integral part of the umpires' Blue for Kids charity. "It makes you proud of being an umpire because you're channeling the contacts and the nice people that you meet on the road into something positive and productive." Nelson has also served as secretary-treasurer of the World Umpires Association, the current union.

Source

Wright, Dave. "Jeff Nelson's Comeback: Satisfying but Tiring." Ballparkdigest.com, September 1, 2007. (October 25, 2010.) http://www.ballparkdigest.com/news/index.html?article_id=214.

Brian O'Nora

BORN: February 7, 1963
FIRST MAJOR LEAGUE GAME: August 4, 1992
FAVORS: Pitchers, strongly
THEY HATE HIM IN: Ballpark EMT units

	2007	2008	2009	2010	Totals
Games	18	34	35	34	121
Innings	163.17	292	300.17	304.67	1,060
R/9	10.26	8.63	8.58	9.01	8.97
BB/9	5.30	5.30	5.43	5.26	5.32
K/9	12.13	13.38	13.97	14.09	13.56
K/BB	2.29	2.52	2.57	2.68	2.55

O'Nora missed half of 2007 due to an undisclosed problem. He returned healthy in 2008, but on May 31 pulled a hamstring running from first base to right field to make a call. He left the game and missed a week. On June 24, less than a month later, he suffered one of the goriest on-field wounds in recent memory. Miguel Olivo of the Kansas City Royals hit a ground ball that shattered his bat, and the barrel hit O'Nora on the left side of the head. Blood poured from O'Nora's scalp. He staggered to the Royal dugout, where outfielder Jose Guillen pressed a towel to O'Nora's head to stanch the flow. Diagnosed with a mild concussion, O'Nora returned in three days and worked the rest of the season without interruption. It looked like he was going to get through 2009 unscathed, but on October 1 he was hit on the right knee by a wild pitch from Kip Wells of the Cincinnati Reds, ending his regular season a few games early. He was able to work the National League Division Series between St. Louis and Los Angeles a week later.

On August 26, 2009, O'Nora was one of the few umpires *not* injured in a game between Tampa Bay and Toronto. Jerry Crawford started at home plate, was hit in the mask by a foul ball in the bottom of the first, developed back spasms, and left in the second. Tom Hallion relieved Crawford behind home plate and lasted until the final pitch of the sixth inning, when he was hit in the chest and knocked flat by a Scott Kazmir fastball. The woozy Hallion moved to third base, and O'Nora took over behind home plate. (Crawford said he would have come back on the field if Hallion had been unable to continue.) So fans at the Rogers Centre that night saw something more unusual than a no-hitter: three home plate umpires in one game.

O'Nora has remarkably consistent plate judgment. His BB/9 has varied by just 17 points over the years under study. His BB/9 is also remarkably low. His aggregate score of 5.32 is second lowest of all umpires, behind only Doug Eddings. O'Nora's strikeout rate has been rising at a faster pace than the major league average, but has never been above average, suggesting he might have an aversion to calling third strikes. Even so, his K/BB is extremely favorable to pitchers—fifth highest of all umpires—due to that very low walk rate. Perhaps because he's so stingy with walks, O'Nora's R/9 is four percent below the major league norm, even after a fluky 2007 in which his R/9 was six percent above average. Smart hitters come to bat ready to swing when O'Nora stands behind home plate.

The stocky O'Nora is slow to anger, compiling a 1.3 percent ejection rate over his career. The last time one of his calls led to an ejection was on July 26, 2008, when manager Trey Hillman of the Kansas City Royals thought his batter should have been safe at first and O'Nora said no. When Hillman didn't take that for an answer, O'Nora booted him. O'Nora had two ejections in 2009, but both sprang from an event that had nothing to do with him. On August 11 a beanball exchange between Detroit and Boston erupted into violence after Tiger pitcher Rick Porcello hit Red Sox batter Kevin Youkilis in the shoulder. It was the second night in a row that Youkilis had been hit by a Tiger pitcher. (The Tigers' Miguel Cabrera had already been hit twice and forced out of the lineup by Red Sox hurlers.) Youkilis rushed the mound and threw his helmet at the retreating Porcello. After the obligatory emptying of dugouts and bullpens, O'Nora sent both Youkilis and Porcello to the showers. O'Nora didn't eject anybody in 2010.

On June 13, 2010, O'Nora called the second major league game pitched by the Washington Nationals' Stephen Strasburg, perhaps the most heralded pitching prospect since Dwight Gooden in the early 1980s. Although Strasburg was wild and departed in the sixth inning, O'Nora was sufficiently impressed to speak publicly about what he saw. "He is the real deal. They said he has a good curveball, which he does. He reminds me a lot of Randy Johnson when he was in his prime. Randy had more of a slider. Strasburg throws hard. He has a different gear than anybody else."

SOURCE

Associated Press. "Plate Umpire O'Nora Hit by Broken Maple Bat." *USA Today*, June 25, 2008. (October 25, 2010.) http://www.usatoday.com/sports/baseball/2008-06-25-umpire-injured_N.htm.

Al Porter

BORN: December 18, 1977
FIRST MAJOR LEAGUE GAME: April 5, 2010
FAVORS: Too early to tell
THEY HATE HIM IN: Nowhere yet

	2007	2008	2009	2010	Totals
Games	0	0	0	9	9
Innings	0	0	0	78.67	78.67
R/9	0.00	0.00	0.00	8.69	8.69
BB/9	0.00	0.00	0.00	4.92	4.92
K/9	0.00	0.00	0.00	13.84	13.84
K/BB	0.00	0.00	0.00	2.81	2.81

Philadelphia native Porter made his major league debut in Pittsburgh on April 5, 2010. He worked third base for the Pirates' opening day 11–5 victory over the Los Angeles Dodgers. After finishing the three-game series, he returned to the minors. He got his first opportunity to work home plate in the majors on June 6, 2010, in a game between the Chicago Cubs and Houston Astros. The Astros won, 6–3, behind starting pitcher Brett Myers and left fielder Carlos Lee, who followed an RBI single by Lance Berkman with a two-run homer to give Houston a lead it never relinquished. Porter didn't call a third strike until the bottom of the sixth, when his victim was the pitcher Myers. It was his only called third strike of the day.

Porter was working home plate during a game between Pittsburgh and Houston on August 15, 2010, when Carlos Lee swung hard at a pitch and hit Porter in the head with his follow-through. Porter remained conscious, but had to be helped off the field and needed five stitches to close the wound. It was just his seventh major league game calling balls and strikes.

If starts behind home plate are an indication of favor, the Lords of Baseball consider

Porter the umpiring corps' 2010 rookie of the year. His nine games and 78.67 innings topped all Triple-A call-ups working their first big league game in 2010. Pitchers should be recommending a full promotion for him. At 4.92, his BB/9 is 19 percent lower than average, contributing to an R/9 slightly below average. Of course, his sample size is small, so pitchers could be in for a big surprise if Porter sees more action.

When he isn't filling in for an indisposed major league umpire, Porter works in the International League. On July 14, 2010, he was the second base umpire for the Triple-A All-Star game in Allentown, Pennsylvania, not far from his hometown.

Source

"Hatboro-Horsham Hatters Baseball: Former HH Star Alan Porter Gets Call to the Big Leagues." LeagueLineup.com, April 4, 2010. (October 25, 2010.) http://www.leaguelineup.com/welcome.asp?url=hatters.

David Rackley

BORN: October 11, 1981
FIRST MAJOR LEAGUE GAME: August 13, 2010
FAVORS: Too early to tell
THEY HATE HIM IN: Also too early to tell

	2007	2008	2009	2010	Totals
Games	0	0	0	2	2
Innings	0	0	0	17.5	17.5
R/9	0.00	0.00	0.00	3.60	3.60
BB/9	0.00	0.00	0.00	5.66	5.66
K/9	0.00	0.00	0.00	17.49	17.49
K/BB	0.00	0.00	0.00	3.09	3.09

In his third full season as an International League umpire, Rackley was finally named a Triple-A call-up. On August 13, 2010, he was assigned to work a series between the Pittsburgh Pirates and Houston Astros with fellow rookie Al Porter under the watchful eyes of crew chief Jerry Layne and veteran Hunter Wendelstedt. It was a thoughtful way to break Rackley into the majors. He lived in League City, an easy drive from Houston, so family members could be there for his big day. And he already knew Wendelstedt because they both have taught at the Wendelstedt Umpire School.

After debuting at first base, Rackley got to work behind the plate in his second major league game. His first big league called strikeout was Pedro Alvarez of the Pirates at the hands of Houston's Bud Norris. Jeff Keppinger of the Astros received Rackley's first big league walk. There were 23 strikeouts in the game, but Rackley called only two of them. His other start behind home plate was also in Houston, on October 1. Again Norris started for the Astros. Norris had racked up 14 strikeouts and earned the win in Rackley's home plate debut. The second time around he tallied six strikeouts in six innings and absorbed the loss as Casey Coleman and the Chicago Cubs shut out the Astros, 2–0.

SOURCE

Fowler, Ryan. "Minor League Umps Share Dream of Bigs." *Toledo Free Press,* May 9, 2008. (October 25, 2010.) http://www.toledofreepress.com/2008/05/09/minor-league-umps-share-dream-of-bigs/.

Tony Randazzo

BORN: January 11, 1965
FIRST MAJOR LEAGUE GAME: August 13, 1999
FAVORS: Pitchers, but hitters don't mind
THEY HATE HIM IN: Boston and Colorado

	2007	2008	2009	2010	Totals
Games	33	0	34	34	101
Innings	303.83	0	300.17	300.83	904.83
R/9	10.01	0.00	9.32	8.68	9.34
BB/9	6.01	0.00	5.01	5.00	5.34
K/9	12.97	0.00	13.67	14.27	13.64
K/BB	2.16	0.00	2.73	2.86	2.55

There's a considerable gap between what the data suggest about Randazzo and what players and managers say about him. The data suggest he has a very large strike zone tempered by a reluctance to call strike three and is more patient than the average umpire in arguments. Stories from players and managers suggest that Randazzo has a tight, sometimes arbitrary strike zone and an aggressive attitude. Most observers would conclude that the anecdotal evidence, being partial and partisan, carries less weight and should be discounted, if not discarded. But it's possible that both accounts are correct. This study does not speak to pitch-by-pitch consistency, nor does it measure how often an umpire rubs teams the wrong way. Randazzo could well have a generous but inconsistent strike zone and a forbearing but irritable disposition.

Randazzo missed 2008 due to neck surgery. It's reasonable to assume that for much of 2007, and perhaps even before that, he was in considerable pain. That could explain the gripes about his strike zone and disposition. Of his 24 career ejections, seven came in 2006 and 2007, but he had none in 2009 or 2010, which supports the proposition that a pain-free Randazzo is a more consistent and friendly Randazzo. And some of Randazzo's pre–2008 ejections do come off as tantrums by a frazzled soul at wit's end with its aching body, none more blatantly than a twin ejection at the end of a comfortable 16–9 win by the Colorado Rockies over the visiting Pittsburgh Pirates on June 7, 2006. Rockie reliever

Ray King struggled in the ninth and blamed it on Randazzo's strike zone. Rather than shrug it off and resume the game, Randazzo walked up the base line, intercepted the departing King, and allegedly bumped King before ejecting him. When Rockie manager Clint Hurdle protested, Randazzo bumped and ejected him too. "He shouldn't have walked up the line," said King. "He gets right up in your face hoping I'd agitate him." After the game, Randazzo refused comment, and his crew chief, Joe West, said, "I'm not taking questions. We have a plane to catch."

One more example. Randazzo worked home plate for the June 15, 2007, game between the San Francisco Giants and Boston Red Sox. In the bottom of the first, he called a third strike on Boston's David Ortiz, who stood in the box and excoriated him. Randazzo let it go and Ortiz stalked off to the dugout, where he threw down his helmet and bat. *That's* when Randazzo ejected him. "If he wants to throw me out, he should throw me out when I'm right in his face. Not when I'm in the dugout. What did I do for him to throw me out? Throw my helmet and bat down? I didn't throw it to him," Ortiz complained the next day, adding, "The strike zone was ridiculous." Randazzo again had no comment.

Randazzo's strike zone after his return from surgery would have delighted Ray King, who retired in 2008. The Chicago-born umpire's 2009 BB/9 of 5.01 was 22 percent below the norm and second lowest in the majors, behind only Charlie Reliford (since retired). His 2010 BB/9 was nearly identical to 2009's, but owing to the reduction in walks across the major leagues, it was "only" 17 percent below the norm — still good for second lowest of the year, this time behind Brian Runge. At the same time, Randazzo joined the trend toward more strikeouts, increasing his K/9 by 1.3 between 2007 and 2010. His K/9 was below average in all three years studied — hence the suspicion that he doesn't like to call third strikes — but because his BB/9 was so low in 2009 and 2010, his overall K/BB ranks fourth highest.

Despite the ample strike zone, Randazzo's R/9 was right at average, suggesting that pitchers do not take full advantage of his generosity. In 2009, the hitters' slash stats when Randazzo worked the plate were a healthy .269/.326/.436. Their 2010 slashes came down to .258/.312/.408, but both the batting average and slugging percentage remained above the major league norm. Evidently batters come to the plate swinging, knowing that if they keep the bat on their shoulders Randazzo is likely to put them behind in the count. In 2009 Randazzo finished 37th in innings worked but 43rd in pitches seen. In 2010 he finished 32nd in innings pitched but 38th in pitches seen.

Randazzo's father founded the National Italian-American Sports Hall of Fame in Chicago.

Source

Goldberg, Jeff. "Ortiz Still Upset About Ejection." *Hartford Courant,* June 17, 2007. (October 25, 2010.) http://articles.courant.com/2007-06-17/features/0706170243_1_ramirez-homers-ejected-david-ortiz.

Ed Rapuano

BORN: September 30, 1957
FIRST MAJOR LEAGUE GAME: May 11, 1990
FAVORS: Hitters, but pitchers don't mind
THEY HATE HIM IN: Philadelphia and Milwaukee

	2007	2008	2009	2010	Totals
Games	35	35	35	35	140
Innings	304.33	318.17	310.33	309.17	1,242
R/9	8.69	9.67	9.08	8.91	9.09
BB/9	6.54	6.34	6.73	5.85	6.36
K/9	13.87	12.33	13.75	14.88	13.70
K/BB	2.12	1.94	2.04	2.54	2.15

Early in Rapuano's career he was considered a top-flight umpire, especially when it came to ball-and-strike judgment. He submitted a resignation during the umpires' misguided rebellion of 1999 but it wasn't accepted, a sign of the high regard management had for him. But of late Rapuano has shown a more nettlesome side, as evidenced by an ejection rate that rose from 1.7 percent through 2006 to 2.1 percent from 2007 through 2010 — not a big percentage jump, but an increase at a time when the major league ejection rate is declining. During the period under study, a couple of confrontations reflected poorly on Rapuano.

On August 9, 2009, Rapuano was behind the plate for a game between Florida and Philadelphia. The visiting Marlins had a 3–1 lead in the sixth, but in the bottom of the inning the Phillies put two runners aboard for slugger Ryan Howard. Rapuano called Howard out on a close pitch to end the inning. The Phils took the field and pitcher Rodrigo Lopez ran up a quick 0–2 count on the Marlins' first batter, Wes Helms. Lopez's next pitch was a slider inside, but the Phillies' Shane Victorino, watching from center field, thought it was strike three and threw up his hands in disgust. Rapuano whipped off his mask, strode toward the outfield, pointed to Victorino, and ejected him. Victorino had never been ejected before and obviously hadn't said a word to Rapuano. He was still surprised after the game. "He's one of those guys you can play grab-ass with and have fun with out there on the field. I think that's why it's more frustrating to me, that it was him that got my first ejection from a major league baseball game."

On May 21, 2010, Rapuano was behind the plate for an interleague game between Milwaukee and Minnesota. Brewer starter Dave Bush struggled in the first inning, loading the bases and going 3–0 on the Twins' Michael Cuddyer. His next pitch looked a little low and Rapuano called it ball four to force in a run, prompting an outburst from Bush. Rapuano whipped off his mask, made a beeline for the mound, and gave Bush an expletive-laden lecture. Denard Span, the Twin who scored from third, said "I touched home, went in and scored and nobody gave me high-fives. Everybody was watching what was going on in the field. I was like, 'Hello, I just scored here,' but nobody was paying attention to me." Span said, "I've never seen an umpire charge the mound," and evidently none of his teammates had either. Rapuano did not eject Bush, but he pushed the Brewer hurler further off-kilter. Bush failed to get another out as six more Twins scored.

From 2007 through 2009 Rapuano had a small strike zone. His BB/9 was above average and, except for 2007, his K/9 was below average. In 2010 Rapuano jumped on the pro-pitcher bandwagon, reducing his BB/9 by nearly an entire walk and increasing his K/9 by more than a strikeout. For the first time during the period under study, his K/BB exceeded the average. But even after 2010, Rapuano has a hitters' strike zone, as he ranks 24th in BB/9, 45th in K/9, and 49th in K/BB among the 77 umpires who worked 500 or more innings behind the plate from 2007 through 2010. All of those numbers favor hitters.

Rapuano's R/9 does *not* favor hitters. Despite his reluctance to give pitchers the close ones, in 2007 the hitters' slash stats when he stood behind the plate were .256/.326/.409, below the norm on all counts. In 2008 they improved to .273/.337/.432, and his R/9 went up by a run. In 2009 they went back down to .255/.328/.418, and his R/9 dropped nearly 60 points. In 2010 the hitters' slash stats declined to .261/.319/.395, above the norm for batting average but below the norm (by six and eight points, respectively) for the more important indices, on-base percentage and slugging percentage. Batters might benefit from being more selective when Rapuano wears the mask.

Except for 2000, when he worked in 127 games, Rapuano has participated in 130 or more games each year since 1996, making him one of the game's more durable umpires. In 1996 he suffered a broken collarbone and was back in action nine days later. He was hit in the chin by a foul off the bat of Oakland's Kevin Kouzmanoff on April 20, 2010, and had to leave the game, but a CT scan revealed nothing serious. Again he missed just a few games.

Rapuano called balls and strikes on June 16, 2010, when Jamie Moyer of the Phillies became the oldest pitcher ever to beat the New York Yankees. The 47-year-old Moyer went eight innings. Rapuano dunned him for just one walk (Alex Rodriguez) and called four of his five strikeouts.

Source

McCalvy, Adam. "Bush, Home Plate Umpire Exchange Words." MLB.com, May 22, 2010. (October 25, 2010.) http://milwaukee.brewers.mlb.com/news/article.jsp?ymd=20100522&content_id=10310652&vkey=news_mil&fext=.jsp&c_id=mil.

Rick Reed

BORN: March 3, 1950
FIRST MAJOR LEAGUE GAME: May 9, 1979
FAVORED: Hitters
THEY HATED HIM IN: The ICU

	2007	2008	2009	2010	Totals
Games	33	13	11	0	57
Innings	291.67	115.5	97.17	0	504.33
R/9	9.91	8.57	9.26	0.00	9.48
BB/9	6.54	7.25	6.95	0.00	6.78
K/9	13.27	12.86	15.10	0.00	13.53
K/BB	2.03	1.77	2.17	0.00	2.00

A pair of strokes forced Reed to retire after 2009. He suffered the first one on May 24, 2008. The next night, despite dizziness and slurred speech, he worked home plate for a game between the New York Mets and Colorado Rockies. After a day off for travel, he worked third base in the Atlanta-Milwaukee game of May 27. "I was a little dizzy, not talking real well, had a hard time running to my position," he recalled. After the game the Brewers' trainer sent him to the hospital, where he received the diagnosis. "It was a significant stroke," Reed admitted. He missed the rest of the 2008 season.

In February 2009 he had a second stroke. But he was determined to work again. "I have a passion for the game. I still enjoy what I do. It's not something everyone can do." His employers were more cautious. "Every neurologist I've gone to has cleared me. Baseball's doctors said no." But then, "I saw two neurologists that baseball wanted me to see. They sided with me," and the Lords of Baseball relented. Reed was about ready to return in May when a stress fracture in his foot set him back. He didn't work a major league game until August 22. He finished the last six weeks of the season — 41 games in 44 days — before calling it a career. His last game, which he worked at home plate, was a big one: Kansas City at Minnesota, with the Twins hoping to force a playoff for the division title against Detroit, Reed's hometown team. The Twins won.

Reed worked home plate in his first major league game. The visiting Cleveland Indians beat Paul Molitor, Robin Yount, and the Milwaukee Brewers, 8–7. Sal Bando received Reed's first walk. Andre Thornton was the victim of his first called strike three. Eight days later, Reed was sent down to the minor leagues. He didn't get another shot at the big time until July 3, 1980, more than a year after his debut, and didn't work home plate in Detroit until that August 29. Did he find it hard to make calls against his hometown Tigers? "The first time the Tigers yelled at me for a call, that took care of any bias I might have." He worked first base for the last regular season game at Tiger Stadium. "I grew up in the place, getting there as the gates would open, and all of those memories came back on that last day," he told the *Toledo Blade* in 2010. "After the game, I stood on the field next to Ernie Harwell the whole time. That was special." Reed worked home plate for the first regular season game at Comerica Park on April 11, 2000. "I remember having to snow-blow my driveway before I left for the park," he said.

At the end of his career Reed had a small strike zone. His overall 6.78 BB/9 was eight percent higher than average for 2007 through 2009. His 13.53 K/9 was just one percent below average, but would have been much lower if not for a huge spike in 2009. The combination of a high BB/9 and low K/9 should have favored hitters, but they weren't able to take advantage, compiling a 9.48 R/9 that was almost exactly average for that three-year span. And his R/9 would have been even lower if not for an incredible game on August 22, 2007, when the Texas Rangers scored 30 runs against the Baltimore Orioles, an American League record. (Three Orioles also scored, for a 33-run game.) Without that game Reed's 2007 R/9, which was two percent above average, would have been five percent *below* average.

Reed was comparatively placid, compiling a career ejection rate of 1.8 percent. His last ejection came on September 8, 2009. The victim was Wladimir Balentien of the Cincinnati Reds. The journeyman outfielder struck out on three pitches, the last one swinging, so theoretically he shouldn't have had a beef with Reed. But he didn't like that the first pitch of the sequence was ruled a strike, and said so as he left the batter's box. Reed took exception to Balentien's words and ran him. Not that it mattered. Balentien was the second out in the ninth inning and a few moments later the Reds lost to the Colorado Rockies, 3-1.

Over his career, Reed worked 3,391 regular season games, 863 of them behind home plate, plus 14 Division Series games, 16 League Championship Series games, the seven-game 1991 World Series, and two All-Star games. "I had 28 years in the big leagues and they were all special, especially the last 41 games. I was able to come back and have some of my hard work appreciated," he told his hometown newspaper in 2010.

Reed had a speaking role as the home plate umpire in *The Love of the Game*, a 1999 baseball movie starring Kevin Costner. "I can't even tell you how much I enjoyed that. Kevin Costner had a lot of friends and neighbors and they'd stop by the set. I remember [model] Elle Macpherson came by. Everybody on the set was impressed by that."

SOURCE

Caputo, Pat. "Inspirational Umpire Rick Reed Retires After 28 Years." *Oakland* (Michigan) *Press,* May 15, 2010. (October 26, 2010.) http://www.theoaklandpress.com/articles/2010/05/15/sports/columns/doc 4bef4d28b8a44151470841.txt.

Mike Reilly

BORN: July 2, 1949
FIRST MAJOR LEAGUE GAME: April 11, 1977
FAVORED: Hitters, strongly
THEY HATED HIM IN: Ryan Zimmerman's fan club

	2007	2008	2009	2010	Totals
Games	34	34	34	33	135
Innings	309.17	303.83	300.67	293	1,206.67
R/9	10.04	9.51	9.88	10.04	9.87
BB/9	6.64	6.40	7.27	7.06	6.84
K/9	12.66	13.74	15.89	13.67	13.98
K/BB	1.91	2.15	2.19	1.93	2.04

With the retirement of Ed Montague and Randy Marsh after 2009, Reilly became the third-oldest umpire in the major leagues, trailing Derryl Cousins and Jerry Crawford. Only Crawford and Joe West had been in the majors longer. Rumor had it that Reilly asked for permission to retire on his birthday in 2010, but the Lords of Baseball replied that if he started the season, they expected him to finish it. The hale Reilly, who worked in 166 games in 1978 and hadn't missed any significant time since 2005, saw the season through.

The pride of Battle Creek, Michigan (he was nicknamed Corn Flakes by the late Detroit Tiger announcer Ernie Harwell) was a resolutely pro-hitter umpire. The only pitcher-friendly number in the chart above is his 2009 K/9, the highest among his peers. That exceptional number drives up his overall K/9 for the period under study to 13.98, one percent above average. Otherwise, he's all about the hitters. His BB/9 is consistently higher than average: by nine percent in 2007, three percent in 2008, 13 percent in 2009 (fifth highest in the majors), and ten percent in 2010 (fourth highest in the majors). For the entire period under study, Reilly's walk rate ranks eighth highest. His R/9 fully reflects the small strike zone. It is above average every year, and in 2010 it rose while just about everybody else's fell; he was one of just five umpires with an R/9 higher than 10.00. From 2007 through 2010, only eight umpires posted a higher R/9 than Reilly.

Reilly's hitter-friendly approach was never more evident than during a nine-day stretch in 2007. On July 19 he called a game between the New York Mets and Los Angeles Dodgers. The teams combined for 22 runs on 35 hits as neither starter, Tom Glavine for the Mets and Derek Lowe for the Dodgers, lasted beyond the third inning. On July 23 Reilly worked the plate at Angel Stadium in Anaheim, where the Oakland Athletics and Angels combined for 18 runs and 24 hits. Reilly tossed 11 walks into the mix (he called five strike threes), and neither starter — Chad Gaudin for the A's, Bartolo Colon for the Angels — made it through the fourth. On July 27, the Florida Marlins and San Francisco Giants scored 22 runs on 29 hits, with Reilly calling 14 walks. This time, one starter (Rick VandenHurk of the Marlins) made it through five innings. Three games, 62 runs, 88 hits, and 31 walks!

Reilly's career ejection rate was a laid-back 1.3 percent. He had no more than one ejection in a season after 2004, and had no more than two ejections in a season after 1998. Reilly's lone ejection of 2009 (and the last of his career) came on August 22 in a game between the Milwaukee Brewers and Washington Nationals. With two strikes on him, Washington's Ryan Zimmerman tried to check his swing on a breaking ball from starter Mike Burns of the Brewers. Reilly said Zimmerman failed. Manager Jim Riggleman argued on Zimmerman's behalf, and Reilly sent him to an early shower.

As a longtime Michigan resident, Reilly was questioned closely about the June 2, 2010, blown call by Jim Joyce that denied Detroit Tiger pitcher Armando Galarraga a perfect game. Speaking to the *Battle Creek Enquirer*, Reilly expressed support for the beleaguered Joyce and opposed changing the call: "If we start doing that, what are we going to do with all the other calls that have impacted games through the years?" Then Reilly said something unexpected. "After what happened, I was hearing people saying that the umpire union is against instant replay. But I believe if you took a poll, it would be 75–25 in favor of using instant replay. I am in favor of using instant replay. Technology is so much better than it was when I first started. I think it can be used fairly quickly now."

Reilly spoke from conviction, having been involved in one of the botched 2008 calls that led to the implementation of replay review for disputed home runs. On May 18 he was working third base and had the closest view when Carlos Delgado of the New York Mets hit a long fly down the left field line that went over the fence near the foul pole. Reilly ruled the ball fair, but Derek Jeter of the Yankees argued it was foul. The umps congregated, and home plate umpire Bob Davidson reversed Reilly's call. Replays showed Reilly had been correct, which became a double embarrassment for Davidson when he ejected Met coach Jerry Manuel for arguing precisely that. To his credit, Davidson apologized for his mistake after the game. Said Reilly, "My three partners were adamant that the ball was foul. It was a tough call to make."

Reilly was named a crew chief in 2000. To honor him in his final season, Major League Baseball named him the crew chief for the 2010 All-Star game.

SOURCE

Broderick, Bill. "Reilly Speaks Out." *Battle Creek Enquirer*, June 4, 2010. (June 24, 2010.) http://www.battlecreekenquirer.com/article/20100604/NEWS01/6040315/Reilly-speaks-out.

Charlie Reliford

BORN: September 19, 1956
FIRST MAJOR LEAGUE GAME: May 29, 1989
FAVORED: Pitchers
THEY HATED HIM IN: The plumbing business

	2007	2008	2009	2010	Totals
Games	25	28	22	0	75
Innings	222.5	245.67	195	0	663.17
R/9	9.59	10.40	7.85	0.00	9.38
BB/9	4.98	6.85	4.94	0.00	5.66
K/9	13.43	13.70	13.85	0.00	13.65
K/BB	2.70	2.00	2.80	0.00	2.41

"Umpiring is like a toilet. Nobody notices you until you stop functioning." So quipped Reliford at an event near his hometown of Ashland, Kentucky in January 2010. Reliford officially retired from umpiring a couple of months later and became an umpire supervisor. Over his career he worked 2,278 regular season games, 566 of them behind home plate. He worked in four Division Series, three League Championship Series, and two World Series (2000 and 2004). He also worked the All-Star games of 1996 and 2007.

A nagging back injury and other ailments caused him to lose time every year after 2001, and of the four umpires who retired before the 2010 season (Randy Marsh, Ed Montague, and Rick Reed were the others), he was by far the youngest. He didn't even get to leave on his own terms. He tore a calf muscle working home plate in the July 31, 2009, game between the Kansas City Royals and Tampa Bay Rays and gimped off the field in the seventh inning, never to work again.

In two of the three years charted above, Reliford had an amazingly low BB/9 of fewer than five walks per game. His 2007 BB/9 was third lowest in the majors and 19 percent below average. His 2009 BB/9 was lowest in the majors and 23 percent below average. But in 2008 he shrank his strike zone considerably, granting batters two extra walks per game. Hard to know what happened there, but even with that season thrown in, his cumulative BB/9 over his final three years was ten percent below average. Despite that low BB/9, Reliford wasn't a huge strikeout guy. In fact, his K/9 progression very closely mirrors the major league average: one percent above normal in 2007, dead-on average in 2008, one percent below normal in 2009, and dead-on average overall. No umpire more closely embodied the major league average in K/9 over those three years than Reliford.

Reliford's R/9 roughly tracked his K/BB ratio. In 2007 his K/BB was 24 percent higher than average, which would lead you to expect a lower than average R/9. Reliford's 2007 R/9 was indeed low, but by only one percent. In 2008 his K/BB dropped to nine percent below average owing to all those extra walks, and his R/9 jumped to 11 percent above normal. In his final season his K/BB was the highest in the league at 2.80, and his R/9 dropped to a puny 7.85, 16 percent below normal. Overall, Reliford's 2007–2009 R/9 was one percent below average.

When it came to game management, Reliford had a slightly quick fuse, compiling a 2.4 percent ejection rate over his career. By his last three seasons he had calmed significantly, however, ejecting just one in 2007, two in 2008, and none in 2009 for a one percent rate. Ron Gardenhire, manager of the Minnesota Twins, was his last ejection. Gardenhire hotly disputed a reversed call in a July 9, 2008, game between the Twins and Boston Red Sox. With runners on second and third, Boston's Jason Varitek hit a sinking fly to center field that Denard Span of the Twins appeared to catch. Reliford ruled it so, anyway. With the runners on the move, Span threw the ball in and the Twins apparently pulled a triple play. But the umpires huddled and reversed the call, saying Span trapped the ball and the lead Red Sox runner had scored. Gardenhire's wrath earned him Reliford's thumb. Replays proved that Reliford and his crew were right to reverse the call.

"When I first came to the big leagues, a huddle was unheard of," Reliford later told his hometown paper, the *Ashland Independent*. "We have a signal on my crew where we can say, 'I think I have different information, if you want it.' But I tell them to never come running over because you might just be complicating the problem."

A member of baseball's rules committee, Reliford at first resisted the introduction of replay review for disputed home runs. He then became the first to use it. On September 4, 2008, Alex Rodriguez of the New York Yankees hit what looked to second base umpire Reliford and the rest of his crew like a home run at Tampa Bay's Tropicana Field. Tampa manager Joe Maddon disagreed. "We made the decision to use the technology and go look at the replays. And the replays we reviewed were conclusive that the call we made was correct," said Reliford. Although the process went smoothly, Reliford wasn't sold on it. Nonetheless, "Given the difficulty of the new stadiums, the microscopic perspective of baseball, it's turned out remarkably well. I'd be hard-pressed to say that some day it's not going to expand."

Years from now, Reliford may be best remembered as the home plate umpire who stepped between Roger Clemens of the New York Yankees and Mike Piazza of the New York Mets after Clemens hurled the barrel of a shattered bat at Piazza during game two of the 2000 World Series.

SOURCE

Maynard, Mark. "Umpire Ready for Another Trip Home." *Ashland* (Kentucky) *Independent,* December 7, 2009. (October 26, 2010.) http://dailyindependent.com/localsports/x546119777/Umpire-ready-for-another-trip-home.

D.J. Reyburn

BORN: October 13, 1976
FIRST MAJOR LEAGUE GAME: June 10, 2008
FAVORS: Pitchers, so far (his sample is small)
THEY HATE HIM IN: The Dominican Republic and Pittsburgh

	2007	2008	2009	2010	Totals
Games	0	5	9	24	38
Innings	0	44.5	78	215.5	338
R/9	0.00	10.31	6.58	8.90	8.55
BB/9	0.00	6.88	4.50	5.76	5.62
K/9	0.00	13.75	13.50	14.45	14.14
K/BB	0.00	2.00	3.00	2.51	2.52

If you're an avid hot stove league fan, you may recall that in January 2010 former major leaguer Jose Offerman, manager of the Dominican League's Licey Tigers, punched an umpire. Do you remember the name of the umpire? It was widely reported as Daniel Rayburn. In fact it was D.J. (for Daniel James) Reyburn, a 5'9", 175-pound Triple-A call-up from Grand Rapids, Michigan. After Licey partisans threatened his life, Reyburn and three other American umpires resigned and returned home. Although Offerman apologized, he was banned for life from the Dominican League.

From his very first big league appearance behind home plate, a June 13, 2008 match-up between the Washington Nationals and Seattle Mariners, Reyburn has been accused of having too big a strike zone. The chart above includes every game he has called in the major leagues, and though the sample size is small, the numbers suggest that he does give pitchers the corners. For the years 2008 through 2010 his 5.62 BB/9 is 11 percent lower than average and his 14.14 K/9 is one percent higher than average. His 2.52 K/BB over the three-year span is 12 percent higher than average, and would give him the eighth largest strike zone in the majors if he worked the minimum 500 innings. His R/9 corresponds with his strike zone, as his 8.55 career number is seven percent below average.

Four of Reyburn's five big league ejections have stemmed from his strike zone judgment. On August 9, 2009, he tossed Alex Gonzalez of the Cincinnati Reds for arguing a strikeout. Gonzalez's entire at-bat consisted of a checked swing and two corner pitches ruled strikes. Replays showed that Reyburn was right on all three calls, but it didn't stop Gonzalez from complaining. On April 28, 2010, two Pittsburgh Pirate batters earned ejections from Reyburn over called strikeouts in an extra-inning game against the Milwaukee Brewers. Reyburn rang up Ryan Church on a full-count fastball, and replays backed him up. Two innings later he called out Andy LaRoche on a 1–2 slider, but that one looked outside. On July 20, 2010, Reyburn notched his one ejection unrelated to plate judgment. He was working first base when Pittsburgh manager John Russell claimed a ball that dribbled into fair territory after Milwaukee's Craig Counsell swung at it was fair, and Counsell should be out. Reyburn correctly called that the ball hit Counsell's leg first, and therefore was foul. On August 15, 2010, Reyburn aroused the ire of the Cincinnati Reds for tossing slugger Joey Votto in the first inning for questioning a pitch call, but again replays showed Reyburn was correct.

Although five ejections are a lot for an umpire with less than a full season of major league games to his credit, the Lords of Baseball understood that Reyburn was being tested — and that with the possible exception of the pitch to LaRoche, he was passing. Based on plate innings, they made him the seventh busiest Triple-A call-up, a sign that they consider him a legitimate prospect for a major league job, possibly as early as 2012 although more likely a bit later.

As a Michigan native, Reyburn grew up rooting for the Detroit Tigers. But he told his local newspaper he'd have no problem making calls against the Tigers. "It's not like Morris, Trammell, and Whitaker are out there," he said. He called his first game involving the Tigers on June 8, 2009. They were trounced 6–1 by the Chicago White Sox, managing just two hits off Jose Contreras and reliever Matt Thornton. Reyburn called three walks in four innings on Tiger starter Jeremy Bonderman. The Tigers did better the second time Reyburn called a game involving them, a June 12, 2010, contest with Pittsburgh. (It was also Reyburn's first chance to call a major league game in his home state.) Carlos Guillen hit a walk-off homer in the bottom of the tenth and the Tigers won, 4–3, to run their interleague record at home to 31–6 since 2006.

Source

"Jose Offerman Punches Ump! Full Video." YouTube.com, January 17, 2010. (October 26, 2010.) http://www.youtube.com/watch?v=Wu4-p_OjzfY.

Jim Reynolds

BORN: December 22, 1968
FIRST MAJOR LEAGUE GAME: June 4, 1999
FAVORS: High strike pitchers and hitters
THEY HATE HIM IN: Los Angeles

	2007	2008	2009	2010	Totals
Games	35	35	29	28	127
Innings	312.33	312.33	253.33	252.17	1,130.17
R/9	10.46	10.34	10.02	8.53	9.90
BB/9	5.99	5.85	6.71	6.10	6.10
K/9	14.03	13.14	15.56	15.10	14.37
K/BB	2.34	2.25	2.32	2.55	2.36

Reynolds attended the University of Connecticut with Dan Iassogna. After graduating they went to umpire school, then worked their way up the minors and arrived in the big leagues within three months of each other. "What's been really nice is having a best friend go through this journey with me," Reynolds told baseball blogger Cecilia Tan in March 2010. When it comes to calling games, however, Iassogna and Reynolds might as well not know each other. Iassogna goes from clearly pro-hitter one year to clearly pro-pitcher the next. Reynolds is also inconsistent, but not the same way: His strike zone is clearly pro-pitcher, but run production when he's behind the plate is clearly pro-hitter. Reynolds has the eighth highest R/9 for the period under study at the same time he's in the top third in K/BB.

When we look at Reynolds's slash stats, it's clear that hitters like his strike zone more than pitchers. They batted a healthy .274/.337/.425 with him behind the plate in 2007, an even healthier .285/.343/.445 in 2008, and .279/.343/.442 in 2009. Those are Steroid Era numbers, but there's an even more telling statistic: Reynolds had the 14th highest home run rate among major league umpires in 2007, the second highest in 2008, and the seventh highest in 2009. We can infer from this that from 2007 through 2009, Reynolds not only had a big strike zone, but a *high* strike zone. In effect, he told pitchers to forget the knee-high strike, but if you throw one above the belt you'll get the call. In 2010 his slash stats went down to .252/.317/.405, which goes a long way toward explaining why his R/9 crashed. But in spite of the big drop, his home run rate remained four percent higher than average.

Reynolds has a much more easygoing temperament than his buddy Iassogna. His career ejection rate is a below-average 1.8 percent, and has dropped to 1.2 percent since 2007. But after an ejection-free 2009, Reynolds brought out his thumb three times in 2010. On May 11 he called Grady Sizemore of the Cleveland Indians safe on a steal of third. The call was correct, but Kansas City Royal manager Trey Hillman argued until Reynolds tossed him. On June 23 the Los Angeles Dodgers were trailing the Los Angeles Angels by a run in the ninth and had runners on first and second with two out. Jamey Carroll blooped a single to left. As the runner on second came around to score, the runner on first, Russell Martin, overran second. Angel left fielder Juan Rivera threw behind Martin. Reynolds, manning second, ruled that Martin was tagged out. Home plate umpire Mike DiMuro then declared that the lead runner failed to cross home plate before Reynolds called the third out. When Martin tossed his helmet in rage, Reynolds ejected him, a gratuitous gesture because the game was over and lost. On September 10 Reynolds was the first base umpire in a game between Atlanta and St. Louis. He ejected Terry Pendleton, the Braves' batting coach, for disputing that the Cardinals' Albert Pujols checked his swing on a two-strike pitch.

"As an umpire, I'm going to miss stuff," Reynolds admitted in his March 2010 interview. "But we are not involved in the outcome. If I miss a call, I miss a call. It's not because I wanted one team or the other to win." Some fans claimed that Reynolds missed a call during the fourth game of the 2010 American League Championship Series. He was stationed in right field. In the second inning, New York's Robinson Cano hit a long fly to the wall. Nelson Cruz of the Texas Rangers tried to make a leaping catch, but a fan blocked his glove. Cruz pointed to the stands, asking Reynolds for an interference call. Reynolds ruled that the ball was over the wall for a home run. Texas manager Ron Washington questioned Reynolds, but did not ask for a replay review. "He asked me, 'What did you have?' I said, 'Ron, the ball was in the stands.' From the angle I had, I was very confident that the ball was in the stands," Reynolds said. Replays indicated that Reynolds was correct. The Rangers won anyway, 10–3, and later won the series.

Reynolds was beaned by a warm-up pitch from Blaine Boyer of the St. Louis Cardinals on April 30, 2009. Explained the remorseful Boyer, "I told Jason [LaRue, the catcher] I was throwing a cutter, but it never cut." Reynolds collapsed, but rose quickly and finished the game. Afterward, however, "[I] went in the locker room, the adrenaline came down, and then the concussion symptoms came in." He missed three weeks. He made up for lost time with an intense schedule later in the season. Just after the All-Star break he worked home plate three times in seven days, and then put in three games at home plate in *six* days at the end of August and beginning of September. Early in 2010 he suffered another injury, tearing the meniscus in a knee. Surgery delayed the start of his season until May.

Reynolds is one of four board members of Umps Care charities. "It's the greatest thing the MLB umpires do off the field," he said.

Source
Tan, Cecilia. "Umps Care, They Really Do." WhyILikeBaseball.com, March 12, 2010. (October 26, 2010.) http://www.whyilikebaseball.com/2010/03/umps-care/#more-301.

Mark Ripperger

BORN: August 6, 1980
FIRST MAJOR LEAGUE GAME: September 30, 2010

Ripperger

FAVORS: Way too early to tell
THEY HATE HIM IN: Nowhere yet

	2007	2008	2009	2010	Totals
Games	0	0	0	1	1
Innings	0	0	0	9	9
R/9	0.00	0.00	0.00	8.00	8.00
BB/9	0.00	0.00	0.00	5.00	5.00
K/9	0.00	0.00	0.00	12.00	12.00
K/BB	0.00	0.00	0.00	2.40	2.40

Ripperger caught the umpiring bug as a teenager in suburban San Diego. He worked Little League games while in high school. "I fell in love with the job," he told the *San Diego Union-Tribune* in 2008. He fell in love with it enough to attend the Wendelstedt Umpire School twice. Although he showed some promise the first time, he didn't make the cut and failed to land a job. So he tried again the following season. "It was tough competition. I felt like I had a pretty good idea what was going on, and I just missed," he said of his first try. "If I didn't think I was close, I wouldn't have come back."

On April 2, 2009, Ripperger worked home plate in an exhibition game between the Los Angeles Angels and San Diego Padres at PetCo Park. Some 80 friends and family members cheered him on. But he wasn't named a Triple-A call-up that year. "The hardest part is not knowing if you're going to get the call. If you knew you were going to get it, you'd wait. You don't know if you're going to be that next person, and there's a process to be those guys," he said.

In 2010 the process finally smiled on him. He was named a Triple-A call-up, and on the very last day of the 2010 season he got to work home plate for a major league game. With the San Diego Padres on the road and fighting for a playoff spot, Ripperger was sent to Texas for his debut. The Los Angeles Angels beat the Texas Rangers 6–2 behind Dan Haren in a brisk 2:29. The very first batter to step in the box for Ripperger, Peter Bourjos, earned Ripperger's inaugural called strike three. Torii Hunter of the Angels received Ripperger's first major league base on balls.

"You do what supervisors tell you to do, and you work hard, and it's worked for me," Ripperger told the *San Diego Union-Tribune*. Expect the Pacific Coast League umpire to work more big league contests on the West Coast over the next few years.

SOURCE

Jones, Zach. "Waiting His Turn: Umpire Mark Ripperger Hopes He'll Soon Get Chance to Work in the Major Leagues." *San Diego Union-Tribune*, July 13, 2008. (October 26, 2010.) http://legacy.signonsandiego.com/news/northcounty/20080713-9999-lz1mcl3umpire.html.

Brian Runge

BORN: January 5, 1970
FIRST MAJOR LEAGUE GAME: April 23, 1999
FAVORS: Pitchers
THEY HATE HIM IN: Seattle and New York

	2007	2008	2009	2010	Totals
Games	36	34	24	25	119
Innings	315	300.83	211.5	211.83	1,039.17
R/9	10.20	9.30	8.09	9.09	9.28
BB/9	6.23	5.44	5.53	4.80	5.57
K/9	13.71	13.88	14.55	15.25	14.25
K/BB	2.20	2.55	2.63	3.18	2.56

The Runges are the only three-generation family of umpires. Ed Runge, Brian's grandfather, was an American League umpire from 1954 to 1970. He was best known for calling foul an October 8, 1956, drive over the right field fence by the Brooklyn Dodgers' Duke Snider. After that fourth inning scare, pitcher Don Larsen of the New York Yankees went on to finish the only perfect game in World Series history. Paul Runge, Brian's father, was a National League umpire from 1973 to 1997 and a powerful figure in the old umpires' union, serving as its president during the early 1990s. Brian has been in the majors since 1999, so since the end of the Korean War only three major league seasons have passed without a Runge calling balls and strikes.

Brian Runge keeps getting tougher on hitters. In 2007 his strike zone, as measured by K/BB ratio, was a mere one percent larger than average. In 2008 it shot up to 17 percent larger than average. In 2009 it went up again, to 21 percent larger than average. And in 2010 it escaped gravity, measuring 35 percent larger than average. Runge's 2010 K/BB of 3.18 was the highest single season K/BB since the 3.24 attained by Doug Eddings in 2007. Overall, Runge grades out as having the third highest K/BB for the period under study, behind only Eddings and Bill Miller. But it's very hard to imagine the trend continuing. If his K/BB goes much higher, pitchers will be able to throw to the on-deck circle and get a strike.

Despite his enormous strike zone, Runge's R/9 is average. From 2007 through 2009 his R/9 fell as his strike zone grew, but in 2010 it rose by an entire run per game. Hitters had success swinging for the fences when Runge was behind the plate in 2010, posting a .422 slugging percentage and a home run rate of 2.10, nine percent higher than average. Runge's HR/9 was above average every year of the period under study, suggesting that the additional strike zone he's been giving pitchers is above the belt, where hitters can wallop the ball if they can catch up to it.

Runge's career ejection rate is a remarkably low 0.7 percent, less than one-third the major league average. He has worked more than 1,300 regular season games but has accumulated only nine ejections. The grandson seems to have embraced Grandfather Ed's wisdom: "[An umpire] should never go in for that nose-to-nose stuff. He ought to hear the man out for a reasonable while, then turn and walk away. Unless a player or manager uses bad language, there's no need to chase him." This from a man whose lifetime ejection rate was three times higher than Brian's! Paul Runge compiled a 0.9 percent lifetime ejection rate, in line with his son's.

Runge's generosity to pitchers has annoyed some hitters, as evidenced by a row Runge got into with Seattle's Ichiro Suzuki on September 26, 2009. After getting ahead in the count 2–0, Ichiro let three pitches from Toronto's David Purcey go by, all of which Runge called strikes. The stunned Ichiro leaned over home plate and drew a line in the dirt to show Runge how far outside he thought the last pitch had been. Runge gave Ichiro the thumb, the first time the Seattle star had ever been tossed from a game — including his tenure in the Japanese major leagues, which began in 1991.

Runge was involved in an even bigger ball-or-strike controversy on June 24, 2008. It may have been the worst meltdown a Runge has ever had on the diamond. Runge called a strike on Carlos Beltran of the New York Mets, and Met manager Jerry Manuel stormed from the dugout to dispute it. Whether or not the pitch was low quickly became secondary as Runge argued heatedly first with Beltran, then Manuel. He bumped Manuel in the chest, which shocked everyone in the park. Then he booted both Manuel and Beltran — two ejections in a moment after only five in a thousand-game career. That night Runge called his father. They had a heart-to-heart talk, and the next day Runge apologized to Manuel. Nonetheless, the Lords of Baseball suspended Runge one game for his aggression.

Runge took a foul ball to the mask on July 28, 2010, while working home plate in a game between the Seattle Mariners and Chicago White Sox. He dropped to a knee but quickly stood up and gave no sign of serious injury. He likely suffered a mild concussion, as he missed the next month of the season.

On July 10, 2009, Runge was behind the plate for San Francisco Giant fireballer Jonathan Sanchez's no-hitter against the San Diego Padres. Many observers thought the last pitch, which Runge called strike three to Padre shortstop Everth Cabrera, was outside.

SOURCE

Associated Press. "Indignant Ichiro Ejected from Game for First Time in Career." *Japan Times,* September 28, 2009. (October 26, 2010.) http://search.japantimes.co.jp/cgi-bin/sb20090928a1.html.

Paul Schrieber

BORN: June 30, 1966
FIRST MAJOR LEAGUE GAME: June 6, 1997
FAVORS: Hitters, strongly
THEY HATE HIM IN: New York

	2007	2008	2009	2010	Totals
Games	31	30	33	16	110
Innings	277.83	270.33	298.17	139.83	986.17
R/9	9.82	9.65	9.60	8.37	9.50
BB/9	8.00	7.86	7.24	7.40	7.65
K/9	13.09	12.68	13.82	13.45	13.25
K/BB	1.64	1.61	1.91	1.82	1.73

Which umpire has the smallest strike zone? Paul Schrieber.

Schrieber has the highest BB/9 of any umpire for the period under study. He also has the lowest K/BB ratio. He didn't arrive at these extremes through one or two aberrant seasons. His strike zone is consistent, and his definition of a strike is clearly narrower than that of his peers. His BB/9 is well above average every season, with his lowest seasonal result, 7.24 in 2009, still 13 percent above average. His K/BB was 25 percent lower than average in 2007 and 26 percent lower than average in 2008. It was 12 percent lower than average in 2009 — still an upper-deck shot from the norm — before returning to a more characteristic 23 percent below average in 2010. Another mark of consistency is that Schrieber's K/9 was lower than average all four years, although his 13.82 in 2009 was just one percent below average.

You would think an umpire with so tight a strike zone would have a stratospheric R/9, but that's not the case with Schrieber. His 2007 R/9 was two percent above normal, his 2008 R/9 was three percent above normal, and his 2009 R/9 was three percent above normal before his 2010 R/9 dropped below normal. Hitters do well when he's behind the plate, but they're hardly marauding Cossacks swooping down on village pitchers. They're more like the gangs in *West Side Story:* menacing until they start to dance.

Schrieber is one of two active umpires from Eugene, Oregon, along with Dale Scott. Although Scott is seven years older than Schrieber, the two knew each other growing up, and some of the equipment Schrieber wore through the minors was a gift from Scott. "I admire Dale greatly. He's where I want to be," Schrieber told the *Eugene Register-Guard* in 2007. Scott returned the compliment, noting that Schrieber was a catcher at Portland State University before he started umpiring. "Some ex-players can transition to umpiring, others are horrible at it. He obviously transitioned very well," said Scott.

At two-thirds the norm, Schrieber's career ejection rate reinforces the image of the easygoing Oregonian working comfortably with the strong, at times overbearing, personalities on the field. But his ejection rate has increased to 2.4 percent since 2007, and on May 13, 2009, Schrieber committed a serious breach of baseball etiquette by touching a player. In the seventh inning of a slow, tense game between the Detroit Tigers and Minnesota Twins (it eventually went 13 innings and nearly five hours), Schrieber called strike three on a low, outside breaking ball to the Tigers' Magglio Ordonez. When Ordonez remained in the box to protest, Schrieber stepped forward, put his left arm on Ordonez's back, and steered the Tiger batsman toward the dugout. That brought Tiger manager Jim Leyland to home plate. He hectored Schrieber with such vitriol that Schrieber threw him out.

After the game, Ordonez said a player is "not supposed to do that. If you touch [an umpire], you get suspended. I'd be home." Schrieber recognized the double standard too, and apologized the next day. "In yesterday's game, after I called Magglio Ordonez out on strikes, I inadvertently placed my hand on his back and ushered him away from home plate so I did not have to eject him for arguing balls and strikes. I should not have placed my hands on him, period. For doing so, I apologize to both Magglio Ordonez and the Detroit Tigers." Ordonez and Leyland readily accepted the apology.

Schrieber learned his lesson in time for a confrontation with David Wright of the New York Mets on May 9, 2010. The Mets trailed the San Francisco Giants 6–5 in the ninth and had the tying run on second with no outs when Wright took a 3–2 fastball inside. Although Schrieber can be depended on to call the close ones for the hitter, this time he didn't, and Wright went nuts. But instead of guiding Wright to the dugout, Schrieber ejected him. "It was a disagreement," said Wright, for whom it was also the fourth strikeout of the game, the eighth in his last two games, and the 13th in his last 24 at-bats, more likely the real issue.

Schrieber admits that he still gets nervous before games. "Nervousness is a desire to do well. Once I get on the field, I'm cool." He also needs time to unwind after games, especially if he's uncertain about a call he made. "It's hard to turn it off. You're trying to be perfect, when you can't." Or, to put it another way, "I do not take things for granted. I always want to get better."

For undisclosed reasons, Schrieber missed the remainder of the 2010 season after July 3.

SOURCE

Beck, Jason. "Ump Apologizes for Contact with Ordonez." MLB.com, May 14, 2009. (October 27, 2010.) http://mlb.mlb.com/news/article.jsp?ymd=20090514&content_id=4726530&vkey=news_mlb&fext=.jsp&c_id=mlb.

Dale Scott

BORN: August 14, 1959
FIRST MAJOR LEAGUE GAME: August 19, 1985
FAVORS: Pitchers, slightly
THEY HATE HIM IN: Boston and Anaheim

	2007	2008	2009	2010	Totals
Games	35	33	35	35	138
Innings	317.17	288.17	308	312	1,225.33
R/9	9.53	9.56	9.03	9.49	9.40
BB/9	5.99	6.53	5.79	6.40	6.17
K/9	13.31	14.55	13.68	14.97	14.12
K/BB	2.22	2.23	2.36	2.34	2.29

Scott's strike zone changes from year to year. In 2007 it was nearly neutral, with a BB/9 two percent lower than average and a K/9 right at average. In 2008 it appeared to shrink as Scott called more walks (five percent above the average), but he also saw more strikeouts, and the contradictory trends canceled each other out: His R/9 and K/BB ended up virtually identical to those he compiled in 2007. Then came 2009, and Scott turned into a pitchers' umpire, calling ten percent fewer walks than average. His K/9 tumbled too, but because his BB/9 took a proportionally larger drop, his K/BB rose and his R/9 fell. In 2010 he bucked the trend and called more walks, but his strikeout rate soared to nearly 15.00, which kept his K/BB at its 2009 level. Even so, the extra walks contributed to a 46 point increase in his R/9. So over four years he went from a neutral strike zone to one that slightly favored hitters to one that strongly favored pitchers to one that favored hitters again.

When the numbers are totaled, Scott comes close to neutral. His R/9 is one percent above the norm, his BB/9 is one percent below the norm, and his K/9 is two percent above the norm. His most extreme departure from middle ground is his K/BB, which is three percent above the norm. Because his K/BB favors pitchers a tad more than his R/9 favors hitters, Scott is rated a pitchers' umpire. But if his 2011 is similar to his 2010, his five-year rating could slip to the hitters' side.

Scott's temper can be short. He has a 2.4 percent career ejection rate. More recently, however, he has shown greater patience. In 2007 he had just one ejection. In 2008 and 2009 he had just two. In 2010 he amassed three ejections by mid–May, raising concerns that he might be flashing back to 1993, when he had 14 ejections. But then things got better, and he had only one ejection the rest of the year. Perhaps his May 12, 2010, confrontation with the Boston Red Sox proved cathartic. The Sox trailed the Toronto Blue Jays in the ninth, and David Ortiz represented the tying run. Scott called Ortiz out on a pitch off the outside corner. Ortiz argued until manager Terry Francona stepped in. Notably, Scott declined to eject either. But when the next batter checked a swing only to have it called a strike by Scott, Francona argued again, and this time Scott tossed him. If Scott watched replays of those two calls, it must have hurt: He missed them both.

Scott also had an embarrassing moment in the 2009 postseason. In the fourth game of the American League Championship Series between the New York Yankees and Los Angeles Angels, Scott was working second base when Angel pitcher Scott Kazmir picked off the Yankees' runner at second, Nick Swisher. Scott was in position, and Swisher's lead hand was tagged several inches from the bag, but Scott inexplicably called Swisher safe. The only thing that rescued Scott from a media firestorm was an even worse performance by Tim McClelland, who missed two calls that game, including one a few moments later in which Swisher was safe but called out, effectively canceling Scott's earlier miscue.

Despite occasional lapses like these, Scott is well-respected by the Lords of Baseball, who made him a crew chief in 2001. "Dale turned out to be probably one of the best umpires we have. I think he has the best mechanics, the best style of the guys we've got," former umpire (and umpire supervisor) Marty Springstead told the *Eugene Register-Guard* in 2007. Scott downplays his high standing within the profession. "I still learn. The moment you think you have this thing down, you're in trouble."

Scott may have first impressed baseball executives in 1988, his third season with the American League. On May 30 he became the last umpire to eject Billy Martin. Walt Weiss of the Oakland Athletics beat out what looked like a one-hopper to Yankee second baseman Bobby Meacham. Martin, serving his last stint as Yankee manager, thought Meacham caught the ball on the fly. Rick Reed, the second base umpire, ruled that the ball hit the ground first. According to Martin, first base umpire Scott admitted he hadn't seen the play, but emerged from a conference with Reed and the rest of the crew saying he *had* seen the play and Reed was correct. Martin accused Scott of lying. To show his contempt he picked up two handfuls of dirt and threw them at Scott. In a statement the next day, Martin further accused Scott of baiting him: "I couldn't get any dirt off the ground. He told me, 'Throw some more dirt on me,' and I did." Scott showed restraint throughout this zoo monkey episode, helping the Lords of Baseball cope with a deteriorating individual (the hard-drinking Martin was fired three weeks later) and an umpires' union threatening to eject Martin every time he took the field.

On April 27, 1994, Scott called a no-hitter by the Minnesota Twins' Scott Erickson.

Source

Hines, Michael. "Blues with the Clues." *Eugene Register-Guard,* July 12, 2007. (October 27, 2010.) http://www.thefreelibrary.com/Blues+with+the+clues.-a0166549790.

Todd Tichenor

Born: December 15, 1976
First Major League Game: June 8, 2007
Favors: Hitters, strongly
They hate him in: Boston and Minnesota

	2007	2008	2009	2010	Totals
Games	5	12	35	32	84
Innings	43.5	103.83	317.33	276	740.67
R/9	10.55	9.71	8.22	10.53	9.43
BB/9	6.21	6.50	6.52	7.08	6.71
K/9	10.97	13.26	14.04	12.98	13.35
K/BB	1.77	2.04	2.15	1.83	1.99

The only active umpire born in Nebraska, Tichenor is a Triple-A call-up who spent all of 2009 and 2010 in the majors, meaning the Lords of Baseball consider him a strong candidate for a permanent big league job, perhaps as soon as 2011.

Tichenor's home-away numbers contain puzzling swings and streaks. In 2008, the home team won nine of the 12 games he called. In 2009 Tichenor went in the other direction, calling only 12 wins for the home team in 35 opportunities, a win percentage of just

.343. But in 2010 the home team won the first 15 games he called. After that they went 6–10 (he had one relief appearance at home plate, replacing heat-stricken Wally Bell in a July 30 game in Kansas City). There's no evidence these wild deviations result from any conscious bias on Tichenor's part.

Through 2009 Tichenor had participated in 227 major league games and compiled an ejection rate of four percent, high even for a new umpire trying to establish himself. But six of his nine ejections came in two games, so if you saw it as a new umpire having one bad moment every hundred games or more, he looked a lot better. Unfortunately, those two bad moments were *very* bad.

On August 7, 2008, Tichenor was working home plate for only the 12th time in the majors. The San Diego Padres were in New York to play the Mets and trailed 3–2 in the eighth. After the Padres went down in the top of the inning, manager Bud Black signaled to Tichenor that he wanted a double switch. New pitcher Bryan Corey would bat second and Edgar Gonzalez, who had pinch hit for the previous pitcher, would bat ninth and play second base. But a dispute arose over the nature of Black's signal, a hand gesture with two fingers extended. According to Black, he rotated his hand to indicate the double switch. But according to Tichenor and his crew chief, Gerry Davis, Black chopped his hand, which Tichenor interpreted as Black wanting a straight switch of Corey for Gonzalez — which didn't make sense, as it brought the pitcher to the plate sooner and the Padres didn't have another second baseman. If the Shea Stadium scoreboard operator posted Black's intentions correctly, why didn't Tichenor understand them? No matter. Tichenor ejected both Black and bench coach Craig Colbert for arguing about what the hand signal meant.

May 28, 2009, was Tichenor's other bad day. He tallied four ejections in *one inning* while working home plate for Boston and Minnesota. The Red Sox had a 2–1 lead in the top of the seventh and runners on first and third with one out. Dustin Pedroia flied to right, and the runner on third, Jeff Bailey, tagged up. But Twin right fielder Jason Kubel made a remarkable throw to catcher Mike Redmond, who appeared to tag out Bailey. Tichenor ruled Bailey safe. Redmond threw up his arms in disgust and was instantly ejected. Recounted the Twin catcher, who had never been ejected before, "I just said, 'I got his arm.' I didn't swear at him or anything. It was a quick gate. In 11 years in the big leagues, I've done a lot worse out there and stayed in the game. Obviously, he had a short fuse." Minnesota manager Ron Gardenhire took up Redmond's cause and was ejected as well.

Then in the bottom of the seventh, Boston pitcher Josh Beckett didn't get a call from Tichenor on a strike-two pitch. Beckett shouted obscenities at Tichenor, causing Red Sox catcher Jason Varitek to stand up and block Tichenor's view of the fulminating hurler. Tichenor tossed Varitek. Red Sox skipper Terry Francona rushed out to protest Varitek's ejection and was ejected as well. Said crew chief Jerry Layne after the game, "Major League Baseball will review the report that Todd puts together. I don't know what was said. I just know it was very emotional at the moment. The umpire did his job." Evidently so: There were no ramifications for Tichenor.

Tichenor did not eject anybody in 2010.

If Tichenor does become a full-fledged major league umpire, Beckett won't be the only pitcher unhappy about it. In his 84 starts behind home plate, Tichenor has shown a small strike zone that favors hitters. His career walk rate is eight percent above average and his career strikeout rate is three percent below average, giving him a 1.99 K/BB that ranks 11th lowest among the 77 umpires who called 500 or more innings from 2007 through 2010. Tichenor's 2010 R/9 was the highest in the majors, a substantial 34 points higher than the next umpire, Mark Carlson.

SOURCE

Cafardo, Nick. "Ejections Appear Way Off Base." *Boston Globe,* May 29, 2009. (October 27, 2010.) http://www.boston.com/sports/baseball/redsox/articles/2009/05/29/ejections_appear_way_off_base/.

Chris Tiller

BORN: October 25, 1978
FIRST MAJOR LEAGUE GAME: May 28, 2008
FAVORS: Too early to say
THEY HATE HIM IN: Baltimore

	2007	2008	2009	2010	Totals
Games	0	6	4	2	12
Innings	0	52.5	34	18	104.5
R/9	0.00	8.23	6.62	10.00	8.01
BB/9	0.00	6.69	7.68	6.00	6.89
K/9	0.00	12.69	11.38	11.00	11.97
K/BB	0.00	1.90	1.48	1.83	1.74

Tiller is a Triple-A call-up who usually works in the Pacific Coast League. In 2009 he was the youngest umpire to call a major league game (he is 15 days younger than Dan Bellino). Tiller started 2010 in the bigs, put in one game behind the plate (Detroit versus Kansas City on April 8), and then was sent down. When the Lords of Baseball needed a pair of minor league umpires in early June 2010, Al Porter and Victor Carapazza got the opportunities. Three opportunities opened up after the 2010 All-Star break, but they went to Porter, Carapazza, and Manny Gonzalez. Tiller didn't get another shot at calling a big league game until August 19. It appears he has fallen behind several other minor league umps in the competition for a big league spot.

Tiller so far has displayed an iPod-sized strike zone. For 2008 through 2010, his aggregate BB/9 is ten percent above average and his aggregate K/9 is nearly 17 percent below average. His 1.74 K/BB would rank at the bottom of the list with Paul Schrieber's and Jerry Crawford's if he worked enough innings. But Tiller hasn't come close to working enough innings, and it would be unfair to draw conclusions from his limited sample size. Besides, several pitchers have flourished with him calling balls and strikes. Ricky Nolasco of the Florida Marlins hurled a shutout against the San Francisco Giants in Tiller's fifth major league start at home plate, and two of Tiller's four home plate assignments in 2009 included multi-pitcher shutouts: Mark Buehrle and Bobby Jenks for the Chicago White Sox on May 7, and Kevin Correia and Edward Mujica for the San Diego Padres on September 2.

Tiller has just one major league ejection. He got manager Dave Trembley of the Baltimore Orioles on May 3, 2009, for arguing a called third strike. At first he half-gestured that Trembley was gone, but after an approving nod from crew chief Jerry Layne, he went all the way. Replays showed that Tiller got the call right.

Tiller met Bruce Weber, author of *As They See 'Em*, the classic tome about umpires, in 2005. "I'm not in it for the glory of being a minor league umpire. I want to get to the major leagues," Tiller declared. He shared with Weber a performance evaluation by his supervisors: "You are umpiring with a greater deal of confidence compared to last year," it said in part. You can only wonder how much confidence Tiller has these days.

Source

Weber, Bruce. "In the Minor Leagues, Umpires Also Dream." *New York Times*, July 28, 2005. (October 27, 2010.) http://www.nytimes.com/2005/07/27/sports/27iht-UMPS.html?_r=1&pagewanted=all.

Tim Timmons

BORN: December 30, 1967
FIRST MAJOR LEAGUE GAME: September 3, 1999
FAVORS: R/9 says hitters, K/BB says pitchers
THEY HATE HIM IN: The Tea Party

	2007	2008	2009	2010	Totals
Games	33	34	34	32	133
Innings	291.5	315.17	302.5	286.83	1,196
R/9	9.23	9.85	10.86	8.19	9.56
BB/9	6.27	5.45	6.90	5.08	5.93
K/9	13.09	14.19	14.04	13.49	13.72
K/BB	2.09	2.60	2.03	2.65	2.31

Except for his K/9 totals in 2008 and 2009, Timmons's numbers jump around. They also defy the tendency of small strike zones to correspond with high R/9s and of large strike zones to correspond with low R/9s. In 2007 his BB/9 was three percent above average and his K/9 was two percent below average, indicating that his strike zone favored hitters. But hitters compiled an R/9 five percent *below* normal. In 2008 his BB/9 plunged to 13 percent below average and his K/9 rose to four percent above average, indicating that his strike zone strongly favored pitchers. But hitters compiled an R/9 five percent *above* average.

In 2009 Timmons's BB/9 was eight percent above average and his K/9 was one percent above average, suggesting his strike zone had shrunk again but he wasn't averse to calling strike three. Did hitters prosper? Yes, but way out of proportion to the increase in his BB/9, as his R/9 was 16 percent above the norm and fifth highest among his peers. In 2010 his BB/9 plunged by nearly two walks a game (only Tony Randazzo and Brian Runge had lower BB/9s for the year), and once again the effect on his R/9 was way out of proportion, as it declined by an astonishing 2.67 runs; Timmons went from having the fifth highest R/9 in 2009 to the 12th lowest R/9 in 2010.

When you total out Timmons's stats, you get contrary results. His overall R/9 is three percent above average, favoring hitters, but his K/BB is four percent above average, favoring pitchers. That makes him one of the more anomalous home plate umpires out there.

Timmons's career ejection rate is 3.5 percent, more than 50 percent higher than average, and it shows no sign of following the downward trend of the last few years. In 2010 he had seven ejections, more than any umpire except Bob Davidson, Joe West, and Paul Emmel. None of the ejections were multiple, meaning there were seven separate incidents that motivated Timmons to banish someone from the game. Four concerned ball-and-strike calls, two were connected to interference calls, and one had to do with a dropped third strike and the resulting play at first. In every instance, replays showed that Timmons got the call right or the call was too close to contest.

Peremptory as he may be, Timmons seldom loses his cool in a confrontation. His ejectees almost always linger after he's told them to go away, and while they shout and gesticulate, he stands quietly with his arms folded, unflinching, as if asking "Why are you getting so excited?" Occasionally he pulls out the lineup card or another piece of paper and writes something on it. Eventually the ejectee gets tired of talking to a wall and either leaves or accepts the escort offered by the crew chief (Tim Tschida in 2010).

Timmons has made a big mark on the business of umpiring. He was one of the founders of the minor league umpires' union, called the Association of Minor League Umpires. Timmons was president of the fledgling union when it signed its first contract with organized baseball. "It was a good thing to get it done and I think everybody is happy. This puts more money in our pockets and they've improved the living conditions," Timmons said. When Timmons filled the major league vacancy created by the departure of Al Clark in 2001, World Umpires Association president John Hirschbeck said, "Now we've got two union presidents."

Named to the 2009 All-Star game crew, Timmons and his mates hosted President Barack Obama for a ten-minute meeting in their cramped locker room. "He asked most of the questions, like how much time we umpires spend on the road. For the leader of the free world to take the time to talk to us lowly umpires was just incredible. I barely remember it, I was just in awe. I've never met a sitting president, so this was definitely a lifetime highlight. [Obama] just strikes you as a cool guy who just wants to sit around and talk baseball," Timmons said.

Timmons called Randy Johnson's 300th career win on June 4, 2009.

SOURCE

Schwarz, Alan. "Umpires Get Chance to Meet America's First Fan." *New York Times,* July 15, 2009. (October 27, 2010.) http://bats.blogs.nytimes.com/2009/07/15/umpires-get-chance-to-meet-americas-first-fan/.

Tim Tschida

BORN: May 4, 1960
FIRST MAJOR LEAGUE GAME: July 24, 1985
FAVORS: Hitters, strongly
THEY HATE HIM IN: Boston

	2007	2008	2009	2010	Totals
Games	35	34	32	33	134
Innings	310.33	299.33	283	302	1,194.67
R/9	9.83	10.16	11.54	7.72	9.79
BB/9	6.35	7.16	8.05	5.60	6.77
K/9	11.92	14.82	13.55	14.16	13.60
K/BB	1.88	2.07	1.68	2.53	2.01

Tschida has called two no-hitters. The first came on May 1, 1991, when Nolan Ryan struck out 16 Toronto Blue Jays en route to his seventh no-no. In the second inning Tschida called strike three on all three Toronto batters, which may have encouraged the Blue Jays to hack: Ryan got 11 of his last 21 outs on swinging strikeouts. (The more likely explanation for the K's is that Ryan had fantastic stuff.) Then on September 14, 2008, Tschida called the first no-hitter by a Chicago Cub since 1972 as Carlos Zambrano dominated the Houston Astros. Tschida dinged Zambrano for a walk in the fourth, but the Cub hurler hit a batter in the fifth, so Tschida's call did not prevent a perfect game.

Prior to 2010, pitchers had reason to doubt that even a shutout was possible when Tschida stood behind the plate, much less a no-hitter. From 2007 through 2009 Tschida compiled an R/9 of 10.49, higher than all but three other umpires. His BB/9 rose from an already high 6.35 to 7.16 to 8.05, third behind Tim McClelland and Jerry Crawford. Meanwhile, his three-year K/9 moseyed along at 13.41, two percent below average. What a difference a year can make. In 2010 Tschida climbed aboard the pro-pitcher bandwagon and had the kind of season you would expect from Doug Eddings or Bill Miller. He went from the second highest R/9 to the fifth lowest, and for the first time during the period under study his K/BB rose above average. For all that, he remains a great friend to hitters. His aggregate R/9 and BB/9 both rank 11th out of 77. His K/9 is down at 53rd. And his K/BB, the best indicator of strike zone size, is 65th, lower than the K/BB of all but 12 other umpires. Unless Tschida's 2010 results were due to a new philosophy of balls and strikes, look for him to rack up higher BB/9s and R/9s in the next few years.

Tschida's career ejection rate is 2.4 percent, higher than average. But if you take out 1998, when he led the American League with 14 thumbings, his career rate comes down to a shade below average. Since 2007 his ejection rate has dropped to about one percent. It's probably no coincidence that the tranquil Tschida, a crew chief since 2007, was put in charge of Bob Davidson, Alfonso Marquez, and Tim Timmons in 2010. All three have high ejection rates at a time when the overall rate is going down. The one ejection Tschida received credit for in 2010 should have been attributed to Timmons, as Seattle manager Don Wakamatsu overstayed his welcome while complaining to Tschida about a strike call Timmons had made.

Tschida worked in the majors for 14 years before he made national headlines, and as usual for an umpire, he made headlines for blowing a call. He was working second base in the fourth game of the 1999 League Championship Series between the Boston Red Sox and New York Yankees. The Sox were trailing 3–2 in the eighth and had Jose Offerman at first with one out. John Valentin hit a roller to Yankee second baseman Chuck Knoblauch, who lunged in hopes of tagging Offerman, then threw to first to get Valentin. Knoblauch missed Offerman cleanly — from some angles it looked like he missed by more than a foot — but Tschida ruled that Knoblauch tagged Offerman to start an inning-ending double play. The Red Sox pleaded with Tschida to reverse the call, which would have brought Nomar Garciaparra to the plate with the tying run in scoring position, but Tschida refused. The goof proved a momentum changer, as the Yankees scored six runs in the top of the ninth to win 9–2 and take an insuperable 3–1 series lead over Boston. "No, I didn't make the right call," Tschida apologized afterward.

As befitting a veteran of more than 3,000 major league games, Tschida is emerging as a spokesman for his fellow umpires, particularly on the issue of instant replay. After Jim Joyce's blown call at first base spoiled the perfect game of Detroit's Armando Galarraga on June 2, 2010, Tschida told an interviewer, "Our job is different today, but no matter what your profession is in this world, your job is different today too. No one's immune to that. You can change with it or you can refuse to grow. The growth part is optional. I think we'd like to grow a little bit." Tschida agreed that the commissioner of baseball shouldn't have changed Joyce's call, but added that "It's refreshing to see that the expansion of replay is at least going to be looked into."

Tschida attended the same St. Paul, Minnesota high school as fellow umpire Mark Wegner and Minnesota Twins catcher Joe Mauer.

SOURCE

"Umpire Tim Tschida Discusses Umpiring and Technology." AOLVideo.com, June 11, 2010. (October 27, 2010.) http://video.aol.ca/video-detail/umpire-tim-tschida-discusses-umpiring-and-technology/1476474145/?icid=VIDLRVSPR08.

John Tumpane

BORN: May 4, 1983
FIRST MAJOR LEAGUE GAME: August 2, 2010
FAVORS: Way too early to tell
THEY HATE HIM IN: Also way too early to tell

	2007	2008	2009	2010	Totals
Games	0	0	0	2	2
Innings	0	0	0	17.5	17.5
R/9	0.00	0.00	0.00	9.53	9.53
BB/9	0.00	0.00	0.00	3.71	3.71
K/9	0.00	0.00	0.00	17.47	17.47
K/BB	0.00	0.00	0.00	4.71	4.71

It didn't take long for Tumpane, a Triple-A call-up assigned to the Pacific Coast League, to make his mark on a major league game. Brought up on August 2, 2010 to work a series between Kansas City and Oakland, he was sent to second base by crew chief Gary Darling. His debut was going smoothly until the bottom of the fourth. The A's had runners on first and second and no one out when Matt Watson lined one into left. The runner on second scored. The runner on first, speedy Rajai Davis, held at third. But Watson kept going, trying to stretch the single into a double. The relay reached Royal second baseman Chris Getz in plenty of time. Getz reached to tag Watson, but Tumpane ruled that Watson eluded the tag and was safe. An infuriated Getz argued with the newbie ump—and while he yammered away, Davis snuck home with another run. Getz knew better than to blame Tumpane. "I got caught up in the situation. It really is inexcusable," he admitted.

A couple of days later, Tumpane called his first big league game behind home plate. The Athletics edged the Royals, 4–3. The first batter of the game was Chris Getz. Tumpane gave him a walk on four pitches, the only base on balls he called on Oakland pitchers all game. An inning later, Alex Gordon of the Royals became the first major league batter Tumpane called out on strikes.

Brought back for the final weekend of the 2010 season, Tumpane called the last game of the year for the Chicago White Sox and Cleveland Indians. The White Sox held on for a 6–5 win. There were 21 strikeouts in the game, but Tumpane called only four.

Raised in the Chicago metropolitan area, the 6'2", 185-pound Tumpane told the *Washington Times* in 2006 that "The adrenaline gets going as soon as I walk out of the tunnel onto the field. You get a beautiful facility, a big crowd, the lights are on. It's time to go to work. When you are standing there for the national anthem, it is amazing to think, 'This is my job.' I love my job."

He worked third base for the Triple-A All-Star game on July 14, 2010.

Source

Siegel, Jon. "A Tough Calling." *Washington Times,* July 27, 2006. (October 28, 2010.) http://www.washingtontimes.com/news/2006/jul/27/20060727-010620-1020r/?page=1.

Larry Vanover

BORN: August 22, 1955
FIRST MAJOR LEAGUE GAME: June 25, 1991
FAVORS: His R/9 says hitters by a lot, his K/BB says pitchers by a little
THEY HATE HIM IN: San Diego

	2007	2008	2009	2010	Totals
Games	36	32	34	30	132
Innings	319.5	285	295	265.17	1,164.67
R/9	11.38	10.20	8.60	9.30	9.91
BB/9	5.86	6.76	5.95	5.74	6.07
K/9	13.55	13.39	14.74	13.95	13.90
K/BB	2.31	1.98	2.48	2.43	2.29

"I just had to let him know what I was thinking. He was real inconsistent all game." So said catcher Yorvit Torrealba of the San Diego Padres on June 14, 2010, after home plate umpire Larry Vanover called him out on a close pitch, then tossed him when he argued and his batting helmet struck Vanover's forehead. Torrealba's starting pitcher that night, Jon Garland, chimed in, "I probably already have umpires dislike me because of what I've already said, but I do think there are umpires out there trying to incite players. I think they look for it, look to get players fired up. Not all of them, but some do, and it's wrong." Torrealba was suspended three days for touching Vanover. "I don't see umpires getting fined and I don't see umpires getting suspended. They make a lot of mistakes," he said.

Mistakes or not, Vanover's numbers do provoke some head scratching. Despite having the second highest R/9 in the majors in 2007, his BB/9 was four percent below average and his K/9 was two percent above average, both of which favor pitchers. In 2008 his BB/9 rose to eight percent above normal and his K/9 dropped slightly, both of which favor hitters. This time Vanover's R/9 corresponded, so in all, his 2008 was a solid win for hitters. But then in 2009 he took a drastic swing toward pitchers, R/9 plunging 1.6 runs per nine innings, BB/9 dropping more than eight-tenths of a walk, and K/9 soaring by a strikeout and a third. In 2010 his strike zone remained pitcher-friendly, though not as pitcher-friendly as the year before, and his R/9 rose by seven-tenths of a run per nine — in a year when run production across the majors dropped by nearly half a run per nine. When Vanover's four-year totals are compared to those of his colleagues, he comes out seventh highest in R/9, highly favorable to hitters. But his BB/9 ranks 50th out of 77, his K/9 is 32nd, and his K/BB is also 32nd; those numbers mildly favor pitchers. He may be a high-strike umpire. In three of the four years under study his home run rate was higher than average, suggesting pitchers serve up more belt-high offerings than usual when Vanover is behind the plate.

Vanover has a little less tolerance for dissent than his colleagues, posting a 2.5 percent career ejection rate. And his fuse is getting shorter: Since 2007 his ejection rate has risen above three percent. Four days after booting Torrealba, Vanover tallied yet another ejection, running manager Ken Macha of the Milwaukee Brewers for disputing a call made by another umpire, Mark Carlson, on a tag play. Carlson sought advice from the other umpires, and collectively they got the call right. After Macha walked up the first base line hectoring Carlson, who bore the rant patiently, Macha addressed an assemblage of three umps. Vanover quickly became the focus of Macha's attention, tempers flared, and Vanover sent Macha to an early shower.

Vanover was one of 22 umpires whose resignation was accepted by Major League Baseball in 1999, blowback from a misconceived negotiating ploy by the leadership of the umpires' union. Lacking job skills outside his profession, Vanover struggled financially. He had to sell his home, and at one point received funds from the Baseball Assistance Team, whose primary purpose, according to its web page, is "to aid those members of the 'baseball family' most in need." Vanover denied to the *New York Times* that he applied for the aid, but did admit hardship: "People are losing homes. I'm working, trying to support my wife and two kids, keep my head above water. I want to go back to work. That's all I want to do." He was rehired in 2002, having missed two full seasons.

The New York Yankees owe Vanover a debt of gratitude, for without him they might not have secured Joe Girardi as their current manager. Girardi piloted the Florida Marlins in 2006 but had trouble coping with team owner Jeffrey Loria, who sat in a box by the dugout and heckled the home plate umpires. On August 6, 2006, the Marlins were clinging to a 3–1 lead against the Los Angeles Dodgers in the seventh inning. The Dodgers loaded the bases. Taylor Tankersley came in to pitch for the Marlins and walked in a run on a questionable call by Vanover. Loria heaped abuse on Vanover, causing Girardi to step out of the dugout and tell Loria to knock it off. After the game (which the Marlins lost) the clubhouse was closed for 90 minutes while Girardi held a closed-door meeting with Loria, then talked to the players. Although all parties denied discord, few observers were fooled. Despite earning Manager of the Year honors, Girardi was fired after the season, making him available to the Yankees when they wanted someone to replace Joe Torre.

Source

Jenkins, Chris. "Suspended Torrealba Rails Against Ump." *San Diego Union-Tribune*, June 16, 2010. (October 28, 2010.) http://www.signonsandiego.com/news/2010/jun/16/padres-torrealba-draws-three-game-suspension/.

Mark Wegner

BORN: March 4, 1972
FIRST MAJOR LEAGUE GAME: May 20, 1998
FAVORS: R/9 says pitchers, K/BB says hitters
THEY HATE HIM IN: Anaheim and San Francisco

	2007	2008	2009	2010	Totals
Games	33	34	35	26	128
Innings	294.5	307.33	318.17	230.17	1,150.17
R/9	9.57	9.22	8.91	8.95	9.17
BB/9	6.02	7.17	6.31	7.00	6.60
K/9	15.46	13.85	14.00	12.98	14.13
K/BB	2.57	1.93	2.22	1.85	2.14

At 5'8" and a trim 180 pounds, Wegner was physically overmatched on June 2, 2007, when Lou Piniella, manager of the Chicago Cubs, argued a call. It was the bottom of the eighth, the game was tied, and the sinking Cubs badly needed a win, as pitcher Carlos Zambrano and catcher Michael Barrett had engaged in a demoralizing dugout brawl the day before. Angel Pagan had tried to take third on a passed ball by Atlanta catcher Jarrod Saltalamacchia, but Saltalamacchia fired a bullet to third and Wegner called Pagan out. Piniella leaned his pot belly into Wegner's chest and flung down his hat so he could go nose-to-nose. The unwavering Wegner stared through his sunglasses at Piniella, who stepped back and repeatedly kicked dirt on Wegner. Crew chief Bruce Froemming interceded, but could barely budge the apoplectic Cub skipper.

It was the sort of tirade that's parodied in baseball movies. Piniella knew it, too. "I was going to argue if he was out, safe, or whatever," he said after admitting Wegner got the call right. Piniella was trying to fire up his talented but unfocused team. And the hoary motivational tool worked. The Cubs got hot and went on to win their division. A grateful Piniella vowed never to kick dirt on an umpire again. "I wrote [Wegner] a note and I apologized to him," he said. "My sandbox days are over. No hat, no dirt, no nothing."

Wegner is himself a feisty guy. His career ejection rate of 3.2 percent is much higher than average. And since 2007 his ejection rate has climbed to 3.5 percent. It's not just that Wegner has a short fuse. He can be combative as well. On May 20, 2010, Wegner ejected Giant manager Bruce Bochy for arguing balls and strikes with two outs in the ninth inning of a one-run game, then apparently grabbed his crotch in response to a remark from San Francisco's Juan Uribe, who struck out to end the game. "[Wegner] told me that the pitch was down the middle of the plate. Tell me it was to the left. Tell me it was to the right. But don't tell me it was down the middle because it wasn't. Then he got angry at me and I don't know why," Uribe maintained.

That wasn't Wegner's first testosterone-fueled response to a challenge. On September 16, 2009, he worked third base during a game between the Los Angeles Angels and Boston

Red Sox. The Angels had a one-run lead in the bottom of the ninth but the Red Sox had the bases loaded. Home plate umpire Rick Reed ruled that Red Sox batter Nick Green successfully checked a swing for ball three, then ruled ball four on the next pitch to force in the tying run. The following hitter singled to win the game. Afterward, the Angels filed down the same hallway as the umpires and openly jeered Reed for costing them a win. They kept their distance, though — until Wegner turned around and confronted them. "There's a little lesson in professionalism for Mark Wegner that needs to be discussed," Angel manager Mike Scioscia huffed.

Then there was the June 28, 2007, game in which Frank Thomas, playing for the Blue Jays, hit his 500th career home run. A joyous occasion — until home plate umpire Wegner ejected him for questioning a called third strike in the ninth inning. "I'm probably the first to get 500 home runs and get thrown out of the ballgame," Thomas rued.

But Wegner also has moments of humility. After blowing a double play call in an April 17, 2010, game between San Francisco and Los Angeles, Wegner admitted that "he [Giant baserunner Eugenio Velez] should've been called out." Fortunately the call didn't make a difference as the Giants led 7–0 at the time of the mistake and eventually won 9–0.

Going by the number of runs scored when he works home plate, Wegner charts as a pitchers' umpire. His R/9 was below average every year under study except 2010, when it was barely one percent above average. Going by BB/9 and K/9, however, Wegner has been shrinking his strike zone, which favors hitters. His K/9 was 16 percent above average in 2007, highest in the majors. But in 2008 it plunged by a strikeout and a half. His K/9 remained at that level in 2009, then took another dip in 2010, to just under 13, nine percent below average and fourth lowest among umps who worked 150 innings or more behind the plate. Meanwhile, his BB/9 has been yo-yoing: just below average in 2007, way above average in 2008, just below average in 2009, way above average in 2010. Wegner's overall K/BB ratio of 2.14 favors hitters by four percent.

A Twin Cities native, Wegner worked what was supposed to be the last game at the Metrodome on October 4, 2009, only to have the Twins tie for the division title and play one last home game in the old yard without him. He also worked the first series in the Twins' new home, Target Field.

Wegner missed all of September 2010. The reason was not disclosed.

Source

Muskat, Carrie. "MLB Suspends Piniella for Tirade." MLB.com, June 3, 2007. (October 28, 2010.) http://mlb.mlb.com/news/article.jsp?ymd=20070603&content_id=2002607&vkey=news_chc&fext=.jsp&c_id=chc.

Bill Welke

BORN: August 22, 1967
FIRST MAJOR LEAGUE GAME: June 4, 1999

FAVORS: R/9 says hitters, everything else says pitchers
THEY HATE HIM IN: Baltimore

	2007	2008	2009	2010	Totals
Games	34	34	33	30	131
Innings	304.67	300.5	294.67	272.33	1,172.17
R/9	9.07	10.48	10.78	8.66	9.77
BB/9	5.32	6.59	5.83	5.29	5.77
K/9	14.15	13.96	14.14	14.24	14.12
K/BB	2.66	2.12	2.43	2.69	2.45

Bill is the younger brother of Tim Welke. They are almost exactly ten years apart, and worked on the same crew in 2005, 2008, 2009, and 2010. They are not the only umpiring brothers in major league history. From 1987 through 2003, John Hirschbeck and his brother Mark served as umpires. (John is still around, but Mark Hirschbeck retired prematurely due to a disability.) Born, raised, and still living in southwestern Michigan, the Welke brothers spoke to a crowd in Kalamazoo shortly before spring training in 2010 and shared memories of arriving in the big leagues. Bill recalled his 13th game, a July 25, 1999, contest between the Cleveland Indians and New York Yankees. Working second base, he called a Yankee baserunner out on a close play. "All of a sudden, I heard a buzz. As umpires, we're trained to focus on the play, and what's going on on the field, and we can really tune out what's going around, but the first time you experience 50,000 people chanting 'Welke sucks, Welke sucks,' it's like the stadium was rocking and my first thought was that they're never gonna call me up here." (Actual attendance that day was 54,944, and they did call him up.)

Neither hitters nor pitchers would be inclined to say Bill Welke sucks, because he gives each a reason to like him. For hitters it's his R/9, which is five percent above average and 12th highest overall, even after a harsh 2010 in which he shed more than two runs per nine innings. His slash stats were consistently favorable to hitters until 2010:

Year	Batting Average	On-Base Percentage	Slugging Percentage
2007	.275	.336	.420
2008	.276	.341	.423
2009	.277	.336	.442
2010	.261	.320	.395

Pitchers can point to Welke's strike zone, as overall he calls seven percent fewer walks than the average umpire, and he sees two percent more strikeouts than the average umpire. His 2007 K/BB was tied for fifth highest, his 2010 K/BB was tied (with his brother) for 11th highest, and his four-year K/BB of 2.45 is a pitcher-friendly ten percent above the norm, 11th highest out of 77 umpires. Like several other umpires, Welke probably prefers high strikes to low ones, forcing pitchers to bring the ball up where hitters can blast it.

Welke's career ejection rate is 3.7 percent, substantially higher than average. His ejection rate for the years under study is three percent, lower than his career figure but still 50 percent above the norm. Welke seems to get involved in a lot of ball-and-strike arguments. His three 2010 ejections concerned disputed pitch calls. In all cases, replays showed he called the pitch correctly. Welke seldom loses his cool, however, and even plays peacemaker at times. On September 7, 2007, he was stationed at first base for a game between Boston and Baltimore. In the fourth inning, Coco Crisp of the Red Sox reached third base and started dancing around to distract Oriole pitcher Daniel Cabrera. Crisp succeeded, and Cabrera was called for a balk, giving the Red Sox a 3–0 lead. Cabrera threw his next pitch behind batter Dustin Pedroia's head. The Red Sox poured out of their dugout. The umpires kept them back, but when Oriole catcher Ramon Hernandez taunted the Red Sox, the human tide grew too strong to contain. Welke found Cabrera and grabbed him by the front of the jersey, pushing him away from the action. No peewee at 6'2" and 240 pounds, Welke was nonetheless shunted aside by the 6'9" Cabrera, although Welke held on so tightly that he tore Cabrera's jersey.

Like many umpires, Welke has no objection to increasing the use of instant replay. "It's either gonna show I'm right or it's gonna fix something that I have wrong, and there's nothing wrong with either being proven right or correcting an error. I'd hate to make a call that could affect maybe the World Series and be wrong and everybody in the world knows it but me, standing out there."

SOURCE

Shebest, Pam. "Welke Brothers Share Entertaining Stories of Big-League Umpiring." *Kalamazoo Gazette*, February 6, 2010. (October 28, 2010.) http://www.mlive.com/news/kalamazoo/index.ssf/2010/02/welke_brothers_share_entertain.html.

Tim Welke

BORN: August 23, 1957
FIRST MAJOR LEAGUE GAME: June 14, 1983
FAVORS: R/9 says hitters, everything else says pitchers
THEY HATE HIM IN: The *Sports Illustrated* editorial boardroom

	2007	2008	2009	2010	Totals
Games	25	34	28	35	122
Innings	228.5	306	238.33	315.67	1,088.5
R/9	9.93	9.38	11.29	9.89	10.06
BB/9	5.91	6.03	7.25	5.59	6.14
K/9	13.55	14.59	14.58	15.05	14.50
K/BB	2.29	2.42	2.01	2.69	2.36

Welke was on the cover of the October 19, 1998, edition of *Sports Illustrated*. Masked and on one knee, he's pointing ominously at someone, perhaps in the first base dugout. The headline under his outstretched arm reads "Kill the umps!" He wasn't named on the cover or in the article, but he took the caption personally. "I was hurt and disappointed by your use of my picture on the cover of your October 19 issue, which bore the headline 'KILL THE UMPS!'" he wrote the magazine [capitals his]. "I perceive the play, apply the rules and make the decision, all in real time. Under these circumstances, questionable calls sometimes happen, just like rainouts and brawls. My role is to decide what is right. I cannot, like Solomon, split the baby. On any call, half the players and fans will be disappointed. The dismay I felt when you used my picture was brought home when my nine-year-old son asked me, 'Dad, does this mean they want to kill you?'"

Welke is not the heavy-handed type. The older brother of fellow umpire Bill Welke and a crew chief since 2000, he has a career ejection rate of two percent, slightly below average. Since 2007 his ejection rate has dropped to one percent. On May 21, 2010, Welke collected his first ejection since 2007, sending Jerry Hairston Jr. to an early shower for questioning a called third strike. Welke didn't hesitate; he thumbed Hairston as soon as the San Diego Padre hitter wheeled around to protest. At the time, the Padres were losing to the Seattle Mariners by 11 runs, so even if merited (which it wasn't) the argument was pointless. "I like Welke. He should have thrown me out," Hairston confessed later. "I thought the pitch call was bad. But when I saw it later on a replay, I'm thinking, 'Jerry, Jerry, Jerry.'" Welke's other three 2010 ejections stemmed from an August 3 beanball war between Boston and Cleveland. If you don't count those, since they had nothing to do with a call he made, his ejection rate since 2007 drops to a microscopic 0.4 percent.

Welke's K/9 is consistently above average, so Hairston probably isn't the only hitter who's had a beef with his strike zone. Welke's 2009 BB/9 was uncharacteristically high — seventh highest in the majors — and that inflated his overall BB/9. But in 2007, 2008, and 2010 his BB/9 was three percent or more below average, so for the most part he matches a higher than average K/9 with a lower than average BB/9, both of which favor pitchers. Welke's overall K/BB ratio is six percent higher than average, further evidence that he defaults to strikes. But check out his R/9. In 2008 it was exactly average. In every other year under study, it's been above average — 21 percent above average in 2009, when it was third highest in the majors, and 12 percent above average in 2010, when it was seventh highest in the majors. It's possible the 6' 3" Welke prefers the high strike. In 2009 his home run rate of 2.40 per nine innings was 11th highest, and in 2010 his HR/9 was seventh highest, suggesting pitchers need to bring the ball up to get a call from him. Overall, Welke has the fifth highest R/9 of the 77 umpires who called 500 or more innings from 2007 through 2010.

Injuries have taken a toll on Welke. On August 24, 2009, he was hit in the mask by a foul off the bat of Vladimir Guerrero. He remained in the game until the inning ended, then departed and missed two weeks. On May 4, 2010, he was hit in the mask by a foul ball off the bat of Cincinnati's Drew Stubbs. After walking it off, he stayed in the game. Then on July 10, 2010, Jason Donald of the Cleveland Indians hit yet another foul ball that caught him in the mask. Again Welke remained in the game. He took his first turn behind the plate after the All-Star break, then went on vacation and didn't return until August. These repeated head blows can't be good for a 27-year major league veteran in his fifties.

In February 2010, Welke told a hometown audience of his first encounter with umpire-baiting Billy Martin. The New York Yankees were playing the Kansas City Royals in Welke's rookie season, 1983. Mickey Rivers hit a fly ball that bounced past the center fielder to the wall. He circled the bases for an inside-the-park home run. Welke saw that Rivers missed second, and so did George Brett, who had the pitcher throw over on appeal. Welke called Rivers out. "I see this short little guy who's got a number one on his chest," Welke said. "So I'm thinking to myself, 'I hope he stops. I hope he doesn't run into me, or my career's gonna be done now.'" But of course Martin gets in his face. "He sprints out, stops just before me, puts his finger under my chin and says, 'Let me tell you one thing, young man. I saw him miss second base too, and I'm gonna fine him $100.'" When Welke laughed, Martin shouted, "Don't you laugh, we're on TV!"

Only problem with the story is that it can't be true. Mickey Rivers last played for Billy Martin and the Yankees in 1979.

Source

Welke, Tim. Letter to the Editor. *Sports Illustrated,* November 16, 1998. (October 28, 2010.) http://sports illustrated.cnn.com/vault/article/magazine/MAG1014539/index.htm.

Hunter Wendelstedt

Born: June 22, 1971
First Major League Game: April 19, 1998
Favors: Pitchers
They hate him in: Remedial classes at umpire school

	2007	2008	2009	2010	Totals
Games	33	35	36	35	139
Innings	296.17	312.33	310.83	302.83	1,222.17
R/9	8.63	9.91	9.27	8.02	8.97
BB/9	5.50	6.31	6.49	5.80	6.03
K/9	11.79	14.09	13.58	14.24	13.44
K/BB	2.14	2.23	2.09	2.46	2.23

Harry Hunter Wendelstedt III, known as Hunter, carries on one of the most famous names in umpiredom. His father, Harry Hunter Wendelstedt Jr., known as Harry, umpired 4,500 National League games from 1966 through 1998 and is best remembered for refusing to grant first base to Dick Dietz of the San Francisco Giants after Dietz was hit by a Don Drysdale pitch with the bases loaded on May 31, 1968. By ruling that Dietz hadn't tried to evade the pitch, Wendelstedt gave Drysdale an opportunity to extend his scoreless inning streak, which Drysdale did to the record length of 58.67 (later surpassed by Orel Hershiser). Harry Wendelstedt continues to exert tremendous influence over umpire training through the Wendelstedt Umpire School, which by Hunter's count has produced "well over 100" major league umpires.

Hunter's happiest umpiring memory is working with his father. They became the only father-son team to umpire a big league game on August 10, 1998, when the Florida Marlins met the San Diego Padres. Harry called balls and strikes and Hunter patrolled second base. In all, father and son worked 18 National League games together, including consecutive doubleheaders between Philadelphia and Florida on September 26 and 27, 1998. Marring the family's bliss was the death of Harry Hunter Wendelstedt Sr., father of Harry and grandfather of Hunter, after that first game. "My dad was so very proud. He watched the game on television," Harry recalled. "It was the most exciting and the saddest moments on the same day." Today Hunter wears uniform number 21, just like his dad.

Wendelstedt's aggregate plate numbers are lower than the major league average. His four-year BB/9 and K/9 are both three percent lower than the norm. Because they're an equal amount below average, his K/BB is right at average. Wendelstedt's aggregate R/9 is four percent lower than the norm, but his year-to-year swings have been large. His 2007 R/9 of 8.63 was fifth lowest in the majors, 11 percent lower than the norm. In 2008 his R/9 leaped to 9.91, six percent *higher* than the norm. Wendelstedt's R/9 came closest to matching the league norm in 2009, when it fell 64 points from 2008. In 2010 Wendelstedt joined the march toward pitching as his R/9 plunged by a run and a quarter to seventh lowest among umpires with 150 or more innings called, nine percent below average.

Even within seasons, Wendelstedt's numbers can swing like monkeys through the forest. In 2009 he called four games in which there were more walks than strikeouts, three of those in his first six starts behind home plate. But on June 15, in a game between the Los Angeles Angels and San Francisco Giants, Wendelstedt didn't call a single walk, yet watched 17 strikeouts. And how about this variation in his first 12 starts of 2010:

	Innings	R/9	BB/9	K/9	K/BB
First 6 starts	52.17	11.73	7.42	12.25	1.65
Second 6 starts	51.5	7.34	6.47	13.81	2.13

In fairness, one of those first six starts included a 20–0 pasting of the Pittsburgh Pirates by the Milwaukee Brewers.

According to Wendelstedt, "The difference between a good Triple-A umpire and a major league umpire is the ability to handle the situations that arise on the field. Most umpires at that level can call balls and strikes, safes and outs, fairs and fouls. It is the ability to defuse a situation, attempt to keep people in the game, but eject when necessary." Yet his career ejection rate is 3.2 percent, much higher than average, and has remained at that level since 2007 despite the downward trend among his peers. (His father's career ejection rate was 1.9 percent.) Why the high ejection rate from the scion of a highly-regarded umpiring family? One anonymous team's answer was revealed in May 2010: "Inconsistent zone, both in-game and from game to game, seemingly losing focus at times by balling pitches over middle and calling strikes on pitches well off plate. Seems to want hitter to put ball in play." This analysis jibes not only with Wendelstedt's higher than average ejection rate (inconsistency and occasional loss of focus would upset players and managers), but with his lower than average BB/9 and K/9 (evidence that he *does* want hitters to put the ball in play).

Although he was born in Atlanta, Wendelstedt loves working in San Diego and San Francisco. He also likes Wrigley Field and Fenway Park. In May 2009 he told the *North County* (San Diego) *Times* that umpiring is "one of the greatest jobs in the world. The only negative is the time away from loved ones. It's everything I thought it would be and more."

SOURCE

Warren (Umpire In Chief). "Interview with Hunter Wendelstedt." Umpire-Empire.com, February 11, 2009. (October 29, 2010.) http://www.umpire-empire.com/forum/showthread.php?t=2400.

Joe West

BORN: October 31, 1952
FIRST MAJOR LEAGUE GAME: September 14, 1976
FAVORS: Hitters, slightly
THEY HATE HIM IN: Every corner of the universe, it would seem

	2007	2008	2009	2010	Totals
Games	36	33	34	36	139
Innings	320.67	299	300.17	332.83	1,252.67
R/9	8.98	10.14	9.53	8.06	9.15
BB/9	6.29	5.63	7.14	6.11	6.29
K/9	12.66	13.12	14.48	13.06	13.31
K/BB	2.01	2.33	2.03	2.14	2.12

If you're asked to name a current umpire, chances are you'll say Joe West. For better or worse — largely for worse, according to his legion of critics — West has become the most famous umpire in baseball. He's been around since 1976 and has worked 4,186 regular season games. In 2009 he took over the presidency of the World Umpires Association and led negotiations that produced a five-year labor agreement. And Joe West is *out there*. At an admitted 275 pounds he is the heaviest umpire, and he is confrontational to the point of belligerence, compiling a lifetime ejection rate of 3.3 percent, 50 percent higher than the norm. What's more, he freely violates the profession's taboo against seeking the limelight, employing a personal publicist and basking in controversy.

It's no surprise that someone who enjoys playing the villain as much as West is disliked by fans and pundits. But he isn't popular with players either. In *Sports Illustrated*'s 2003 poll of 550 players, West was voted the fourth worst umpire in the majors, behind C.B. Bucknor, Bruce Froemming (since retired), and Joe Brinkman (since retired). He finished fourth from the bottom again in *Sports Illustrated*'s poll of 470 players in 2006, although this time he also appeared on the best umpire list, albeit with just two percent of the vote. And in June 2010 *ESPN The Magazine* conducted a poll of 100 players (50 from each league) and 35 percent of them named West the worst umpire in the game, behind only Bucknor. They also said West was quickest to eject someone. That widespread animosity helps explain the response from two highly-respected pitchers to a couple of notorious incidents involving West in 2010.

On April 8, during the first full week of the season, West told the *Bergen* [New Jersey] *Record* that games between the New York Yankees and Boston Red Sox went too slowly: "They're two of the best teams in baseball. Why are they playing the slowest? It's pathetic and embarrassing." Then, for good measure, he called their pace "a disgrace to baseball." The sin was not that he spoke the truth (the Yankees and Red Sox do play the slowest games in the majors), but that he expressed a preference. Umpires, like judges, are held to a high standard of neutrality. West's outburst prompted a rebuttal from Yankee closer Mariano Rivera, who in 16 big league seasons has never been ejected. "It's incredible. If he has places to go, let him do something else. What does he want us to do, swing at balls?" Added Rivera, "He has a job to do. He should do his job."

An even more cutting reaction came from pitcher Mark Buehrle of the Chicago White Sox, who had never been ejected from a game until May 26, 2010, when West, working first base, called balks on Buehrle's pickoff move *twice*. After the first balk, West ejected White Sox manager Ozzie Guillen. After the second, Buehrle dropped his glove in disbelief and West tossed him. "Eleven years in the big leagues, I've used the same move. I still don't know what he called a balk on. I honestly don't think I balked either time," Buehrle said. "I think he's too worried about promoting his CD. And I think he likes seeing his name in the papers a little too much instead of worrying about the rules."

Buehrle was referring to West's avocation as a country-western singer. Born in North Carolina and often called "Country Joe" or "Cowboy Joe," West has performed with a number of Nashville luminaries and has held the stage at the Grand Ole Opry. He has also cut a couple of CDs, *Blue Cowboy* and *Diamond Dreams*. Sample titles from the latter effort include "Extra Innings," "Out at Home," and "The Men in Blue." Critics have been slow to appreciate West's artistry. In May 2010 the *Cleveland Plain Dealer* ran a review titled "As a country singer, Joe West is a good umpire."

West's entrepreneurial streak extends to umpire gear. He is best known for inventing the West Vest, a chest protector manufactured by Wilson Sporting Goods. According to one of West's web sites, the gold version of the hard shell protector ($154.99) was introduced at the 1992 World Series (guess who called balls and strikes in game three that year) and is today worn by more big league umpires than any other chest protector. The West Vest Umpire Mask, replete with deerskin padding, is yours for $82.

In three of the four years studied, West's R/9 and strike zone size didn't match. What's worse, the mismatches weren't consistent. In 2007 and 2010 he had a pitcher-friendly R/9 but a hitter-friendly strike zone. In 2008 he had a hitter-friendly R/9 but a pitcher-friendly strike zone. The way his R/9 bobs up and down makes it impossible to guess whether he prefers high strikes or low strikes, inside strikes or outside strikes. Perhaps that is part of what makes him so unpopular with players. What is clear, however, is that his strike zone is small; 2008 was the only season it favored pitchers, and his four-year K/BB ratio ranks 54th out of 77, placing it in the third that most favors hitters. When it comes to plate judgment, he is more likely to make pitchers mad than hitters.

After 33 seasons (he missed 2000 and 2001 because the Lords of Baseball accepted the 1999 resignation he submitted along with most other umpires), West's enthusiasm for his job is undiminished. He became a crew chief in 2003. He seldom misses games, and in 2010 he worked more innings behind the plate than any other umpire. On June 29, 2010, he called a game at Yankee Stadium for the first time since his comment about the length of Yankee-Red Sox games. He was booed. "I hear 'em every time I go out there," he scoffed. Cliff Lee and the Seattle Mariners beat the Yankees and Phil Hughes, 7–4. Time of game? A snappy 2:30.

Sources

Elsesser, Stephen. "Ozzie, Buehrle Ejected for Arguing Balks." MLB.com, May 26, 2010. (October 29, 2010.) http://mlb.mlb.com/news/article.jsp?ymd=20100526&content_id=10449660&vkey=news_cws&fext=.jsp&c_id=cws.

Roberts, Jeff. "Ump Calls Yanks, Sox 'a Disgrace to Baseball.'" *Bergen Record,* April 8, 2010. (October 29, 2010.) http://www.northjersey.com/sports/pro_sports/90192892__It_s_a_disgrace_to_baseball_.html.

Mike Winters

BORN: November 19, 1958
FIRST MAJOR LEAGUE GAME: July 9, 1988
FAVORS: Pitchers, but hitters don't mind
THEY HATE HIM IN: Major League Baseball's human resources department

	2007	2008	2009	2010	Totals
Games	32	31	31	33	127
Innings	280.5	270.5	273.5	292.17	1,116.67
R/9	9.59	9.18	9.05	9.70	9.39
BB/9	5.87	5.82	5.66	6.84	6.06
K/9	13.83	13.48	13.23	16.23	14.23
K/BB	2.36	2.32	2.34	2.37	2.35

Milton Bradley is a talented player, but no angel. Over 11 major league seasons he has worn out his welcome with eight different teams. Three times he has led all players in annual ejections. But according to Ellis Burks, who played with Bradley in Cleveland, "He's not a bad guy at all. With Milton, if you don't bother him, he won't bother you." In the second half of the 2007 season, Bradley was playing for San Diego, and evidently no one was bothering him. He was hitting .313 with 11 home runs in 42 games for the offense-starved contender. But in the Padres' September 23, 2007 home game against the Colorado Rockies, umpire Brian Runge called him out on strikes to end the fifth inning. That annoyed Bradley. He stood at the plate a long moment, then tossed his bat.

When Bradley batted again in the eighth, Runge asked whether Bradley meant to throw the bat at him. Bradley said no. Runge said another umpire told him that Bradley *had* thrown the bat at him. After Bradley slapped a base hit he asked the first base umpire, San Diego area native Mike Winters, whether he had said anything to Runge about the thrown bat. According to Padre first base coach Bobby Meacham, Winters's response was "the most disconcerting conversation I have heard from an umpire to a player. There's no possible way a man is going to stand there and take what he said to Milton." Although Meacham would not be specific, he alleged that Winters called Bradley something profane. The insult kindled Bradley's anger, and when Winters's collar heated too, Bradley lost control and stepped toward Winters. Padre manager Bud Black pulled Bradley away, but Bradley resisted, got his legs tangled with Black's, and fell awkwardly, tearing the anterior cruciate ligament of his right knee. His season ended, and without him the Padres lost a one-game playoff for the National League wild card spot eight days later.

Umpires are given broad discretion to manage games smoothly and efficiently. When their action produces the opposite result they are often reprimanded, occasionally fined, but hardly ever suspended. (Prior to the Bradley-Winters incident, the last umpire to serve a suspension was John Hirschbeck in 2003 for making personal threats against Rob Manfred, the labor relations attorney for the Lords of Baseball.) Baseball executives spent two days investigating the incident, reportedly interviewing the two principals plus Meacham and Rockie first baseman Todd Helton, a presumably dispassionate witness (although another account had Helton declining to cooperate). The investigators concluded that "the umpire's role is to defuse, not escalate, a situation, and that wasn't done," according to one anonymous major league official. Winters was suspended without pay for the remainder of the season (five games) and barred from postseason work until 2008.

Crew chief Bruce Froemming defended Winters after the game by saying "[Bradley] got grumpy with Mike Winters. Winters told him to knock it off and he continued it. There is no covering up what he did. He had to be physically restrained." But after the suspension was announced, Froemming had no comment. Nor did union president John Hirschbeck. Four days after the incident, Larnell McMorris, spokesman for the World Umpires Association, issued an apology on Winters's behalf. "He sincerely regrets what happened on the field that day. Sometimes, regrettable situations just come out of nowhere and spiral out of control, and everyone involved later wishes that the entire thing can be undone and everyone can go back to the beginning and start over," McMorris said.

The evidence suggests that Winters does have a short fuse. His career ejection rate is 2.9 percent, a third higher than the norm. Since 2007 his ejection rate has fallen to 2.5 percent, thanks to a peaceful 2009 in which he didn't toss anybody. He's one of only four 20-year veterans not to be a crew chief. Another is Jim Joyce, who reportedly does not want the job. The other two are Bill Hohn and Bob Davidson, also notorious for their tempers.

Behind the plate, Winters was a model of consistency from 2007 through 2009. His R/9, BB/9, K/9, and K/BB all fell within a fairly narrow range. In 2010 Winters kept his K/BB steady, but all his other numbers jumped. In the first three years of this study his combined BB/9 and K/9 never reached 20. In 2010 they soared over 23, an extraordinary figure, propelled by the highest K/9 for any umpire in the last four years and the eighth highest BB/9 of the season. Boy, did he make pitchers work. He was 50th in innings called in 2010, but was 34th in total pitches seen. Tired pitchers may account for the rise in his R/9 to the highest in four years — during a season when run production across the majors fell sharply. Winters has a solidly pro-pitcher strike zone, ranking 24th largest out of 77 umpires. But if he continues to make pitchers work as hard for him as they did in 2010, look for his R/9 to remain above average in the next few seasons.

Winters was behind home plate when Kevin Gross of the Los Angeles Dodgers threw a no-hitter against the rival San Francisco Giants on August 17, 1992.

Sources

Pugmire, Lance. "Umpire Winters is Suspended." *Los Angeles Times,* September 27, 2007. (October 29, 2010.) http://articles.latimes.com/2007/sep/27/sports/sp-umpire27.

Schwarz, Alan. "Bradley's Season is Over, but Fight with Umpire is Not." *New York Times,* September 25, 2007. (October 29, 2010.) http://www.nytimes.com/2007/09/25/sports/baseball/25bradley.html.

Jim Wolf

BORN: July 24, 1969
FIRST MAJOR LEAGUE GAME: September 2, 1999
FAVORS: Pitchers, slightly
THEY HATE HIM IN: Major League Baseball's ethics department (if there is one)

	2007	2008	2009	2010	Totals
Games	33	35	34	31	133
Innings	291	307	290.5	277.83	1,166.33
R/9	9.00	9.62	10.13	7.74	9.14
BB/9	5.38	6.51	6.63	5.67	6.06
K/9	13.39	14.10	13.82	14.67	13.99
K/BB	2.49	2.17	2.08	2.59	2.31

In 2008 and 2009 Jim Wolf moved from a solid pitchers' umpire to a hitters' umpire. His K/BB progressively shrank and his R/9 rose. But in his first five home plate appearances of 2010 he went back to being the pitchers' friend of 2007. Over 47 innings he compiled a K/9 of 16.47 and a BB/9 of 5.55, giving him a K/BB ratio of 2.97. His R/9 shriveled to 5.94. Look what these starting pitchers accomplished with Wolf calling balls and strikes:

Pitcher	Date	IP	H	R	ER	BB	K	W/L/ND
Mike Pelfrey	April 9	6.0	4	2	2	4	4	W
Colby Lewis	April 14	5.1	3	2	2	4	10	W
Ervin Santana	April 18	9.0	4	1	1	0	6	W
Ricky Romero	April 18	8.0	5	1	1	2	6	L
Colby Lewis	April 30	9.0	3	0	0	1	10	ND
Cliff Lee	April 30	7.0	3	0	0	0	8	ND
Nick Blackburn	May 4	9.0	11	3	3	1	2	W

If you were tracking this, and you knew Wolf's next home plate assignment would be on May 9 in Oakland, a pitchers' park, and that the starters would be rising stars James Shields of the Rays and Dallas Braden of the Athletics, you would predict — not with certainty, but with confidence — that it would be a low-scoring game. And you would be right — righter than you imagined. Because that night Braden threw the 19th perfect game in major league history. "You do get caught up in it a little bit," Wolf marveled afterward.

Wolf's younger brother Randy has been a major league pitcher since 1999. The Lords of Baseball have prohibited Wolf from calling games his brother pitches except in spring training. Jim Wolf didn't call a single pitch from Randy Wolf until March 15, 2008, when Randy threw four innings of an exhibition game against the Milwaukee Brewers. "They were too busy swinging the bat for me to really have to worry about getting any called strikes," quipped Randy, who added, "He just throws it back harder than most umpires. I've always heard that from guys."

There has been some debate about Wolf calling games pitched by his brother. It's an integrity issue: Do you trust the umpire or not? Those supportive of Jim Wolf argue that if the Lords of Baseball doubt his integrity, he shouldn't be umpiring at all. Otherwise, trust him to do his job, just as teammates trust the catching brothers Bengie, Jose, and Yadier Molina to call tough pitches against each other. Randy Wolf addressed the issue head-on in 2004. "For my brother and I, it [would be] just like any other game. I'd have to throw strikes and he's got to call balls and strikes. The only difference is it will be scrutinized. The microscope would be a little bit bigger on every call." How does his brother feel? "Nobody likes to have their integrity questioned," Randy answered. Would Randy, who has never been ejected from a game, get upset if his brother called a close pitch against him? "I've never shown up an umpire. I don't think I'd start with him," he said.

Few players do start with Jim Wolf, although there are amusing Internet videos of him staring down managers Bobby Cox of Atlanta and Frank Robinson of Washington. Wolf has a very slow fuse, sporting a career ejection rate of just 1.2 percent, little more than half the major league average. And in a June 2010 poll of 100 players conducted by *ESPN The Magazine,* Wolf was rated the third best umpire of all, behind only Jim Joyce and Tim McClelland.

Much as he may conform to the old stereotype of the laid-back Southern Californian, Wolf will do what he considers necessary to keep a game under control. On October 7, 2010, in the second game of the American League Division Series between Texas and Tampa Bay, home plate umpire Wolf deferred to first base umpire Jerry Meals on a 2–2 checked swing by Michael Young of the Rangers. Meals ruled no swing, infuriating Tampa pitcher Chad Qualls, who badly wanted the strikeout. On the very next pitch, Young hit a three-run homer to give the Rangers a 5–0 lead. Rays manager Joe Maddon came out to talk to Qualls. He shouted at Meals from the mound. Crew chief Tim Welke said that Wolf and Meals "showed a lot of restraint," but eventually Maddon went too far (he later confessed that he was trying to provoke an ejection in hopes it would fire up his players) and the normally tolerant Wolf made him the first manager ejected from a postseason game in five years.

Source

Bostrom, Don. "Wolf: Brother Won't Compromise Integrity." *Allentown Morning Call,* April 17, 2004. (October 29, 2010.) http://articles.mcall.com/2004-04-17/sports/3544289_1_jim-wolf-randy-wolf-plate-umpire.

Appendices

Appendix 1. Highest and Lowest Runs per Nine Innings (R/9), 2007
Minimum 150 Innings

Umpire	Innings	2007 R/9
Gerry Davis	310.83	11.81
Larry Vanover	319.5	11.38
James Hoye	315	11.00
Brian Gorman	302.17	10.96
Sam Holbrook	307.5	10.77
Greg Gibson	302.67	10.65
John Hirschbeck	233.17	10.54
Phil Cuzzi	305.33	10.52
Jim Reynolds	312.33	10.46
Dana DeMuth	307.17	10.43
Chad Fairchild	255.5	10.43
Angel Hernandez	314.5	10.36
2007 Average R/9		9.67
Randy Marsh	318.83	8.98
Derryl Cousins	298.83	8.91
Mark Carlson	305.83	8.89
Rob Drake	317.83	8.83
Marvin Hudson	296.5	8.74
Ed Rapuano	304.33	8.69
Doug Eddings	309.17	8.67
Hunter Wendelstedt	296.17	8.63
Mike Everitt	301.67	8.47
Laz Diaz	324.33	8.27
Andy Fletcher	161.67	7.18
Jeff Nelson	182.33	5.82

Appendix 2. Highest and Lowest Runs per Nine Innings (R/9), 2008
Minimum 150 Innings

Umpire	Innings	2008 R/9
Angel Campos	232.5	11.30
Jerry Crawford	194.33	11.21
Chad Fairchild	318.17	11.17
Sam Holbrook	307.5	10.83
Tim McClelland	298.33	10.77
Randy Marsh	168	10.66
Bill Welke	300.5	10.48
Charlie Reliford	245.67	10.40
Jim Reynolds	312.33	10.34
Gary Darling	293.67	10.33
Scott Barry	261.33	10.23
Larry Vanover	285	10.20
2008 Average R/9		9.38
Jeff Nelson	293.33	8.56
Marty Foster	300.33	8.51
Ed Montague	229	8.29
Mike Estabrook	199	8.23
Ted Barrett	305	8.17
Bruce Dreckman	312.67	8.03
Bob Davidson	306	8.03
Paul Emmel	300	8.01
Bill Miller	322.17	7.96
Andy Fletcher	305.83	7.89
Ron Kulpa	294.67	7.61
Bill Hohn	235.5	7.41

Appendix 3. Highest and Lowest Runs per Nine Innings (R/9), 2009
Minimum 150 Innings

Umpire	Innings	2009 R/9
Tim McClelland	315.67	11.55
Tim Tschida	283	11.54
Tim Welke	238.33	11.29
Jeff Nelson	294.83	11.02
Tim Timmons	302.5	10.86
Bill Welke	294.67	10.78
Dan Iassogna	308.5	10.47
Jerry Crawford	208	10.43
Chuck Meriwether	302.5	10.23

Bob Davidson	290.17	10.20
Laz Diaz	293	10.20
Brian Knight	310.17	10.18
2009 Average R/9		9.33
Mark Carlson	308	8.50
Ted Barrett	299.17	8.48
Marvin Hudson	320	8.41
Brian Gorman	293.67	8.40
Sam Holbrook	313	8.40
Chad Fairchild	315.67	8.38
Chris Guccione	296.33	8.23
Todd Tichenor	317.33	8.22
Brian Runge	211.5	8.09
Jerry Layne	296	7.97
Charlie Reliford	195	7.85
Jeff Kellogg	300.83	7.75

Appendix 4. Highest and Lowest Runs per Nine Innings (R/9), 2010
MINIMUM 150 INNINGS

Umpire	Innings	2010 R/9
Todd Tichenor	276	10.53
Mark Carlson	305.5	10.19
Ted Barrett	305.5	10.08
Angel Campos	218.17	10.07
Mike Reilly	293	10.04
Derryl Cousins	302.33	9.94
Tim Welke	315.67	9.89
Marvin Hudson	302.67	9.84
Marty Foster	220.67	9.79
Sam Holbrook	245.17	9.76
C.B. Bucknor	315.5	9.73
Scott Barry	293	9.71
2010 Average R/9		8.86
Tim Timmons	286.83	8.19
Chris Guccione	312	8.13
Joe West	332.83	8.06
Angel Hernandez	312.5	8.04
Mike Estabrook	291.5	8.03
Hunter Wendelstedt	302.83	8.02
Jim Wolf	277.83	7.74
Tim Tschida	302	7.72
Doug Eddings	305.83	7.47

Paul Nauert	294.17	7.25
Greg Gibson	322.83	7.00
James Hoye	306.5	6.78

Appendix 5. Highest and Lowest Walks per Nine Innings (BB/9), 2007
MINIMUM 150 INNINGS

Umpire	Innings	2007 BB/9
Paul Schrieber	277.83	8.00
Gerry Davis	310.83	7.44
Jerry Layne	180.5	7.23
Angel Hernandez	314.5	7.04
Greg Gibson	302.67	6.99
Dana DeMuth	307.17	6.97
Lance Barksdale	309.33	6.84
Chuck Meriwether	304	6.66
Mike Reilly	309.17	6.64
Sam Holbrook	307.5	6.61
Jim Joyce	298.17	6.58
Rick Reed	291.67	6.54
Ed Rapuano	304.33	6.54
2007 Average BB/9		6.12
Hunter Wendelstedt	296.17	5.50
Fieldin Culbreth	301.17	5.50
Gary Darling	290.33	5.46
Laz Diaz	324.33	5.44
Marty Foster	281.67	5.43
Mark Carlson	305.83	5.41
Jim Wolf	291	5.38
Bill Welke	304.67	5.32
Mike Everitt	301.67	5.31
Brian O'Nora	163.17	5.30
Charlie Reliford	222.5	4.98
Andy Fletcher	161.67	4.79
Doug Eddings	309.17	4.63

Appendix 6. Highest and Lowest Walks per Nine Innings (BB/9), 2008
MINIMUM 150 INNINGS

Umpire	Innings	2008 BB/9
Lance Barksdale	297.17	8.00
Paul Schrieber	270.33	7.86

Umpire	Innings	BB/9
Jerry Crawford	194.33	7.69
Jerry Layne	276.5	7.55
Tim McClelland	298.33	7.39
Marvin Hudson	305	7.35
Chad Fairchild	318.17	7.30
Alfonso Marquez	319.17	7.22
Mark Wegner	307.33	7.17
Tim Tschida	299.33	7.16
Randy Marsh	168	7.13
Adrian Johnson	322	7.04
2008 Average BB/9		6.24
Paul Emmel	300	5.46
Ted Barrett	305	5.46
Tim Timmons	315.17	5.45
Paul Nauert	307.33	5.45
Brian Runge	300.83	5.44
Laz Diaz	302.33	5.42
Bill Miller	322.17	5.39
Brian Gorman	288.33	5.34
Brian O'Nora	292	5.30
Eric Cooper	300.5	5.30
Gary Cederstrom	313	5.23
Jeff Nelson	293.33	5.12

Appendix 7. Highest and Lowest Walks per Nine Innings (BB/9), 2009
MINIMUM 150 INNINGS

Umpire	Innings	2009 BB/9
Tim McClelland	315.67	8.44
Jerry Crawford	208	8.18
Tim Tschida	283	8.05
Jeff Nelson	294.83	7.39
Adrian Johnson	316.67	7.33
Mike Reilly	300.67	7.27
Tim Welke	238.33	7.25
Paul Schrieber	298.17	7.24
Jeff Kellogg	300.83	7.21
Scott Barry	346.33	7.20
Joe West	300.17	7.14
Dana DeMuth	297	7.12
2009 Average BB/9		6.42
Doug Eddings	311.17	5.67
Mike Winters	273.5	5.66

Umpire	Innings	BB/9
Mike Estabrook	209.33	5.63
Brian Gorman	293.67	5.61
Bill Miller	318	5.60
Jerry Meals	303.83	5.60
Chad Fairchild	315.67	5.59
Angel Campos	242.17	5.57
Brian Runge	211.5	5.53
Brian O'Nora	300.17	5.43
Tony Randazzo	300.17	5.01
Charlie Reliford	195	4.94

Appendix 8. Highest and Lowest Walks per Nine Innings (BB/9), 2010
MINIMUM 150 INNINGS

Umpire	Innings	2010 BB/9
Angel Campos	218.17	7.30
Jerry Crawford	206	7.25
Todd Tichenor	276	7.09
Mike Reilly	293	7.06
Kerwin Danley	295	7.02
Mark Wegner	230.17	7.00
Adrian Johnson	297.83	6.98
Jerry Layne	278	6.93
Mike Winters	292.17	6.84
Mark Carlson	305.5	6.83
Alfonso Marquez	308.5	6.80
Ron Kulpa	316.67	6.79
2010 Average BB/9		6.05
Paul Emmel	300.17	5.46
Dana DeMuth	298.67	5.45
Paul Nauert	294.17	5.42
Phil Cuzzi	309.17	5.41
Wally Bell	302.5	5.36
Bill Welke	272.33	5.29
Brian O'Nora	304.67	5.26
Mike Estabrook	291.5	5.22
Bill Miller	297	5.15
Tim Timmons	286.83	5.08
Tony Randazzo	300.83	5.00
Brian Runge	211.83	4.80

Appendix 9. Highest and Lowest Strikeouts per Nine Innings (K/9), 2007
MINIMUM 150 INNINGS

Umpire	Innings	2007 K/9
Mark Wegner	294.5	15.46
Tom Hallion	291.5	15.28
Andy Fletcher	161.67	15.20
Doug Eddings	309.17	14.99
Chad Fairchild	255.5	14.90
Bill Miller	313.5	14.50
Laz Diaz	324.33	14.46
Bill Welke	304.67	14.15
Rob Drake	317.83	14.07
Mark Carlson	305.83	14.07
Jim Reynolds	312.33	14.03
James Hoye	315	14.03
2007 Average K/9		13.34
Dana DeMuth	307.17	12.57
Tim McClelland	333	12.54
Alfonso Marquez	276.5	12.50
Gerry Davis	310.83	12.48
Jeff Kellogg	306.67	12.41
Kerwin Danley	303.5	12.37
Jim Joyce	298.17	12.35
Jerry Layne	180.5	12.32
Brian O'Nora	163.17	12.13
Tim Tschida	310.33	11.92
Hunter Wendelstedt	296.17	11.79
Randy Marsh	318.83	11.69

Appendix 10. Highest and Lowest Strikeouts per Nine Innings (K/9), 2008
MINIMUM 150 INNINGS

Umpire	Innings	2008 K/9
Phil Cuzzi	295.5	15.56
Dan Iassogna	293	15.42
Tim Tschida	299.33	14.82
Angel Campos	232.5	14.79
Ron Kulpa	294.67	14.75
Ted Barrett	305	14.67
Tim Welke	306	14.59
Dale Scott	288.17	14.55
Ed Hickox	285.33	14.51
Jeff Nelson	293.33	14.39
Laz Diaz	302.33	14.32
James Hoye	343	14.22
2008 Average K/9		13.65
Kerwin Danley	220.5	13.06
Angel Hernandez	299.33	13.02
Scott Barry	261.33	13.02
Greg Gibson	333.83	12.91
Jeff Kellogg	301.17	12.79
Jim Joyce	307.17	12.77
Derryl Cousins	317.83	12.77
Paul Schrieber	270.33	12.68
Tim McClelland	298.33	12.37
Ed Rapuano	318.17	12.33
Jerry Crawford	194.33	12.23
Randy Marsh	168	11.95

Appendix 11. Highest and Lowest Strikeouts per Nine Innings (K/9), 2009
MINIMUM 150 INNINGS

Umpire	Innings	2009 K/9
Mike Reilly	300.67	15.89
Jim Reynolds	253.33	15.56
Rob Drake	339.83	15.33
Chris Guccione	296.33	15.19
Jerry Crawford	208	14.80
Andy Fletcher	298.17	14.79
Paul Nauert	303.67	14.79
Marvin Hudson	320	14.77
Paul Emmel	299.67	14.75
Larry Vanover	295	14.74
Gary Cederstrom	281	14.64
Tim Welke	238.33	14.58
Bill Miller	318	14.58
2009 Average K/9		13.97
Jeff Nelson	294.83	13.28
Bill Hohn	210.83	13.28
Lance Barksdale	308.83	13.23
Fieldin Culbreth	300.67	13.23
Mike Winters	273.5	13.23
James Hoye	369	13.15

Umpire	Innings	K/9
Jim Joyce	305.17	13.06
Gerry Davis	303.5	12.93
Ted Barrett	299.17	12.85
Greg Gibson	248.67	12.70
Randy Marsh	286.17	12.49
Bruce Dreckman	232.83	12.14

Appendix 12. Highest and Lowest Strikeouts per Nine Innings (K/9), 2010
MINIMUM 150 INNINGS

Umpire	Innings	2010 K/9
Mike Winters	292.17	16.23
Gary Darling	305.17	15.78
Lance Barksdale	291.33	15.32
Kerwin Danley	295	15.32
Marty Foster	220.67	15.25
Brian Runge	211.83	15.25
Wally Bell	302.5	15.20
Chad Fairchild	288.5	15.16
Jim Reynolds	252.17	15.10
Dan Iassogna	297	15.09
Tim Welke	315.67	15.05
Dana DeMuth	298.67	15.04
2010 Average K/9		14.26
Chris Guccione	312	13.67
Mike Reilly	293	13.67
Tim McClelland	283.17	13.54
Tim Timmons	286.83	13.49
Scott Barry	293	13.42
Gerry Davis	303	13.40
Joe West	332.83	13.06
Alfonso Marquez	308.5	12.98
Mark Wegner	230.17	12.98
Todd Tichenor	276	12.98
Jerry Crawford	206	12.67
Bill Hohn	298.5	12.30

Appendix 13. Highest and Lowest Strikeout-to-Walk Ratio, 2007
MINIMUM 150 INNINGS

Umpire	Innings	2007 K/BB
Doug Eddings	309.17	3.24
Andy Fletcher	161.67	3.17
Charlie Reliford	222.5	2.70
Tom Hallion	291.5	2.68
Bill Welke	304.67	2.66
Mark Carlson	305.83	2.60
Mark Wegner	294.5	2.57
Marty Foster	281.67	2.55
Mike Everitt	301.67	2.55
Jeff Nelson	182.33	2.52
Jim Wolf	291	2.49
Eric Cooper	283	2.46
2007 Average K/BB		2.18
Brian Knight	247.83	1.96
Chuck Meriwether	304	1.96
Mike Reilly	309.17	1.91
Tim Tschida	310.33	1.88
Lance Barksdale	309.33	1.88
Jim Joyce	298.17	1.88
Greg Gibson	302.67	1.83
Dana DeMuth	307.17	1.80
Angel Hernandez	314.5	1.80
Randy Marsh	318.83	1.79
Jerry Layne	180.5	1.70
Gerry Davis	310.83	1.68
Paul Schrieber	277.83	1.64

Appendix 14. Highest and Lowest Strikeout-to-Walk Ratio, 2008
MINIMUM 150 INNINGS

Umpire	Innings	2008 K/BB
Jeff Nelson	293.33	2.81
Ted Barrett	305	2.69
Phil Cuzzi	295.5	2.67
Ron Kulpa	294.67	2.65
Laz Diaz	302.33	2.64
Dan Iassogna	293	2.61
Brian Gorman	288.33	2.60
Tim Timmons	315.17	2.60
Gary Cederstrom	313	2.59
Doug Eddings	306.33	2.57
Brian Runge	300.83	2.55
Paul Emmel	300	2.54
2008 Average K/BB		2.19

Umpire	Innings	K/BB
Mark Wegner	307.33	1.93
Fieldin Culbreth	305.83	1.93
Scott Barry	261.33	1.91
Derryl Cousins	317.83	1.89
Marvin Hudson	305	1.86
Alfonso Marquez	319.17	1.85
Chad Fairchild	318.17	1.82
Jerry Layne	276.5	1.77
Randy Marsh	168	1.68
Tim McClelland	298.33	1.67
Lance Barksdale	297.17	1.66
Paul Schrieber	270.33	1.61
Jerry Crawford	194.33	1.59

Appendix 15. Highest and Lowest Strikeout-to-Walk Ratio, 2009

MINIMUM 150 INNINGS

Umpire	Innings	2009 K/BB
Charlie Reliford	195	2.80
Tony Randazzo	300.17	2.73
Brian Runge	211.5	2.63
Bill Miller	318	2.60
Rob Drake	339.83	2.58
Angel Campos	242.17	2.58
Brian O'Nora	300.17	2.57
Jerry Meals	303.83	2.51
Doug Eddings	311.17	2.48
Larry Vanover	295	2.48
Brian Gorman	293.67	2.47
Paul Emmel	299.67	2.44
Gary Darling	245.33	2.44
2009 Average K/BB		2.18
Fieldin Culbreth	300.67	1.92
Jeff Kellogg	300.83	1.91
Paul Schrieber	298.17	1.91
Lance Barksdale	308.83	1.91
Jim Joyce	305.17	1.87
Scott Barry	346.33	1.86
Adrian Johnson	316.67	1.83
Jerry Crawford	208	1.81
Jeff Nelson	294.83	1.80
Randy Marsh	286.17	1.76

Umpire	Innings	K/BB
Tim Tschida	283	1.68
Tim McClelland	315.67	1.62

Appendix 16. Highest and Lowest Strikeout-to-Walk Ratio, 2010

MINIMUM 150 INNINGS

Umpire	Innings	2010 K/BB
Brian Runge	211.83	3.18
Bill Miller	297	2.92
Tony Randazzo	300.83	2.86
Wally Bell	302.5	2.84
Mike Estabrook	291.5	2.82
Dana DeMuth	298.67	2.76
Paul Emmel	300.17	2.74
Phil Cuzzi	309.17	2.73
Gary Darling	305.17	2.73
Marty Foster	220.67	2.71
Tim Welke	315.67	2.69
Bill Welke	272.33	2.69
2010 Average K/BB		2.36
Ron Kulpa	316.67	2.10
Jeff Nelson	301.5	2.08
Adrian Johnson	297.83	2.06
Mark Carlson	305.5	2.06
Jerry Layne	278	1.98
Bill Hohn	298.5	1.95
Mike Reilly	293	1.93
Angel Campos	218.17	1.92
Alfonso Marquez	308.5	1.91
Mark Wegner	230.17	1.85
Todd Tichenor	276	1.83
Jerry Crawford	206	1.75

Appendix 17. Runs per Nine Innings (R/9), 2007–2010

MINIMUM 500 INNINGS

Umpire	Innings	R/9
1. Gerry Davis	1,200	10.18
2. Tim McClelland	1,230.17	10.14
3. Jerry Crawford	743.83	10.08
4. Angel Campos	746.84	10.07

#	Umpire	Innings	R/9
5.	Tim Welke	1,088.5	10.06
6.	Sam Holbrook	1,173.17	9.94
7.	Larry Vanover	1,164.67	9.91
8.	Jim Reynolds	1,130.17	9.90
9.	Mike Reilly	1,206.67	9.87
10.	Scott Barry	971.83	9.79
11.	Tim Tschida	1,194.67	9.79
12.	Bill Welke	1,172.17	9.77
13.	Chad Fairchild	1,177.83	9.74
14.	Brian Knight	1,119.17	9.74
15.	Randy Marsh	773	9.72
16.	Jerry Meals	1,190.33	9.60
17.	Dana DeMuth	1,198.33	9.57
18.	Brian Gorman	1,181.67	9.56
19.	Tim Timmons	1,196	9.56
20.	Chuck Meriwether	901.5	9.55
21.	Ed Montague	545	9.53
22.	Ed Hickox	922.33	9.52
23.	Paul Schrieber	986.17	9.50
24.	Rick Reed	504.33	9.48
25.	Adrian Johnson	1,078.33	9.47
26.	Kerwin Danley	904.17	9.47
27.	Lance Barksdale	1,206.67	9.46
28.	Eric Cooper	1,164.17	9.46
29.	Dan Iassogna	1,193	9.45
30.	C.B. Bucknor	1,211.17	9.44
31.	Todd Tichenor	740.67	9.43
32.	John Hirschbeck	691.33	9.43
33.	Alfonso Marquez	922	9.41
34.	Dale Scott	1,225.33	9.40
35.	Mike Winters	1,116.67	9.39
36.	Charlie Reliford	663.17	9.38
37.	Wally Bell	1,253.67	9.35
38.	Tony Randazzo	904.83	9.34
	Average R/9		9.31
39.	Brian Runge	1,039.17	9.28
40.	Gary Darling	1,134.5	9.28
41.	Marvin Hudson	1,224.17	9.27
42.	Jim Joyce	1,162.17	9.26
43.	Derryl Cousins	1,223.17	9.24
44.	Tom Hallion	1,193.5	9.21
45.	Ted Barrett	1,216.83	9.21
46.	Greg Gibson	1,208	9.19
47.	Fieldin Culbreth	1,207.33	9.18
48.	Mark Wegner	1,150.17	9.17
49.	Mark Carlson	927.83	9.16
50.	Marty Foster	1,088.17	9.16
51.	Mike Everitt	1,252.67	9.15
52.	Angel Hernandez	1,234	9.15
53.	Joe West	1,252.67	9.15
54.	Jim Wolf	1,166.33	9.14
55.	Laz Diaz	1,222.67	9.13
56.	James Hoye	1,333.5	9.12
57.	Phil Cuzzi	1,213	9.10
58.	Ed Rapuano	1,242	9.09
59.	Rob Drake	1,297.83	9.09
60.	Paul Nauert	1,218.83	9.09
61.	Jeff Kellogg	1,210.67	9.07
62.	Bruce Dreckman	1,094.17	9.01
63.	Brian O'Nora	1,060	8.97
64.	Hunter Wendelstedt	1,222.17	8.97
65.	Mike DiMuro	985.17	8.96
66.	Gary Cederstrom	1,189.33	8.94
67.	Bob Davidson	1,232.83	8.93
68.	Chris Guccione	1,288.83	8.90
69.	Bill Miller	1,250.67	8.83
70.	Paul Emmel	1,156.17	8.80
71.	Jeff Nelson	1,072	8.80
72.	Ron Kulpa	1,121.33	8.79
73.	Doug Eddings	1,232.5	8.76
74.	Jerry Layne	1,031	8.69
75.	Bill Hohn	771	8.40
76.	Andy Fletcher	1,041.83	8.28
77.	Mike Estabrook	728.83	8.13

Appendix 18. Walks per Nine Innings (BB/9), 2007–2010

MINIMUM 500 INNINGS

#	Umpire	Innings	BB/9
1.	Paul Schrieber	986.17	7.65
2.	Jerry Crawford	743.83	7.50
3.	Tim McClelland	1,230.17	7.07
4.	Adrian Johnson	1,078.33	6.94
5.	Jerry Layne	1,031	6.90
6.	Lance Barksdale	1,206.67	6.89
7.	Randy Marsh	773	6.86
8.	Mike Reilly	1,206.67	6.84
9.	Scott Barry	971.83	6.83
10.	Rick Reed	504.33	6.78

#	Umpire	Innings	BB/9
11.	Tim Tschida	1,194.67	6.77
12.	Todd Tichenor	740.67	6.71
13.	Alfonso Marquez	922	6.67
14.	Derryl Cousins	1,223.17	6.67
15.	Gerry Davis	1,200	6.60
16.	Mark Wegner	1,150.17	6.60
17.	Marvin Hudson	1,224.17	6.53
18.	Jeff Kellogg	1,210.67	6.47
19.	Greg Gibson	1,208	6.46
20.	Kerwin Danley	904.17	6.42
21.	Brian Knight	1,119.17	6.41
22.	Sam Holbrook	1,173.17	6.38
23.	Ed Montague	545	6.37
24.	Ed Rapuano	1,242	6.36
25.	Dan Iassogna	1,193	6.36
26.	Jim Joyce	1,162.17	6.35
27.	Fieldin Culbreth	1,207.33	6.34
28.	Bill Hohn	771	6.33
29.	Angel Hernandez	1,234	6.29
30.	Joe West	1,252.67	6.29
31.	Ed Hickox	922.33	6.28
32.	Chad Fairchild	1,117.83	6.27
33.	Jeff Nelson	1,072	6.27
34.	Dana DeMuth	1,198.33	6.27
35.	C.B. Bucknor	1,211.17	6.26
36.	Angel Campos	746.83	6.25
37.	Chris Guccione	1,288.83	6.25
38.	Mark Carlson	927.83	6.25
39.	Ron Kulpa	1,121.33	6.24
40.	James Hoye	1,333.5	6.22
	Average BB/9		6.21
41.	Chuck Meriwether	901.5	6.20
42.	Rob Drake	1,297.83	6.18
43.	Andy Fletcher	1,041.83	6.18
44.	Dale Scott	1,225.33	6.17
45.	Bruce Dreckman	1,094.17	6.14
46.	Tim Welke	1,088.5	6.14
47.	Bob Davidson	1,232.83	6.13
48.	Jim Reynolds	1,130.17	6.10
49.	Mike DiMuro	985.17	6.08
50.	Larry Vanover	1,164.67	6.07
51.	Mike Winters	1,116.67	6.06
52.	Jim Wolf	1,166.33	6.06
53.	Jerry Meals	1,190.33	6.05
54.	Hunter Wendelstedt	1,222.17	6.03
55.	Gary Cederstrom	1,189.33	6.02
56.	Marty Foster	1,088.17	6.01
57.	Tom Hallion	1,193.5	6.00
58.	Wally Bell	1,253.67	5.99
59.	Mike Everitt	1,252.67	5.99
60.	Tim Timmons	1,196	5.93
61.	Ted Barrett	1,216.83	5.91
62.	John Hirschbeck	691.33	5.88
63.	Brian Gorman	1,181.67	5.80
64.	Laz Diaz	1,222.67	5.80
65.	Gary Darling	1,134.5	5.80
66.	Phil Cuzzi	1,213	5.79
67.	Bill Welke	1,172.17	5.77
68.	Paul Emmel	1,156.17	5.66
69.	Charlie Reliford	663.17	5.66
70.	Paul Nauert	1,218.83	5.64
71.	Brian Runge	1,039.17	5.57
72.	Eric Cooper	1,164.17	5.57
73.	Bill Miller	1,250.67	5.56
74.	Mike Estabrook	728.83	5.47
75.	Tony Randazzo	904.83	5.34
76.	Brian O'Nora	1,060	5.32
77.	Doug Eddings	1,232.5	5.32

Appendix 19. Strikeouts per Nine Innings (K/9), 2007–2010

MINIMUM 500 INNINGS

Umpire	Innings	K/9
1. Andy Fletcher	1,041.83	14.59
2. Rob Drake	1,297.83	14.56
3. Tim Welke	1,088.5	14.50
4. Phil Cuzzi	1,213	14.46
5. Angel Campos	746.83	14.42
6. Bill Miller	1,250.67	14.38
7. Jim Reynolds	1,130.17	14.37
8. Dan Iassogna	1,193	14.36
9. Doug Eddings	1,232.5	14.35
10. Paul Emmel	1,156.17	14.33
11. Marty Foster	1,088.17	14.32
12. Brian Runge	1,039.17	14.25
13. Mike Winters	1,116.67	14.23
14. Tom Hallion	1,193.5	14.21
15. Laz Diaz	1,222.67	14.21
16. Ron Kulpa	1,121.33	14.16

17. Wally Bell	1,253.67	14.14
18. Mark Wegner	1,150.17	14.13
19. Mike DiMuro	985.17	14.12
20. Gary Darling	1,134.5	14.12
21. Bill Welke	1,172.17	14.12
22. Dale Scott	1,225.33	14.12
23. Chad Fairchild	1,177.83	14.11
24. Mark Carlson	927.83	14.09
25. Gary Cederstrom	1,189.33	14.05
26. Jim Wolf	1,166.33	13.99
27. Mike Everitt	1,252.67	13.99
28. Mike Reilly	1,206.67	13.98
29. John Hirschbeck	691.33	13.93
30. Marvin Hudson	1,224.17	13.92
31. Jeff Nelson	1,072	13.90
32. Larry Vanover	1,164.67	13.90
33. Ed Hickox	922.33	13.89
34. Mike Estabrook	728.83	13.87
35. Eric Cooper	1,164.17	13.86
36. James Hoye	1,333.5	13.85
37. Ted Barrett	1,216.83	13.82
38. Dana DeMuth	1,198.33	13.81
Average K/9		13.81
39. Brian Gorman	1,181.67	13.80
40. Adrian Johnson	1,078.33	13.80
41. Paul Nauert	1,218.83	13.79
42. Chris Guccione	1,288.83	13.78
43. Tim Timmons	1,196	13.72
44. C.B. Bucknor	1,211.17	13.71
45. Ed Rapuano	1,242	13.70
46. Chuck Meriwether	901.5	13.68
47. Jerry Meals	1,190.33	13.67
48. Charlie Reliford	663.17	13.65
49. Lance Barksdale	1,206.67	13.65
50. Tony Randazzo	904.83	13.64
51. Sam Holbrook	1,173.17	13.62
52. Derryl Cousins	1,223.17	13.60
53. Tim Tschida	1,194.67	13.60
54. Kerwin Danley	904.17	13.59
55. Bob Davidson	1,232.83	13.57
56. Brian O'Nora	1,060	13.56
57. Jerry Layne	1,031	13.54
58. Rick Reed	504.33	13.53
59. Bruce Dreckman	1,094.17	13.45
60. Hunter Wendelstedt	1,222.17	13.44
61. Angel Hernandez	1,234	13.43
62. Ed Montague	545	13.43
63. Brian Knight	1,119.17	13.36
64. Todd Tichenor	740.67	13.35
65. Fieldin Culbreth	1,207.33	13.33
66. Joe West	1,252.67	13.31
67. Jeff Kellogg	1,210.67	13.27
68. Paul Schrieber	986.17	13.25
69. Scott Barry	971.83	13.24
70. Greg Gibson	1,208	13.19
71. Jerry Crawford	743.83	13.13
72. Gerry Davis	1,200	13.06
73. Jim Joyce	1,162.17	13.06
74. Bill Hohn	771	13.05
75. Tim McClelland	1,230.17	13.03
76. Alfonso Marquez	922	13.00
77. Randy Marsh	773	12.04

Appendix 20. Strikeout-to-Walk Ratio (K/BB), 2007–2010

MINIMUM 500 INNINGS

Umpire	*Innings*	*K/BB*
1. Doug Eddings	1,232.5	2.70
2. Bill Miller	1,250.67	2.59
3. Brian Runge	1,039.17	2.56
4. Tony Randazzo	904.83	2.55
5. Brian O'Nora	1,060	2.55
6. Mike Estabrook	728.83	2.53
7. Paul Emmel	1,156.17	2.53
8. Phil Cuzzi	1,213	2.50
9. Eric Cooper	1,164.17	2.49
10. Laz Diaz	1,222.67	2.45
11. Bill Welke	1,172.17	2.45
12. Paul Nauert	1,218.83	2.45
13. Gary Darling	1,134.5	2.44
14. Charlie Reliford	663.17	2.41
15. Marty Foster	1,088.17	2.38
16. Brian Gorman	1,181.67	2.38
17. Tom Hallion	1,193.5	2.37
18. John Hirschbeck	691.33	2.37
19. Andy Fletcher	1,041.83	2.36
20. Tim Welke	1,088.5	2.36
21. Wally Bell	1,253.67	2.36
22. Rob Drake	1,297.83	2.36

#	Name	Value	Ratio	#	Name	Value	Ratio
23.	Jim Reynolds	1,130.17	2.36	50.	Mark Wegner	1,150.17	2.14
24.	Mike Winters	1,116.67	2.35	51.	Sam Holbrook	1,173.17	2.14
25.	Ted Barrett	1,216.83	2.34	52.	Angel Hernandez	1,234	2.13
26.	Gary Cederstrom	1,189.33	2.34	53.	Marvin Hudson	1,224.17	2.13
27.	Mike Everitt	1,252.67	2.33	54.	Joe West	1,252.67	2.12
28.	Mike DiMuro	985.17	2.32	55.	Kerwin Danley	904.17	2.12
29.	Tim Timmons	1,196	2.31	56.	Ed Montague	545	2.11
30.	Jim Wolf	1,166.33	2.31	57.	Fieldin Culbreth	1,207.33	2.10
31.	Angel Campos	746.83	2.31	58.	Brian Knight	1,119.17	2.08
32.	Larry Vanover	1,164.67	2.29	59.	Bill Hohn	771	2.06
33.	Dale Scott	1,225.33	2.29	60.	Jim Joyce	1,162.17	2.06
34.	Ron Kulpa	1,121.33	2.27	61.	Jeff Kellogg	1,210.67	2.05
35.	Jerry Meals	1,190.33	2.26	62.	Mike Reilly	1,206.67	2.04
36.	Dan Iassogna	1,193	2.26	63.	Greg Gibson	1,208	2.04
37.	Mark Carlson	927.83	2.26	64.	Derryl Cousins	1,223.17	2.04
38.	Chad Fairchild	1,177.83	2.25	65.	Tim Tschida	1,194.67	2.01
39.	Hunter Wendelstedt	1,222.17	2.23	66.	Rick Reed	504.33	1.99
40.	James Hoye	1,333.5	2.23	67.	Todd Tichenor	740.67	1.99
41.	Jeff Nelson	1,072	2.22	68.	Adrian Johnson	1,078.33	1.99
				69.	Lance Barksdale	1,206.67	1.98
	Average K/BB		2.22	70.	Gerry Davis	1,200	1.98
42.	Bob Davidson	1,232.83	2.21	71.	Jerry Layne	1,031	1.96
43.	Ed Hickox	922.33	2.21	72.	Alfonso Marquez	922	1.95
44.	Chuck Meriwether	901.5	2.21	73.	Scott Barry	971.83	1.94
45.	Chris Guccione	1,288.83	2.21	74.	Tim McClelland	1,230.17	1.84
46.	Dana DeMuth	1,198.33	2.20	75.	Randy Marsh	773	1.76
47.	C.B. Bucknor	1,211.17	2.19	76.	Jerry Crawford	743.83	1.75
48.	Bruce Dreckman	1,094.17	2.19	77.	Paul Schrieber	986.17	1.73
49.	Ed Rapuano	1,242	2.15				

Index

Main entries are in **boldface**.

Aaron, Henry 48, 96, 111
Abbott, Jim 94
Abreu, Bobby 105
Adrenoleukodystrophy (ALD) 95–96
Air Force, United States 36
Albuquerque Journal 71
Alderson, Sandy 108
All-Star Break 36, 151, 160, 173
All-Star Game 63, 89, 127, 144, 146, 162; Triple-A 44, 132, 138, 165
Allen, Dick 111
Allentown, Pennsylvania 138
Alomar, Roberto 13, 95–96, 108
Alou, Moises 76
Alvarez, Pedro 85, 138
American League Championship Series 41, 71, 115, 117, 119, 121, 151, 157, 164
American League Division Series 33, 52, 84, 86, 88, 181
American Legion 135
Anderson, Brett 32
Anderson, Garret 88
Anderson, Marlon 34
Andrus, Elvis 134
Andujar, Joaquin 61
Angel Stadium 145
Apodaca, Bob 110
Arizona Daily Star 97
Arizona Diamondbacks 55, 84, 103, 107, 110
Arizona State Legislature 116
Arizona Umpiring Academy 68
Arlington, Texas 65, 111
Arroyo, Bronson 119
As They See 'Em: A Fan's Travels in the Land of Umpires 7, 161
Ashland, Kentucky 146
Ashland Independent 147
Associated Press 29
Association of Minor League Umpires 16, 162
AT&T Park 9, 128, 130
Atlanta Braves 25, 41, 45–46, 49, 59, 72, 74, 78, 84, 98, 99, 100, 103, 105, 110, 123, 128, 143, 151, 168, 180
Atlantic League 43
Ausmus, Brad 61
Aybar, Erick 35, 116

Bailey, Jeff 159
Baker, Dusty 70, 74
Baker, Jeff 23
Baker, John 98
Baldelli, Rocco 55
Balentien, Wladimir 144
Balfour, Grant 30
Baltimore Orioles 2, 36, 39, 44, 45, 65, 72, 73, 85, 95–96, 103, 108, 112, 125, 133, 134, 144, 161, 171
Baltimore Sun 96
Bando, Sal 143
Barajas, Rod 55
Barden, Brian 22
Barksdale, Lance 2, **21–22**, 45, 184, 186, 187, 188, 189, 191, 192
Barrett, Lance **22–23**
Barrett, Michael 168
Barrett, Ted **23–25**, 68, 117, 121, 183, 184, 185, 186, 187, 189, 190, 191, 192
Barry, Scott 16, **25–26**, 117, 183, 184, 185, 186, 187, 188, 189, 191, 192
Bartman, Steve 76
Baseball Assistance Team 167
Baseball Digest 7
Baseball Prospectus 2, 12
Baseball Reference 2
Baseball Tonight 81
Baton Rouge, Louisiana 27
Batting Average (definition) 11
Battle Creek, Michigan 145
Battle Creek Enquirer 145
Bautista, Denny 106
Bautista, Jose 93
BB/K (definition) 8
BB/9 (definition) 8
Beal, Damien **26–27**
Beckett, Josh 41, 159–160

Bell, Wally **28–29**, 67, 111, 159, 185, 187, 188, 189, 190, 191
Bellino, Dan 16, **29–31**, 68, 130, 160
Beltran, Carlos 154
Beltre, Adrian 31
Bergen Record 176
Berkman, Lance 28, 29, 43, 137
Berkshire Eagle 44
Berra, Yogi 120
Betancourt, Yuniesky 77
Biel, Jessica 111
Black, Bud 159, 178
Blackburn, Nick 180
Blalock, Hank 55, 106
Blanton, Joe 103
Blaser, Cory **31–32**
Bloomberg.com 90
Bloomquist, Willie 73
Blue Cowboy 176
Blue for Kids 135
Blum, Geoff 77
Bochy, Bruce 57, 107, 127, 168
Bonderman, Jeremy 149
Bonds, Barry 48, 76, 96, 114, 127, 128
Boston Red Sox 2, 6, 24, 26, 31, 33, 36, 41, 45, 51, 68–69, 72, 74–75, 84, 98, 101, 110–111, 112, 113, 117–118, 119, 125, 128, 135, 136, 140, 147, 157, 159, 164, 168–169, 171, 172, 176–177
Bourjos, Peter 152
Bourn, Michael 45
Bowa, Larry 105
Boyer, Blaine 151
Braden, Dallas 180
Bradley, Milton 178
Braun, Ryan 131
Brett, George 120–121, 173
Brinkman, Joe 176
Brock, Lou 27, 42, 128
The Bronx, New York 81, 118
Brooklyn Dodgers 5, 153
Brooks Baseball 2
Brown, Daren 32
Broxton, Jonathan 107

Index

Buchholz, Taylor 106
Buckner, Bill 128
Bucknor, C.B. 15, **32-34**, 52, 91, 176, 184, 189, 190, 191, 192
Buehrle, Mark 45, 130, 131, 161, 176
Burks, Ellis 178
Burnett, A.J. 63
Burns, Mike 145
Burrell, Pat 111
Busch Stadium (old and new) 99, 113
Bush, Dave 141-142
Butler, Pennsylvania 123

Cabrera, Daniel 171
Cabrera, Everth 154
Cabrera, Melky 52
Cabrera, Miguel 109, 136
Cabrera, Orlando 73
Cain, Matt 35, 45, 72
Calling for Christ 24, 68, 117
Cameron, Mike 30, 40, 110, 135
Campos, Angel 16, **34-36**, 126, 183, 184, 185, 186, 188, 190, 192
Cancer 96, 135
Cano, Robinson 11, 61, 122, 151
Cape Cod, Massachusetts 111
Capuano, Chris 85
Carapazza, Victor **36-37**, 130, 160
Carlson, Mark **37-39**, 160, 167, 183, 184, 185, 186, 187, 188, 189, 190, 191, 192
Carmona, Fausto 103
Carpenter, Chris 123
Carroll, Jamey 150
Casey at the Bat 6
Castillo, Luis 76
Causey, Kevin **39-40**
Cederstrom, Gary **40-42**, 185, 186, 187, 189, 190, 191, 192
Chamberlain, Joba 124
Championship, Triple-A 44
Chapman, Aroldis 69
Chicago Bears 91
Chicago Cubs 12, 23, 25, 29, 30, 35, 37, 38, 72, 76, 91, 123, 124, 133, 137, 139, 163, 168
Chicago White Sox 30, 32, 45, 51, 53, 57, 61, 64, 65, 71, 105, 111, 130, 131, 134, 149, 154, 161, 165, 176
Christianity 17, 24
Chunichi Dragons 66
Church, Ryan 149
Cincinnati Reds 35, 39, 49, 56, 69-70, 74, 85, 96, 101, 127, 136, 144, 149, 172
Citi Field 44, 69
Clark, Al 162
Clemens, Roger 29, 118, 124, 148
Clendenon, Donn 65
Cleveland Indians 5, 32, 35, 39, 41, 43, 51, 55, 58, 69, 93, 94, 102, 103, 109, 128, 143, 150, 165, 170, 172, 178
Cleveland Plain Dealer 87, 176
Cobb, Ty 128
Coghlan, Chris 66
Colbert, Craig 159
Coleman, Casey 139
Coleman, Leonard 53, 90
Collins, Dave 111
Colon, Bartolo 145
Colon, Delfin **42-43**
Colorado Rockies 32, 54, 72, 90, 110, 114, 118, 123, 126, 129, 139-140, 143, 144, 178
Columbus, Ohio 102
Columbus Dispatch 69
Comerica Park 109, 143
Concussions 1, 55, 80, 93, 96, 97, 102, 116, 127, 136, 151, 154
Cone, David 25
Conroy, Chris **43-44**
Contreras, Jose 149
Coomer, Ron 91
Cooper, Cecil 43, 45, 130
Cooper, Don 134
Cooper, Eric **44-46**, 185, 187, 189, 190, 191
Coors Field 9, 131
Corey, Bryan 159
Correia, Kevin 161
Cossacks 155
Costner, Kevin 144
Counsell, Craig 40, 149
Cousins, Derryl **46-48**, 49, 145, 183, 184, 186, 188, 189, 190, 191, 192
Cox, Bobby 25, 46, 59, 78, 98, 105, 180
Crawford, Carl 73, 90, 133
Crawford, Jerry 13, 15, **48-50**, 71, 117, 121, 136, 145, 160, 163, 183, 185, 187, 188, 189, 191, 192
Crawford, Shag 50
Crede, Joe 71
Crisp, Coco 110, 171
Cruz, Nelson 151
Cuddyer, Michael 131, 141
Culbreth, Fieldin 41-42, **50-52**, 184, 186, 188, 189, 190, 191, 192
Culbreth, Fieldin IV 52
Cuzzi, Phil **52-54**, 183, 185, 186, 187, 188, 189, 190, 191

Damon, Johnny 41, 86
Danley, Kerwin **54-56**, 83, 134, 185, 186, 187, 189, 190, 191, 192
Darling, Gary **56-58**, 98, 165, 183, 184, 187, 188, 189, 190, 191
Davidson, Bob 15, 23, **58-60**, 97, 132, 146, 162, 164, 179, 183, 184, 189, 190, 191, 192
Davis, Gerry 9, 10, 11, 48, **60-61**, 86, 121, 123, 131, 159, 183, 184, 186, 187, 188, 190, 191, 192
Davis, Rajai 165
Daytona Beach Shores, Florida 94
Dead Ball Era 9
DeJean, Mike 90
Delgado, Carlos 146
DeMuth, Dana 8, **62-63**, 131, 183, 184, 185, 186, 187, 188, 189, 190, 191, 192
Denkinger, Don 13, 109
DeRosa, Mark 133
Desmond, Ian 68
Detroit Tigers 5, 9, 26, 34, 41-42, 44, 47, 51, 59, 78, 82, 86, 94, 103, 109, 114, 118, 119, 121, 136, 143, 145, 149, 155-156, 160, 164
Diamond Dreams 176
Diaz, Laz 12, **63-65**, 85, 91, 183, 184, 185, 186, 187, 189, 190, 191
Dietz, Dick 174
DiMaggio, Joe 48
DiMuro, Lou 65
DiMuro, Mike **65-66**, 67, 124, 151, 189, 190, 191, 192
DiMuro, Ray 66
Dior, Christian 60
Disabled American Veterans 116
Disc Degeneration 37, 97
Dominican League 148
Dominican Republic 71, 148
Donald, Jason 5, 109, 172
Drake, Rob 16, 17, 28, **67-68**, 101, 107, 117, 127, 183, 186, 188, 189, 190, 191
Dreckman, Bruce 15, 42, **68-70**, 183, 187, 189, 190, 191, 192
Drew, J.D. 98

Drysdale, Don 174
Dunn, Adam 130
Durham, Ray 61

Eckstein, David 69
Eddings, Doug 1, 62, **70–72**, 136, 153, 163, 183, 184, 185, 186, 187, 188, 189, 190, 191
Ejection Rate (definition) 12
Elizabethton, Tennessee 64
Ellis, Mark 32, 131
Emmel, Paul 14, 67, **72–73**, 113, 162, 183, 185, 186, 187, 188, 189, 190, 191
Ensberg, Morgan 106
Erickson, Scott 158
Erstad, Darin 43
Escobar, Kelvim 71
Escobar, Yunel 123
ESPN 2, 12, 68, 96
ESPN Insider 100
ESPN the Magazine 15, 33, 91, 109, 121, 176, 181
Estabrook, Mike 9, 10, 11, 16, **74–75**, 79, 183, 184, 185, 188, 189, 190, 191
Estes, Shawn 29
Ethier, Andre 26, 45
Eugene, Oregon 155
Eugene Register-Guard 155, 157
Everett, Carl 114
Everitt, Mike 8, 72, **75–77**, 183, 184, 187, 189, 190, 191, 192

Facebook 64
Fairchild, Chad 16, **77–79**, 107, 183, 184, 185, 186, 187, 188, 189, 190, 191, 192
Feliciano, Pedro 69
Fenway Park 175
Fielder, Prince 85
Fisk, Carlton 111
Fletcher, Andy 9, **79–80**, 183, 184, 186, 187, 189, 190, 191
Florida Marlins 12, 14, 22, 27, 32, 37, 49, 65–66, 76, 84, 93, 98, 103, 105, 110, 128, 141, 145, 161, 167, 174
Florida Times-Union 93
Fonzie's Kids 117
Foreman, George 24
Foster, Marty **81–82**, 96, 183, 184, 187, 188, 189, 190, 191
Fox Sports 41, 115
Francisco, Ben 93
Francona, Terry 26, 31, 75, 84, 111, 119, 135, 157, 159
Frasor, Jason 69

Froemming, Bruce 13, 33, 86, 91, 113, 168, 176, 178
Fuentes, Brian 114
Fullerton, California 117
Furcal, Rafael 45–46

Galarraga, Armando 5, 41, 44, 103, 109, 121–122, 145, 164
Game Management (definition) 12
Garcia, Karim 118
Garciaparra, Nomar 164
Gardenhire, Ron 58, 131, 147, 159
Garko, Ryan 43
Garland, Jon 166
Garza, Matt 82, 94
Gaston, Cito 123
Gathright, Joey 131
Gaudin, Chad 145
Gehrig, Lou 9
Geren, Bob 7, 57, 131
Getz, Chris 165
Gibson, Bob 9, 86
Gibson, Greg 26, **82–84**, 183, 184, 186, 187, 189, 190, 191, 192
Girardi, Joe 69, 81, 167
Glanville, Doug 111
Glavine, Tom 7–8, 77–78, 99, 145
God 24, 36
Golson, Greg 88
Gomes, Jonny 110
Gomez, Carlos 131
Gomez, Chris 112
Gonzalez, Alex 149
Gonzalez, Carlos 11
Gonzalez, Edgar 159
Gonzalez, Fredi 22
Gonzalez, Manuel **84–85**, 160
Gooden, Dwight 137
Google 91
Gordon, Alex 165
Gorman, Brian 15, **85–87**, 133, 183, 184, 185, 187, 188, 189, 190, 191
Gorman, Tom 85–86
Gossage, Goose 120
Grace, Mark 13
Grand Ole Opry 176
Grand Rapids, Michigan 148
Green, Nick 169
Green, Shawn 34
Gregg, Kevin 92
Griffey, Ken, Jr. 111, 130
Gross, Kevin 179
Guccione, Chris 28, **87–88**,
127, 184, 186, 187, 189, 190, 191, 192
Guerrero, Vladimir 172
Guillen, Carlos 34, 149
Guillen, Jose 136
Guillen, Ozzie 51, 53, 105, 176
Guthrie, Jeremy 36
Gwynn, Tony 8, 56

Hairston, Jerry, Jr. 74, 172
Hairston, Scott 55
Halladay, Roy 45, 66, 96
Haller, Bill 66
Hallion, Tom 2, 22, **89–90**, 136, 186, 187, 189, 190, 191
Halls Cough Drops 37
Hamilton, Josh 62
Hammel, Jason 129
Haren, Dan 152
Hart, Corey 40
Harvey, Doug 66
Harwell, Ernie 143, 145
Havana, Cuba 91
Hawkins, LaTroy 125
Hayes, Brett 14
Hayes, Charlie 108
Helena, Montana 111
Helena Independent Record 111
Hell 23
Hell's Kitchen 86
Helms, Wes 22, 66, 141
Helton, Todd 178
Henderson, Rickey 42
Hendrick, George 133
Henry, Doug 61
Hernandez, Angel 34, **90–92**, 183, 184, 186, 187, 189, 190, 191, 192
Hernandez, Felix 31, 32, 130
Hernandez, Livan 80
Hernandez, Ramon 103, 171
Hershiser, Orel 174
Herzog, Whitey 61
Hickox, Ed 14, **92–94**, 186, 189, 190, 191, 192
Hillman, Trey 136, 150
Hiroshima Carp 94
Hirschbeck, John 13, 28, 29, 81–82, 83, 84, **94–97**, 108, 121, 129, 162, 170, 178, 183, 189, 190, 191
Hirschbeck, Mark 13, 96, 170
Hodges, Gil 65
Hohn, Bill 15, **97–98**, 123, 179, 183, 186, 187, 188, 189, 190, 191, 192
Holbrook, Sam 38, 83, **99–100**, 183, 184, 189, 190, 191, 192
Hollywood, California 111

195

Index

Holyfield, Evander 24
Houston Astros 23, 26, 29, 36, 37, 42–43, 45, 49, 61, 77, 106, 123, 124, 130, 137, 138–139, 163
Howard, Ryan 26, 61, 86, 90, 123, 141
Hoye, James 16, 26, 28, 67, 83, **100–102**, 107, 126, 132, 183, 184, 186, 189, 190, 191, 192
Hubbard, Cal 5
Hubbard, Trenidad 27
Hudson, Marvin 12, 14, 30, **102–104**, 183, 184, 185, 186, 188, 189, 190, 191, 192
Hudson, Tim 123
Hughes, Phil 177
Hunter, Torii 75, 152
Hurdle, Clint 140

Iassogna, Dan **104–105**, 150, 183, 186, 187, 189, 190, 192
Ibanez, Raul 73, 100
Iguchi, Tad 34
Immigration Reform and Control Act of 1986 117
Inge, Brandon 119
Instant Replay 16, 26, 32, 35, 38, 41, 43, 51, 53, 55, 59, 61, 71, 73, 74, 75, 81, 86, 88, 90, 91, 103, 109, 111, 112, 116, 119, 121, 128, 131, 149, 157, 161, 162, 172; expanding game use of 6, 122, 146, 164, 171; for home run calls 22, 62, 83, 130, 135, 147–148, 151
International League 23, 27, 30, 36, 40, 44, 84, 138
Internet 1, 7, 12, 180
iPod 160
Irabu, Hideki 108
Iwamura, Akinori 59
Izturis, Maicer 116

Jackowski, Bill 29
Jackson, Austin 44
Jackson, Edwin 107
Jackson, Reggie 122
Jamaica 34
James, Bill 6
Japan 59, 65, 66
Japanese Central League 66
Japanese Major Leagues 94, 154
Jenks, Bobby 131, 161
Jesus Christ 68
Jeter, Derek 22, 81–82, 119, 125, 146
Jimenez, Ubaldo 110
Joe Brinkman Umpire School 117

Johjima, Kenji 69
Johnson, Adrian 16, **106–107**, 185, 188, 189, 191, 192
Johnson, Josh 66
Johnson, Randy 51–52, 84, 103, 110, 137, 163
Joliet, Illinois 38
Jones, Chipper 98
Jones, Cleon 65
Jones, Garrett 85
Joyce, Jim 5, 6, 15, 41, 44, 103, **107–109**, 121–122, 145, 164, 179, 181, 184, 186, 187, 188, 189, 190, 191, 192
Joyner, Wally 7
Jurrjens, Jair 46

K/BB (defined) 9
K/9 (defined) 8
Kalamazoo, Michigan 170
Kansas City Royals 7, 34, 63, 74–75, 77, 112, 120–121, 131, 136, 143, 147, 150, 159, 160, 165, 173
Kazmir, Scott 46, 47–48, 136, 157
Kellogg, Jeff **109–111**, 184, 185, 186, 188, 189, 190, 191, 192
Kemp, Matt 106
Kendall, Jason 75
Kendrick, Howie 73
Kenosha, Wisconsin 64
Keppinger, Jeff 138
Kershaw, Clayton 107
Kiner, Ralph 99
King, Ray 140
Kinugasa, Sachi 94
Kirk, Jim 102
Kline, Steve 127
Knight, Brian 16, 59, 107, **111–113**, 184, 187, 189, 190, 191, 192
Knight, Ray 49
Knoblauch, Chuck 164
Korean War 153
Kouzmanoff, Kevin 142
Krukow, Mike 38
Ku Klux Klan 83
Kubel, Jason 159
Kulpa, Joe 113
Kulpa, Ron 83, **113–114**, 183, 185, 186, 188, 189, 190, 192
Kunkel, Bill 66
Kuroda, Hiroki 130
Kuwait 36

Lachemann, Rene 99
Lane, Jason 106
Langford, Rick 46

LaRoche, Adam 22
LaRoche, Andy 149
Larsen, Don 153
LaRue, Jason 151
LaRussa, Tony 99, 118
Layne, Jerry **114–116**, 121, 138, 159, 161, 184, 185, 186, 187, 188, 189, 191, 192
League City, Texas 138
Lee, Carlos 64, 137
Lee, Cliff 63, 177, 180
Lee, Derrek 35, 76
The Left Field Corner 2
Lester, Jon 36, 112
Letendre, Mark 80
Lewis, Colby 180
Lewis, Fred 27
Leyland, Jim 41, 42, 51, 59, 82, 90, 119, 155–156
Licey Tigers 148
Lieberthal, Mike 111
Lilly, Ted 123
Lincecum, Tim 106
Lind, Adam 30
Little League 152
Lofton, Kenny 41
Lohse, Kyle 68
Loney, James 35, 107
Longoria, Evan 35
Lopez, Jose 73
Lopez, Rodrigo 55, 141
Lords of Baseball 5, 6, 12, 13, 15, 16, 23, 25, 37, 40, 49, 57, 61, 67, 69, 73, 76, 78, 82, 83, 87, 89, 90, 92, 95–96, 100, 101, 107, 108, 116, 126, 133, 137, 143, 145, 149, 154, 157, 158, 160, 177, 178, 180; *see also* Major League Baseball
Loria, Jeffrey 167
Los Angeles Angels (also Anaheim Angels; California Angels) 7, 35, 47, 71, 73, 75, 84, 115, 116, 121–122, 145, 150–151, 152, 157, 168–169, 174
Los Angeles Dodgers 26, 35, 45, 49, 50, 54, 87, 88, 106, 119, 130, 136, 137, 145, 150–151, 167, 169, 179
Los Angeles Times 26, 86
Louisville, Kentucky 89
The Love of the Game 144
Lowe, Derek 74, 145

Macha, Ken 40, 45, 167
MacPhail, Lee 121
Macpherson, Elle 144
Maddon, Joe 22, 35, 47, 83, 92, 148, 181

196

Index

Maddux, Greg 7–8, 25, 125
Maholm, Paul 36
Major League Baseball 1, 2, 26, 37, 38, 53, 54, 57, 61, 82, 86, 89, 93, 108, 129, 130, 141, 146, 159, 167, 177, 179; *see also* Lords of Baseball
Major League Rule Book 5, 104, 107, 120
Major League Umpires Association 15, 76
Manfred, Rob 178
Manuel, Charlie 100, 105, 128
Manuel, Jerry 105, 146, 154
Marichal, Juan 50
Marine Corps, United States 38, 64
Maris, Roger 48, 99
Markakis, Nick 103–104, 112, 134
Marmol, Carlos 123
Marquez, Alfonso 23, 34, 42, **116–118**, 119, 164, 185, 186, 187, 188, 189, 190, 191, 192
Marsh, Randy 15, 22, 114, 117, **118–120**, 121, 145, 147, 183, 185, 186, 187, 188, 189, 191, 192
Martin, Billy 120, 158, 173
Martin, Russell 54, 88, 106, 151
Martin Methodist College 125
Martinez, Buck 59
Martinez, Pedro 62–63, 117–118
Martinez, Tino 73
Matsui, Hideki 61, 118
Matsui, Kaz 45
Matthews, Gary, Jr. 47
Mattingly, Don 107
Matusz, Brian 44
Mauer, Joe 52, 53, 164
May, Milt 90
Mays, Willie 128
McCann, Brian 46, 78, 98
McClelland, Tim 7, 15, 48, 49, 77, 109, 117, **120–122**, 157, 163, 181, 183, 185, 186, 187, 188, 189, 191, 192
McGraw, John 25, 78
McGwire, Mark 48, 99, 128
McLain, Dennis 9
McLaren, John 130
McMichael, Steve 91
McMorris, Larnell 178
McNally, Dave 65
McSherry, John 49
Meacham, Bobby 158, 178
Meals, Jerry 21, **122–124**, 181, 185, 188, 189, 190, 191, 192
Melhuse, Adam 112

Melvin, Bob 73
Meriwether, Chuck **124–125**, 183, 184, 187, 189, 190, 191, 192
Metrodome 135, 169
Mexico 59, 117
Meyer, Dan 98
Miami, Florida 64, 85, 91
Miami Herald 133
Mientkiewicz, Doug 119
Military Times Edge 64
Millar, Kevin 133
Miller, Bill 67, 104, **126–127**, 153, 163, 183, 185, 186, 188, 189, 190, 191
Millwood, Kevin 76
Milwaukee Brewers 27, 30, 37, 39, 40, 44, 45, 49, 78, 85, 96, 131, 133, 141–142, 143, 145, 149, 167, 174, 180
Minnesota Twins 29, 35, 46, 52, 53, 58, 64, 68, 88, 103, 119, 122, 124, 128, 131, 134–135, 141–142, 143, 145, 147, 155, 158, 159, 164, 169
Minute Maid Park 42
MLB.com 31, 62
Molina, Bengie 180
Molina, Jose 180
Molina, Yadier 58, 180
Molitor, Paul 143
Montague, Ed, Jr. 104, **127–129**, 145, 147, 183, 189, 190, 191, 192
Montague, Ed, Sr. 128, 129
Montreal Expos 25, 49, 56
Morales, Franklin 72
Morgan, Keegan 89
Morgan, Nyjer 14, 38
Morneau, Justin 58–59
Morris, Jack 149
Morton, Charlie 123
Moser, Casey **129–130**
Mouth Guard 80
Moyer, Jamie 68, 90, 142
Moylan, Peter 41
Muchlinski, Mike **130–132**
Mujica, Edward 161
MyCentralJersey.com 43
Myers, Brett 137

Nady, Xavier 23
Napoleon Complex 122
Napoli, Mike 47, 115, 122
Nashville, Tennessee 176
Nathan, Joe 53
National Basketball Association 50, 83
National Italian-American Sports Hall of Fame 140

National League Championship Series 76
National League Division Series 69, 89, 96, 123, 136
Nauert, Paul **132–133**, 184, 185, 186, 189, 190, 191
Navarro, Dioner 30
Nelson, Jeff 28, **134–135**, 183, 185, 186, 187, 188, 189, 190, 191, 192
New Haven Register 96
New York Giants 9, 25, 85, 128
New York Mets 29, 34, 44, 49, 65, 69, 78, 86, 93, 102, 105, 123, 127, 128, 143, 145–146, 148, 154, 156, 159
New York Times 2, 49, 76, 167
New York Yankees 9, 22, 25, 29, 47, 51–52, 61, 63, 69, 81, 86, 88, 93, 94, 101, 108, 115, 116, 117–118, 119, 120, 121–122, 124, 125, 142, 146, 147–148, 151, 153, 157, 158, 164, 167, 170, 173, 176–177
Newark Star-Ledger 53
Nix, Jayson 57
Nolasco, Ricky 161
Nomo, Hideo 45
Norris, Bud 138–139
North County Times 175
Norwalk Reflector 78

Oakland-Alameda County Coliseum 131
Oakland Athletics 7, 32, 46, 47, 57, 103, 114, 127, 131, 142, 145, 158, 165, 180
Obama, Barack 63, 162
Offerman, Jose 148, 164
O'Flaherty, Eric 98
Oh, Sadaharu 59
Ohio State University 100, 102
Oliver, Darren 121
Olivo, Miguel 93, 110, 136
Olsen, Scott 68
On-Base Percentage (definition) 11
O'Nora, Brian 32, 70, **135–137**, 185, 186, 188, 189, 190, 191
Orange County, California 70, 115
Ordonez, Magglio 155–156
Ordonez, Rey 29
Ortiz, David 75, 140, 157
Ortiz, Russ 130
Oswalt, Roy 36
Outside the Lines 12
Ozuna, Pablo 71

Index

Pacific Coast League 31, 36, 44, 131, 152, 160, 165
Pagan, Angel 168
Paine Webber 89
Parrott, Harold 5
Pasco, Washington 24
Paul, Josh 71
Paulino, Ronny 66
Payton, Jay 73
Peavy, Jake 76
Pedroia, Dustin 36, 110, 159, 171
Pelfrey, Mike 180
Pena, Carlos 92
Pendleton, Terry 151
Penny, Brad 54, 83
Peralta, Jhonny 43, 44
Perry, Gerald 76, 133
PetCo Park 131, 152
Philadelphia Daily News 114
Philadelphia Inquirer 50
Philadelphia Phillies 26, 32, 34, 50, 55, 61, 63, 64, 68, 69–70, 72, 76, 80, 86, 90, 96, 100, 101, 105, 112, 123–124, 128, 141, 142, 174
Phillips, Richie 13, 49, 57, 95
Piazza, Mike 29, 148
Pierzynski, A.J. 171
Pine Island, Minnesota 135
Pine Tar 120
Pineiro, Joel 22
Piniella, Lou 38, 56–57, 73, 168
Pitch f/x Tool 2
Pittsburgh Pirates 22, 27, 36, 38, 85, 86, 96, 123, 137, 138, 139, 149, 174
Porcello, Rick 26, 136
Port, Mike 55, 87
Porter, Alan 37, 130, **137–138**, 160
Portland State University 155
Posada, Jorge 63, 116, 122
Price, David 55
Prinze, Freddie, Jr. 111
Puckett, Kirby 128
Puerto Rico 42
Pujols, Albert 151
Purcey, David 154

Qualls, Chad 181
Queens, New York 86
QuesTec 6

R/9 (defined) 8
Rackley, David 23, **138–139**
Ramirez, Hanley 105
Ramirez, Manny 118
Randazzo, Tony **139–140**, 162, 185, 188, 189, 190, 191

Rapuano, Ed **141–142**, 183, 184, 186, 189, 190, 191, 192
Ray, Robert 130
Reagan Administration 117
Redding, Tim 35
Redmond, Mike 159
Reed, Jeff 90
Reed, Rick **142–144**, 147, 158, 169, 184, 189, 191, 192
Regions Financial Corporation 89
Reilly, Mike 15, **144–146**, 184, 185, 186, 187, 188, 189, 191, 192
Relaford, Desi 34
Reliford, Charlie 29, 84, 140, **146–148**, 183, 184, 185, 187, 188, 189, 190, 191
Renteria, Rick 55
Retrosheet 2
Reyburn, D.J. 16, **148–149**
Reyes, Jose 93
Reynolds, Jim 2, 44, **150–151**, 183, 186, 187, 189, 190, 192
Reynolds, Shane 124
Rhodes, Arthur 133
Riggleman, Jim 14, 26, 68, 100, 145
Righetti, Dave 127
Ripken, Cal 94
Ripperger, Mark **151–152**
Rivera, Juan 151
Rivera, Mariano 88, 176
Riverfront Stadium 119
Rivers, Mickey 173
Robinson, Frank 180
Robinson, Jackie 120
Rodriguez, Alex 119, 142, 147
Rodriguez, Edwin 14
Rodriguez, Ivan 100
Rogers, Kenny 118
Rogers Centre 136
Rojas, Cookie 12
Rolen, Scott 81
Rollins, Jimmy 34, 55, 61, 123
Romero, Ricky 180
Rose, Pete 64, 128
Roseboro, John 50
Ross, David 100
Rowand, Aaron 107
Runge, Brian 40, 42, 84, 140, **153–154**, 162, 178, 184, 185, 187, 188, 189, 190, 191
Runge, Ed 153–154
Runge, Paul 49, 153–154
Russell, John 149
Ruth, Babe 9, 11, 48
Ryan, Nolan 94, 163

Safeco Field 131
St. Louis Cardinals 9, 22, 58, 61, 85–86, 99, 118, 123, 125, 128, 136, 151
Saint Paul Pioneer Press 68
Saltalamacchia, Jarrod 168
Sanchez, Anibal 110
Sanchez, Gaby 14
Sanchez, Jonathan 154
San Diego Padres 7, 49, 55, 56, 69, 72, 76, 118, 152, 154, 159, 161, 166, 172, 174, 178
San Diego State University 56
San Diego Union-Tribune 152
San Francisco Chronicle 129
San Francisco Giants 25, 36, 38, 45, 48, 50, 57, 72, 76, 80, 106, 114, 125, 126, 127, 128, 129, 140, 145, 154, 156, 160, 168, 169, 174, 179
Santana, Ervin 180
Santana, Johan 123
Santiago, Benito 80
Sarasota Herald Tribune 36
Satan 24
Sauerbeck, Scott 69
Schaefer, Bob 107
Schilling, Curt 33, 69, 84, 114
Schrieber, Paul 1, 30, 117, 121, **154–156**, 160, 184, 185, 186, 187, 188, 189, 191, 192
Scioscia, Mike 71, 115, 116, 169
Scott, Dale 14, 155, **156–158**, 186, 189, 190, 191, 192
Scott, Luke 125
Scully, Vin 87
Seattle Mariners 31, 32, 43, 51, 69, 73, 85, 102, 130, 131, 133, 148, 154, 164, 172, 177
Secret Service 62
Selig, Bud 6, 95
Shea Stadium 29, 86, 102, 159
Sheffield, Gary 51
Shields, James 110, 180
Short Hills, New Jersey 53
Showalter, Buck 134
Silva, Carlos 103
Sizemore, Grady 43, 103, 150
Slash statistics (definition) 11
Slaten, Doug 14
Slugging percentage (definition) 11
Smoltz, John 6
Snider, Duke 153
Solomon (King) 172
Solomon, Jimmie Lee 89
Sonnanstine, Andy 101
Soriano, Rafael 69
Sosa, Sammy 48, 99

198

Index

Soto, Geovany 38
Sounds of the Game 115
Southern University 27
Sowers, Jeremy 55
Spahn, Warren 29
Span, Denard 141–142, 147
Spartanburg Herald-Journal 52
Sports Illustrated 15, 33, 91, 109, 121, 171, 172, 176
Springstead, Marty 157
Staats, Dewayne 73
Star Trek 102
State University of New York–Buffalo 89
STATS, Inc. 7
Steroid Era 9, 60, 100, 150
Strasburg, Stephen 137
Street, Huston 123
Street & Smith's Sports Business Journal 31
Strike zone (defined) 5
Stubbs, Drew 172
Summer Catch 111
Suzuki, Ichiro 11, 102, 154
Suzuki, Kurt 131
Sveum, Dale 40
Swisher, Nick 69, 101, 121, 157

Tacoma, Washington 131
Tacoma News Tribune 69
"Take Me Out to the Ballgame" 61, 91
Tampa Bay Rays (also Tampa Bay Devil Rays) 22, 24, 25, 30, 35, 47, 49, 55, 73, 82, 83, 90, 92, 94, 101, 110, 133, 136, 147–148, 180, 181
Tan, Cecilia 150
Tankersley, Taylor 167
Target Field 133, 169
Tata, Terry 90
Tea Party 161
Teixeira, Mark 53
Tejada, Miguel 103
Terry, Bill 9
Texas Rangers 7, 55, 62, 65, 74, 88, 106, 111, 112, 133, 134, 144, 151, 152, 181
Thomas, Frank 169
Thome, Jim 88, 131
Thomson, Rob 81–82
Thornton, Andre 143
Thornton, Matt 149
Tichenor, Todd 16, **158–160**, 184, 185, 187, 188, 189, 190, 191, 192
Tiger Stadium 66, 143
Tiller, Chris **160–161**
Timmons, Tim 23, **161–163**, 164, 184, 185, 187, 189, 190, 191, 192
Toledo Blade 143
Toronto Blue Jays 33, 45, 47, 49, 51, 55, 68, 69, 74, 75, 80, 81, 92, 93, 123, 130, 136, 154, 157, 163, 169
Torre, Joe 14, 35, 49–50, 107, 167
Torrealba, Yorvit 126, 166–167
Tracy, Jim 32
Trammell, Alan 149
Trebelhorn, Tom 103–104
Trembley, Dave 73, 161
Trinity University 24
Triple-A Call-Up Umpires (defined) 15–16
Tropicana Field 147
Tschida, Tim 23, 49, 134, 162, **163–164**, 183, 184, 185, 186, 187, 188, 189, 190, 191, 192
Tumpane, John **165–166**

Umpire Media Guide 66
Umps Care 66, 124, 151
United States Senate 6
United States Supreme Court 6
University of California–Los Angeles (UCLA) 127
University of Connecticut 104, 150
University of San Diego 66
Upton, B.J. 82
Uribe, Juan 168
U.S. Cellular Field 64
USA Today 6, 119
Utley, Chase 69–70, 105, 123–124

Valentin, John 164
Valenzuela, Mario 59
Vallejo, California 127
VandenHurk, Rick 145
Vanover, Larry **166–167**, 183, 186, 188, 189, 190, 191, 192
Vargas, Jason 43
Varitek, Jason 147, 159
Vaughn, Mo 127
Velez, Eugenio 169
Venezuela 84
Ventura County, California 87
Verlander, Justin 78, 114
Veterans Administration (VA) Hospitals 116
Veterans Affairs, United States Department of 116
Victorino, Shane 141
Virginia Babe Ruth Umpires Association 40
Visalia, California 64
Volstad, Chris 14
Volusia County, Florida 92
Votto, Joey 35, 74, 149
Vuvuzelas 21–22

Wagner, Billy 34
Wakamatsu, Don 43, 164
Washington, Ron 7, 88, 151
Washington Nationals 14, 26, 35, 37, 50, 68, 100, 103, 130, 137, 145, 148, 180
Washington Post 2
Washington Times 165
Watson, Matt 165
Weaver, Jered 130
Weber, Bruce 7, 161
Wedge, Eric 51, 55, 58–59, 69
WEEI 82, 84
Weeks, Rickie 27
Wegner, Mark 42, 134, 164, **168–169**, 185, 186, 187, 188, 189, 190, 191, 192
Weiss, Walt 158
Welke, Bill **169–171**, 183, 184, 185, 186, 187, 188, 189, 190, 191
Welke, Tim 11, 170, **171–173**, 181, 184, 185, 186, 187, 188, 189, 190, 191
Wells, David 122
Wells, Kip 136
Wells, Vernon 51, 68
Wendelstedt, Harry 173–174
Wendelstedt, Harry Hunter, Sr. 174
Wendelstedt, Hunter 42, 138, **173–175**, 183, 184, 186, 189, 190, 191, 192
Wendelstedt Umpire School 133, 138, 152, 174
West, Joe 12, 13, 14, 15, 24, 30, 33, 34, 73, 91, 97, 115, 121, 140, 145, 162, **175–177**, 184, 185, 187, 189, 190, 191, 192
West Side Story 155
West Vest 176–177
Westbrook, Jake 69
Whitaker, Lou 149
Whitestone, New York 86
Wigginton, Ty 36
Williams, Jimy 114
Williams, Mitch 26
Williams, Ted 48
Willits, Reggie 47
Wilson, C.J. 112
Wilson, Jack 51
Wilson, Mookie 128
Wilson Sporting Goods 176

Index

Winn, Randy 59
Winters, Mike 30, 55, 67, **177–179**, 185, 186, 187, 189, 190, 192
Wolf, Jim **179–181**, 184, 187, 189, 190, 191, 192
Wolf, Randy 180
Wolverton, Michael 12
Wood, Kerry 124
World Baseball Classic 59
World Cup 22
World Series 29, 41, 55, 61, 63, 65, 71, 76, 86, 89, 90, 109, 118, 120, 121, 125, 127, 128, 144, 146, 148, 153, 171, 176

World Umpires Association 13, 15, 24, 49, 95, 128, 135, 162, 175, 178
Wotus, Ron 57
Wright, David 156
Wrigley Field 30, 38, 75, 76, 91, 175
Wuertz, Michael 131

Yankee Stadium 25, 119, 177
Yastrzemski, Carl 9
Yost, Ned 75
Youkilis, Kevin 26, 136
Young, Chris 76
Young, Delmon 88

Young, Eric, Jr. 32
Young, Larry 80
Young, Michael 181
Yount, Robin 143
YouTube 30

Zambrano, Carlos 23, 38, 123, 163, 168
Zaun, Gregg 96
Zimmer, Don 117–118
Zimmerman, Ryan 26, 144–145
Zito, Barry 129
Zone Evaluation System 6

www.ingramcontent.com/pod-product-compliance
Lightning Source LLC
Chambersburg PA
CBHW081557300426
44116CB00015B/2923